51 Melbourne	61 Yangon	71 Damascus	81 Caracas	91 New York
52 Mumbai	62 Abu Dhabi	72 Dubai	82 Chicago	92 Québec
53 Osaka	63 Alexandria	73 Jerusalem	83 Havana	93 Quito
54 Perth	64 Algiers	74 Johannesburg	84 Las Vegas	94 Rio de Janeiro
55 Phnom Penh	65 Baghdad	75 Kabul	85 Lima	95 San Francisco
56 Shanghai	66 Beirut	76 Marrakesh	86 Los Angeles	96 Santiago
57 Singapore	67 Cairo	77 Nairobi	87 Mexico City	97 Seattle
58 Sydney	68 Cape Town	78 Tel Aviv-Yafo	88 Mi	98 Toronto
59 Taipei	69 Casablanca	79 Boston	89 M	
60 Tokyo	70 Dar es Salaam	80 Buenos Aires	90 N	DC

100
Great Cities of the World

Published by Gramercy Books, an imprint of Random House Value Publishing, a
division of Random House, Inc., New York.

Gramercy is a registered trademark and the colophon is a trademark of Random
House, Inc.

Random House
New York • Toronto • London • Sydney • Auckland
www.randomhouse.com

Written by Jack Barker, Andrew Evans, Andrew Forbes, Mike Ivory, George
McDonald, Robin McKelvie, Neil Murray, Nicholas T Parsons, Sally Roy, Dave
Scott, Anna Selby, Ann F Stonehouse, Lee Karen Stow and Paul Wade

Design layouts for AA Publishing by Nautilus Design

Printed and bound in Dubai by Oriental Press

A catalog record for this title is available from the Library of Congress.

ISBN 0-517-22736-3

10 9 8 7 6 5 4 3 2 1

100
Great Cities
of the World

GRAMERCY BOOKS

NEW YORK

Contents

Cities are listed in their English name, but are ordered according to their local-language name.

Europe

Asia, Australia, and New Zealand

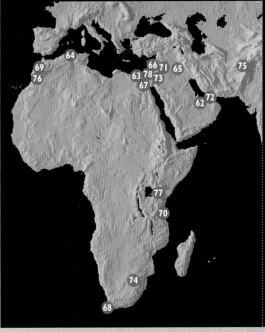

Africa and the Mid-East

The Americas

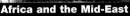

100 GREAT CITIES OF THE WORLD

Europe

The great cities of Europe reflect the wealth and history of the Western World, stemming from the ancient roots of Athens and Rome. They are national treasure houses, cultural magnets developed perhaps over centuries but often perceived as a microcosm of an age. Thus Bruges is celebrated for its medieval structures, Florence for the glory of its Renaissance buildings, St Petersburg for its early 18th-century completeness. Layered with history, many bear with pride the scars of power struggles through the centuries, while some—including Warsaw and Munich—required major reconstruction after the devastation of warfare in the 20th century. The closed world of Communism in Eastern Europe preserved many intriguing cities in the last century, but, newly exposed to consumerism and tourism, cities like Prague and Tallinn are catching up fast. Meanwhile late starters such as Dublin, Reykjavík and Helsinki have reinvented themselves as lively nightlife capitals, or under the European Union umbrella as Cities of Culture.

Amsterdam

statistics

- Population: 740,000
- Number of canals and bridges: 165 and 1,280 respectively
- Estimated number of bicycles: 400,000
- Lowest point below mean sea level: 18ft (5.5m)

A msterdam has always been a city dominated by water and remains so today. The capital and most populous city of the Netherlands stands at the mouth of the River Amstel and on Het IJ, a southern bay of the IJsselmeer. Today this is a freshwater lake, but prior to a great sea barrier being built in the 1930s it was the saltwater Zuiderzee. Much of the city is actually below the level of the nearby North Sea, guarded from the threat of encroaching waters by rigorously maintained coastal and river dikes and dams. The old city's defining feature is the *Grachtengordel* (Canal Belt), a necklace of concentric 16th- and 17th-century canals. Working outward from the centre, they are called Singel, Herengracht, Keizersgracht, and Prinsengracht. These and other major canals are criss-crossed by many smaller ones, effectively dividing the city into a jigsaw puzzle of tiny islands connected by humpback bridges.

The capital of the Netherlands takes great pride in its history and in the legacy of past centuries, represented by some 7,000 buildings that are protected monuments and have contemporary uses ranging from private homes to cafés, restaurants, offices, and even bordellos. Masterpieces and mementoes from its Golden Age fill the halls of the Rijksmuseum (National Museum), which include works by Old Dutch Masters such as Rembrandt, and Johannes Vermeer (1632–75), and of the Scheepvaartmuseum (Maritime Museum) and the Koninklijk Paleis (Royal Palace) on the Dam. More recent treasures are housed in the Van Gogh Museum and the modern art Stedelijk Museum. But Amsterdam is no dry and dusty museumpiece. It has its own tolerant and multicultural lifestyle that embraces legalized prostitution and official acceptance of the public use of "soft" narcotic drugs (under certain conditions).

LEFT: *Looking down into an Amsterdam café.*

BELOW: *Rooftops and decorative gables observed from the 273ft (85m) clock tower of Westerkerk.*

ANNE FRANK

In 1942, eight Jewish refugees entered a specially prepared hiding place in a house on Amsterdam's Prinsengracht. One of them was 13-year-old Anne Frank (1929–45), who began to keep a diary recording her experiences and her thoughts. They lived in oppressive silence and fear until their sanctuary was betrayed to the Nazis in August 1944. Anne died in Bergen-Belsen concentration camp the following year, but her spirit lives on. Today, close to a million people visit Anne's hideaway every year, and she achieved her dream of being a famous writer—*The Diary of Anne Frank* has sold 25 million copies in 60 languages.

ABOVE: *Visitors waiting to see Anne Frank's house.*

THE STORY OF...

Amsterdam took shape towards the end of the 12th century as a settlement of fisherfolk and farmers on the low-lying coast of Holland. It quickly developed as a trading centre for herring and beer, setting the scene for its future mercantile career. Its greatest period was the 17th-century "Golden Age", when profits poured in from trade with the Far East and the Americas, and Dutch Masters such as Rembrandt Hamenszoon van Rijn (1606–69) created paintings that today hang in museums around the world. Wars and a fading of the commercial drive then took their toll, but not before the city had been graced with thousands of gabled canalside dwellings and warehouses.

Amsterdam is more than elegant buildings and scenic canal views. Its live-and-let-live attitude has made it a byword for tolerance and has brought it many foreign refugees fleeing persecution. In recent decades, a permissive attitude towards controversial issues such as prostitution and drug use has given it an international reputation that verges on notoriety.

1207
Some time before this year, fishing and farming families establish a settlement at the mouth of the River Amstel

1275
Count of Holland Floris V grants "Aemstelledame" trading privileges. This first-known documentary reference is now considered Amsterdam's founding date

1578
During the Dutch rebellion against Catholic Spanish rule, Amsterdam turns Calvinist in a revolution called the *Alteratie* (Alteration)

1814
Amsterdam becomes the capital (but not the seat of government) of the Kingdom of the Netherlands

2002
Queen Beatrix's son and heir to the throne, Prince Willem Alexander, marries Máxima Zorreguieta from Argentina in the city

A Commercial Center

Amsterdam may have the reputation of being a paradise for anyone seeking an alternative lifestyle, but alongside this undoubted truth it remains the same shrewd and successful commercial and trading center it has always been. Its port—although it trails behind Rotterdam—is large and busy, and Schiphol Airport is one of Europe's most important and successful air hubs. Many large international companies have chosen to locate their European distribution operations and headquarters in or near Amsterdam, often in the ultramodern business districts on the city's edge. They benefit from a highly educated and cosmopolitan workforce that is invariably fluent in English and proficient in other world languages. Tourism, diamonds, cheese, plants, and flowers (including tulips, of course) are the important driving forces behind the economy.

ABOVE: *The wooden Magere Brug, known as "the Skinny Bridge".*

Athens

statistics

- Population: 10,950,000

- 98 percent of the population are Greek Orthodox

- 21,500 members of the global press travelled to Athens to cover the 2004 Olympic Games

- 10,500 athletes participated in the 2004 Olympic Games

SOCRATES

The Athenian philosopher Socrates (469–399BC), who served as a soldier and retired as a stonemason, dedicated his life to challenging accepted thoughts and views. His reflections centered largely on morality and mankind's place in the world and he drew his audience from Athens' young aristocracy. Socrates' teachings ultimately led to his death when the courts convicted him of corrupting the city's youth. He is believed to have accepted his fate graciously, opting to die at home in the company of his students and friends by taking a fatal dose of hemlock (a poisonous herb).

ABOVE RIGHT: *A guard on sentry duty.*

September 2004 saw the Olympic Games return to Athens, the city where the first modern Olympiad was staged in 1896. A lot has changed since then with the city's wealth of Greek and Roman treasures being joined by the new buildings and infrastructure that heralded the return of the world's leading sporting competition to its spiritual home. Modern-day Athens, a city that combines ancient monuments with contemporary architecture, is powered by tourism and service industries. Located on the southern tip of the Greek mainland adjacent to the country's largest, and most important, trading port of Piraeus, Athens is also at the heart of Greece's shipping industry. While manufacturing is still an important part of the local and national economies, its contribution is beginning to wane. Athenians are hard workers, however in their free time they take advantage of the city's warm climate and embrace outdoor living; on balmy evenings Athens becomes a relaxed oasis of alfresco dining, and on hot summer weekends the locals flock to the beaches of the nearby Aegean Islands.

ABOVE RIGHT: *The Acropolis houses some of the world's finest monuments of antiquity and sits on a rock overlooking the city.* RIGHT: *The cathedral (Metropolis) built between 1840 and 1855.*

Ancient Treasures

While the 2004 Olympic Games improved the infrastructure and running of the city, its main attractions remain rooted firmly in the past. To say that Athens is crucial to the history of Western civilization is to state the obvious, as this is the city of the Acropolis, the Parthenon, and luminaries such as Sophocles (495–406BC) and Euripides (480–406BC). The Acropolis itself has an unmistakable presence as it hangs high above the city, rearing into view at the end of seemingly every street. Its landmark building, the Parthenon—a vast Doric temple constructed entirely from marble and built to house a grand statue of the god Athena dating from 447BC—is equally spectacular in the clear light of a bright Athenian day or when floodlit at night.

The historic treasures of Athens do not end with the Acropolis and often it seems as though history is wherever you look, such as the remains of the old Roman Agora and the Tower of the Winds—a first-century BC tower that functioned as a sundial and weather vane—and the Temple of Olympian Zeus, which had 104 columns (15 remain today) and was the largest temple in Greece in AD102.

BELOW: *The Sanctuary of Zeus.*
BELOW LEFT: *Fireworks display at the opening ceremony of the 2004 Olympic Games which were held in the city.*

THE STORY OF...

Early settlers had established a base on the city's north hill (where the Acropolis is located) by 3000BC. Athens emerged as the cultural center of classical Greece and, although its significance gradually diminished, it continued to flourish during the dominance of the Roman Empire. The collapse of the latter sealed the city's fate, condemning it to become a provincial town absorbed by the Byzantine Empire. In 1204 western crusaders took Athens before it was annexed by the Ottomans in 1456.

With the War of Independence (1821–32) Athens materialized as the capital of an emancipated Greece in 1833. However, autonomy did not end the country's hardships. During World War I, Greece joined the Allies in 1917 and then in 1920 entered a further war with Turkey. World War II saw 40,000 Athenians die during German and Italian occupation. Liberation in 1944 did not end the bloodshed as Greece entered a five-year civil war. Over the last five decades Greece has joined the EU, while Athens has evolved into a city capable of staging the world's biggest sporting event.

BELOW: *Shopping at a market stall in Monastiraki.*

Athens

1821
Greek War of Independence with the Ottoman Empire

1834
Athens becomes Greek capital

1981
Greece joins European Union

1985
Athens becomes first Cultural Capital of Europe

2004
Athens hosts Olympic Games

key dates

Barcelona

Population: 1,582,738

Highest points in Barcelona: Montjuic 670ft (192m) and Tibidabo 1,777ft (542m)

Area: City 39.6 sq miles (99 sq km); metropolitan area 200 sq miles (500 sq km)

8,153 cargo ships, 2,102 ferries, and 708 cruise ships used the Port of Barcelona in 2003

BELOW: *Chimneys on the roof of Gaudí's Casa Milá.*
BELOW RIGHT: *Café terraces on the Passeig de Gracia.*
BELOW LEFT: *A decoration by Gaudi in the Parc Güell.*

SAGRADA FAMÍLIA

Of all Barcelona's exuberant Modernist buildings, Antoni Gaudí's (1852–1926) unfinished Temple Expiatori de la Sagrada Família (Temple of the Holy Family) is the most famous, and a symbol of the city itself. Gaudí became involved with the project in 1891 and dedicated the next 40 years to it. His design perfectly illustrates his obsession with symbolic meaning and organic form, and the themes of the completed sections refer to his ideas of penance in atonement for the materialism of the modern world. Since his death, the fate of the building, where work still continues, has been the subject of much controversy.

Barcelona, capital of the autonomous region of Catalunya, stands on the shores of the northeast Spanish Mediterranean coast. It is home to a prosperous, design-conscious Catalan population, whose pride in its language, culture, and city has been justified by its increasing appeal to tourists from all over the world—a pride fuelled by the overwhelming success of the 1992 Olympic Games. This vibrant metropolis is contained by two hills, Tibidabo to the northwest and Montjuïc to the west, and, historically, has always been defined by the sea.

Today, the major port of Barcelona lies to the west of the city center, while the old port area, the Port Vell, has been transformed into a stylish recreational area linked by walkways via the old fishing quarter of Barceloneta to Port Olímpic, with its modern marinas and beaches, to the east. Behind the Port Vell, lies the heart of historic Barcelona, the Barri Gòtic (Gothic Quarter) and Ciutat Vella (Old City). Here stand the emblems of Barcelona's great past; the Roman walls, the cathedral, the Palau de la Generalitat (Government Building) which is still in use today, and scores of handsome medieval mansions lining narrow picturesque streets. This area is separated from the old Raval quarter by the world-famous promenade known as the Ramblas, which runs down from the Plaça de Catalunya, a huge square that divides old and new Barcelona. Behind the square stretches the Eixample (Extension), a regimented grid of wide streets erected in the 19th century and dissected by the Avenida Diagonal. Gràcia is the Eixample's showpiece neighborhood, an wealthy suburb crammed with lovely buildings, squares, and many of Barcelona's best stores. Some of the city's finest Modernist buildings, such as Gaudí's La Pedrera and his Sagrada Família, are sited in the Eixample, while tucked in northwest Barcelona is the beautiful medieval Pedralbes monastery.

Green Space

Barcelonans are blessed with superb parks for relaxation, ranging from the ex-Olympic site of Montjuïc, with its excellent sporting facilities, to the slopes of Tibidabo, the great inland hill, with its splendid views over the city to the sea. Parc Güell lies east of here, another airy green space that is also home to some of Gaudí's most idiosyncratic architectural creations in the form of mosaic-encrusted sculptures and sinuous buildings and towers. Other open areas are scattered throughout the city, many embellished with sculpture, lakes, and fountains, creating a backdrop to everyday life that reflects the city's obsession with style and design.

RIGHT: *Two women performing the sardana, the national dance of Catalan Barcelona.*
BELOW: *The Palau Sant Jordi stadium forms part of the 1992 Olympic complex in Montjuïc.*

THE STORY OF...

The Romans founded Barcelona around a natural harbor in 15BC, later erecting massive city walls around the town, which were to ensure its survival during the following tumultuous centuries. Roman rule was replaced by Visigothic rule around AD415, but in AD717 Barcelona fell to the Moors, remaining Arab until AD801. The city flourished as a trading center, becoming the capital of independent Catalunya in AD988, a position it held until the early 15th century. The next 300 years saw Barcelona subjugated to Spanish rule and later invaded by Napoleon Bonaparte's (1769–1821) army.

After 1813 Barcelona expanded as an industrial center, its prosperity based on the textile industry. The city was stridently anti-Nationalist during the Spanish Civil War (1936–39), but fell to Francisco Franco (1892–1975) in 1939, when Catalan language, identity, and culture were suppressed. With the restoration of parliamentary democracy in 1975, Barcelona regained its status as capital of an autonomous Catalunya, and its hosting of the 1992 Olympic games marked its re-emergence as one of the Mediterranean's most dynamic cities.

key dates

15BC
Roman colony of Barcino founded

AD988
Barcelona becomes capital of independent Catalunya

1714
Barcelona and Catalunya become a province of Spain

1939
Barcelona falls to Nationalists, Catalan identity and culture suppressed by Franco regime

1977
Re-establishment of Generalitat as parliament of autonomous region of Catalunya

Berlin

statistics

Population: 3.4 million

Municipal area: 347 sq miles (889 sq km), nine times that of Paris

Highest point: Teufelsberg, 394ft (120m)

The city's extensive public transportation system carries more than a billion passengers every year

Germany's capital city lies in the far east of the country, only about 90km (56 miles) from the border with Poland. With a population only half that of London or Paris, Berlin covers a much greater area; within the city limits are forests and farmland as well as lakes and rivers, and even the more densely populated areas are broken up by fine parks and extensive areas of *Kleingärten*, the leafy allotments which are a weekend refuge for many Berliners. Stretching right up to the famous Brandenburg Gate in the very center of the city is the vast Tiergarten, once the hunting park of Prussian royalty. No rival in size to either the Thames or Seine, the River Spree makes an attractive setting for the monumental neoclassical buildings of the central Mitte (Middle) district in the east, before winding westward past the new government quarter, then curving around the gardens of Charlottenburg Palace in the west. Before reunification, Mitte formed the center of East Berlin, its main thoroughfares being Friedrichstrasse and the broad boulevard of Unter den Linden. Cut off from the East, an alternative hub for West Berlin developed around the Zoo railway station, and although Friedrichstrasse has revived as a prime shopping street, the West's Kurfürstendamm avenue has kept its more exclusive reputation. Here, the imposing ruin of the Kaiser Wilhelm Memorial Church stands as a reminder of Berlin's wartime agony. East Berlin's most prominent structure is the TV Tower which is 1,197ft (365m) tall.

Unlike the inhabitants of Munich, intimately connected with their Bavarian hinterland, Berliners are a people apart. Energetic, witty, and irreverent, they have their own dialect, and delight in pricking any sort of pomposity. Every Berlin monument has its nickname: the Memorial Church is known as the "Hollow Tooth", and the "Washing Machine" exactly describes the head of government's new and rather boxy Chancellery. Berlin has always attracted outsiders, from Germany and beyond, particularly students and young people in search of alternative lifestyles. Many congregate in the densely built-up inner borough of Kreuzberg, which is also home to numerous Turks, the city's largest immigrant community.

THE BERLIN WALL

On the night of 13 August 1961, the East German government erected a crude barrier of breeze blocks and barbed wire between the two halves of divided Berlin, its aim being to stop the flight of its population to the freer and more prosperous West. Constant "improvements" to the Wall eventually made it an almost impenetrable barrier of smooth-faced concrete 13ft (4m) high, backed by other fortifications, watch towers, and a "death strip" which not even the numerous security guards were allowed to enter. Many East Germans lost their lives in their attempts to escape, though others succeeded by digging tunnels, swimming across lakes and canals, and even aboard home-made aircraft.

ABOVE: *Waving German flags by the Berlin Wall in 1989.*

Industrial Heartland

As the national capital, Berlin has seen an influx of civil servants and other government employees, but it has long been Germany's most important industrial city, famous for great engineering firms such as Siemens. Many of the inefficient industrial plants of East Berlin failed to survive reunification, and while unemployment remains a major problem, the future of the city's economy seems assured, given Berlin's central location in the expanded European Union.

RIGHT: *The remains of Berlin's neo-Romanesque Kaiser-Wilhelm-Gedächtniskirche, next to a modern addition of glass and steel.*

THE STORY OF...

A relatively insignificant trading city in the Middle Ages, Berlin began its rise to prominence in the 15th century as the seat of the Hohenzollern family, rulers first of Brandenburg, then Prussia, and finally the German Empire itself. The city's glory days began after the unification of Germany in 1871, when it expanded rapidly and great edifices such as the Reichstag—the Parliament building—were erected. World War I brought misery and near starvation to Berliners; the conflict ended with revolution and the abdication of the last Hohenzollern, Kaiser Wilhelm II.

In the short interval before the rise of Nazism, Berlin became a powerhouse of modern culture and was notorious for the extravagance of its nightlife. Then, British and American bombing and Soviet assault in 1945 left most of the city in ruins. Its division into eastern and western sectors by the victors of World War II grew ever starker; a Soviet blockade from 1947–48 was overcome when the western Allies organized the Berlin Airlift and brought in essential supplies, but the city had to wait until 1989 for the infamous Wall to be breached and for East and West to be reunited.

LEFT: *The glass dome of the Reichstag, designed by Sir Norman Foster.*
BELOW LEFT: *The central dome of the neo-Baroque Berliner Dom (cathedral).*

key dates

1244
First mention of Berlin as a town

1871
Berlin becomes capital of Germany and experiences rapid growth

1936
The Nazi regime impresses the world with its lavish staging of the Olympic Games

1989
Fall of the Wall dividing West Berlin from the Communist East

1999
Berlin becomes the seat of government of a reunited Germany

Bratislava

PETRŽALKA

More than a quarter of Bratislava's citizens live on the south bank of the River Danube, in what is claimed to be the biggest housing estate in Europe. Petržalka consists of innumerable multi-storey apartment blocks stretching from the riverside almost to the border with Austria. Construction of these buildings was begun by the communist government in 1976; assembled from concrete panels built on site, they are nicknamed *paneláks*. Should Petržalka ever become a city in its own right, it would be the third largest in Slovakia.

ABOVE: *Urban apartment buildings stretch into the distance.*

Despite its location on the River Danube in the extreme southwestern corner of Slovakia, Bratislava is the country's undisputed capital and by far its largest city. Its port is one of the most important on the Danube. In some ways the city's peripheral position in relation to the rest of the country is an asset; rail and motorway links tie it closely to Central European neighbors such as Austria and the Czech Republic, and the city and surrounding area are more buoyant economically than Slovakia's more remote eastern regions. New business parks and shopping malls spread eastward from the old built-up area over the flat Danube lowlands, where the country's modern international airport is also located. Young at heart, not least because of the 60,000 or so students attending its institutions of higher education, Bratislava is also an old city, with an exquisite and immaculately restored Old Town at the foot of its Castle Hill. Here, streets and squares freed from traffic are lined by the lovely Baroque palaces of the Hungarian aristocracy who once constituted the city's elite. The largest of these edifices, the Grassalkovitch Palace, just outside the line of the old walls, is now the official residence of the country's president.

In summer, café and restaurant life spills out into the open, while in winter people retreat to intimate little wine bars serving the produce of the vineyards that start within the city limits and stretch picturesquely northward along the lower slopes of the Little Carpathians. Bratislava Castle stands on the last of these rocky outcrops, overlooking the broad river; visible from far away, it owes its nickname, the "overturned table", to its four massive corner towers.

ABOVE RIGHT: *Door handle detail in the Town Hall.*

BELOW: *The view from the walls of Bratislava Castle.*

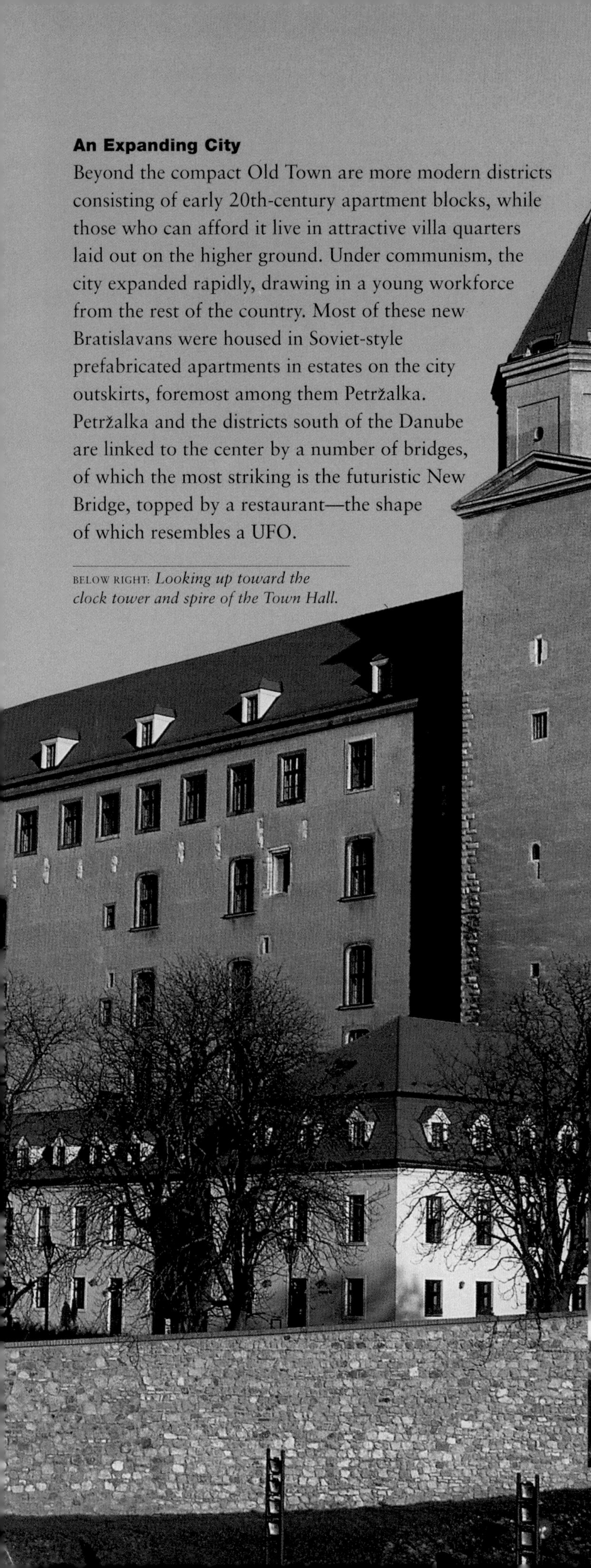

An Expanding City

Beyond the compact Old Town are more modern districts consisting of early 20th-century apartment blocks, while those who can afford it live in attractive villa quarters laid out on the higher ground. Under communism, the city expanded rapidly, drawing in a young workforce from the rest of the country. Most of these new Bratislavans were housed in Soviet-style prefabricated apartments in estates on the city outskirts, foremost among them Petržalka. Petržalka and the districts south of the Danube are linked to the center by a number of bridges, of which the most striking is the futuristic New Bridge, topped by a restaurant—the shape of which resembles a UFO.

BELOW RIGHT: *Looking up toward the clock tower and spire of the Town Hall.*

THE STORY OF...

The strategic heights overlooking the Danube offered a fine defensive site to successive waves of occupiers: Celts, Romans, and Slavs. In the 10th century, the area became part of Hungary, whose kings were to rule it for 1,000 years. As the Hungarian capital after 1536, Pozsony (as it was then known) enjoyed periods of great prosperity, particularly during the reign of Maria Theresa (1740–80). During the Napoleonic wars, the city was occupied twice by the French, and in 1811 the Castle burnt down.

By the beginning of the 20th century, the city's population was mostly German-speaking, and the town itself was known as Pressburg. Renamed Bratislava in 1919, in 1939 it became the capital of the short-lived, Nazi-dominated Slovak State. Its Slovak character was reinforced when its German and Hungarian inhabitants were expelled after World War II. The city's Jewish population had already perished in the Holocaust.

In 1989, Bratislava's inhabitants played a major role in the overthrow of the communist regime in Czechoslovakia.

BELOW: *View of the Old Town with the tower of St. Martin's Cathedral rising up against the skyline.*

key dates

NINTH CENTURY AD
Slav fortress built on Bratislava's Castle Hill

1291
Hungarian King András grants Bratislava full city privileges

1536
With Budapest occupied by the Turks, Bratislava is capital of Hungary

1918
Bratislava becomes part of Czechoslovakia

2004
Slovakia joins EU

Bruges

THE PROCESSION OF THE HOLY BLOOD

A rock-crystal phial inside a gold and silver reliquary in Bruges' Heilig-Bloedbasiliek (Basilica of the Holy Blood) holds a relic that the faithful believe to be drops of Christ's blood from his crucifixion. It is said to have been donated in 1150 by the Count of Flanders, Thierry of Alsace, who was given it as a reward for bravery during the Second Crusade. Each year on Ascension Day, the Catholic Bishop of Bruges leads the *Heilig-Bloedprocessie* (Procession of the Holy Blood) through the streets, followed by re-enactors wearing medieval and biblical garb, in a pageant dating from 1291.

ABOVE: *Girls in traditional costume during the Holy Blood Procession.*

The pride of Belgium's Dutch-speaking Flanders region, Bruges is among Europe's best preserved medieval towns, replete with Gothic monuments from its heyday as a great trading center. It sits in the north of the flat Flemish coastal plain, 9 miles (14km) from the North Sea, and its historic center is all but surrounded by an oval canal that outlines the shape of the vanished city walls. The Markt was the commercial heart in times past, a square surrounded by elegant gabled guildhalls that now mostly house bustling cafés, restaurants, and hotels. Here, too, is the city's most visible symbol, the Belfort (Belfry), a tower rising 276ft (84m) from its foundations in the vast Gothic Hallen (Market Halls), and dating from the 13th to the 15th centuries.

A short street connects the Markt to the Burg, a square that was traditionally Bruges' political heart, where the original castle, also called the Burg, was built in the ninth century. Here stands the ornate Stadhuis (Town Hall), the Landhuis van het Brugse Vrije (Palace of the Liberty of Bruges), and a Romanesque church, the Heilig-Bloedbasiliek (Basilica of the Holy Blood), which houses Bruges' famed relic of Christ's blood.

From these central points, narrow cobbled streets and canals radiate outward to the ring canal and the four surviving fortified city gates of an original nine. In its Groeninge Museum and Memling Museum, and on the walls of some churches, Bruges boasts some of the greatest late medieval European art, the works of the so-called Flemish Primitives. The Catholic cathedral that once stood on the Burg was destroyed in the 1790s during the French occupation, but many other churches, in styles ranging from Romanesque through Gothic to Baroque, grace the city.

Tourism and Lace

In the 19th century, British visitors discovered the eerie romanticism of the medieval town, and since then the popularity of Bruges as an international tourist destination has blossomed. After World War II, income from this source and from a general resurgence of commercial life has enabled the public authorities and private owners to repair the damage done by centuries of neglect—a process that continues to this day. Lace-making, which was an important industry in Bruges during the Middle Ages, has also experienced a revival. In addition to two lace museums, a myriad of stores sell lace souvenirs, but handmade, locally produced lace is expensive and hard to find. Bruges once again has an outlet to the sea, by canal to the harbor at Zeebrugge, and international trade has revived.

LEFT: *Costumes from the Holy Blood Procession which takes place on Ascension Day.*

THE STORY OF...

Signs of human life in this part of the Flemish coastal plain date from the start of the Christian era. It is not until the mid-ninth century, however, that there is evidence of the settlement's growing importance and of its name at the time: Bryggia. Bruges became the seat of the Counts of Flanders and later of the Dukes of Burgundy, who controlled an empire from here. The city became wealthy from textile production and maritime trade. In the Middle Ages, it was a member of the powerful, Baltic-based Hanseatic League and artists like Jan van Eyck (1385–1440) and Hans Memling (c1430–94) worked in the city.

By the 1480s the city's prosperity was waning when the Burgundians gave way to the Habsburgs, who transferred the capital to Ghent and Brussels. With the silting up of the outlet to the North Sea in 1520, Bruges declined. In the 19th century, then one of the poorest places in Belgium, it was rediscovered as a Gothic gem by the tourist industry.

BELOW LEFT: *Lace-making in progress.*

Bruges

key dates

AD850
Although the Bruges area has been settled since at least the first century AD, a castle is first established about this time

1150
Count of Flanders Thierry of Alsace is said to return from the Second Crusade with a relic of Christ's holy blood

1482
Mary, Duchess of Burgundy, dies in a riding accident, bringing to an end the Burgundian line and Bruges' role as the Burgundian capital

1892
Bruges-la-Morte (Dead Bruges), a novel by Georges Rodenbach, is published, starting the romantic legend of the city that leads to it being a center of tourism today

2002
Bruges is one of Europe's Capitals of Culture and builds the new Concertgebouw Concert Hall to celebrate

Brussels

statistics

Population: 117,000
(20,000 in the Old Town)

Number of states
represented at the
European Commission
and Parliament: 25

Magnification of the iron
crystal represented by
the Atomium monument:
165 billion

Number of costumes
belonging to the *Manneken-
Pis* statue (2005): 750
(increasing annually by
12–20)

CAPITAL OF EUROPE

There is, officially, no such thing
as a "capital of Europe." Entirely
unofficially, however, there is no
doubt about what city the citizens of
European Union member states look
to for EU subsidies, rules, and
regulations, and bureaucratic
procedures—and also for advancing
the vision of a peaceful, free, and
united Europe. Brussels is home
to the European Commission, the
European Parliament, and the
Council of Europe, and so it has the
respective headquarters and takes
the title, not so much by design as
by default.

ABOVE: *European Parliament
interior sculpture.*

russels, located in west-central Belgium, on the dividing line between
Germanic northern Europe and the Latin south, is bilingual: French and
Dutch. The main square is called the Grand-Place in French and the Grote
Markt in Dutch, while the Royal Mint Theater opera house is the Théâtre
Royal de la Monnaie in French and the Koninklijke Munttheater in Dutch. In addition
to being the capital of Belgium, it is also the capital of Belgium's Dutch-speaking region
of Flanders. However, there are in fact more French speakers in Brussels—and nowadays,
in keeping with its high international profile, many English speakers too, not to mention
speakers of other languages from around the world. In the space of a few decades,
Brussels has been transformed from a provincial city to a cosmopolitan one.

ABOVE: *Sablon Square antique market.* RIGHT: *Grand-Place flower market.*

The Grand-Place, surrounded by elegant 17th-century
guildhouses, on which stands the Hôtel de Ville (Town
Hall) with its elaborate Gothic tracery, has been the heart
of the city since its early days. It stands in the Basse-Ville
(Lower City), on the low-lying plain of the River Senne
(the river was hidden away under brick arches in the 19th century for health reasons).
Close to the Grand-Place is that endearingly cheeky symbol of Brussels, *Manneken-Pis*,
a bronze sculpture of a little boy, often wearing one of the specially made costumes that
admirers both at home and abroad have donated to him. Historically, the city's rulers
have had their palaces amid the higher ground of the Haute-Ville (Upper City), and so
it is today. The Palais Royal (Royal Palace) and the Palais de la Nation (the Parliament
building), are located there. A bit more distant are the grandiose buildings that house the
European Union's institutions.

Not Just Europe

While the international focus on Brussels rests primarily on its EU role, in the city itself
most of the populace have other things on their mind. Quality of life is taken seriously,
with many fine, hearty restaurants and easy access to the 450 different Belgian beers. The
city is also one of the spiritual homes of art nouveau architecture and design, of surrealist
art, and of comic books raised to the status of an art (the so-called Ninth Art)—the
buildings of Victor Horta (1861–1947), the paintings of René Magritte (1898–1967), and
the antics of Hergé's (Georges Rémi, 1907–83) irrepressible *Tintin* are a testament to this.

THE STORY OF...

Brussels emerges slowly out of the mists of the Dark Ages. Its story begins, perhaps, at the end of the sixth century, when St. Géry is said to have founded a settlement on an island in the River Senne. By AD979 there was a castle on the island, which controlled the river crossing on the important trade route from Bruges to Cologne. At first a fiefdom of the Counts of Leuven, the growing city soon became the most important possession of the Dukes of Brabant, and by the 15th century, of the far more powerful Dukes of Burgundy and their successors, the Habsburg Emperors.

By this route, Brussels became one of the capitals of a vast empire, but declined in influence when the center of power shifted from the Low Countries to Spain. After the Protestant Dutch provinces broke away, Brussels remained the capital of the Spanish and then the Austrian Low Countries, until revolutionary France invaded in 1795. At Waterloo, outside Brussels, Napoleon Bonaparte's (1769–1821) career of conquest came to an end. Brussels has been the capital of Belgium since 1830.

BACKGROUND: *The European Parliament district, Le Caprice des Dieux.*
LEFT: *The* Mannekin Pis *fountain.*

ABOVE: *Locals in costume for the Ommegang Procession in July.*

ABOVE: *The Atomium, built for the 1958 World Fair.*

key dates

AD979
Duke Charles of Lorraine builds a castle in Brussels, and this is now considered the city's founding date

1402
Building of the magnificent Gothic Hôtel de Ville (Town Hall) on the Grand-Place begins

1815
Napoleon is defeated at the decisive Battle of Waterloo, just outside Brussels

1889
Brussels is made a semi-autonomous region of the new federal Belgian state: Brussels-Capital Region

2002
Euro replaces Belgian franc as the unit of currency

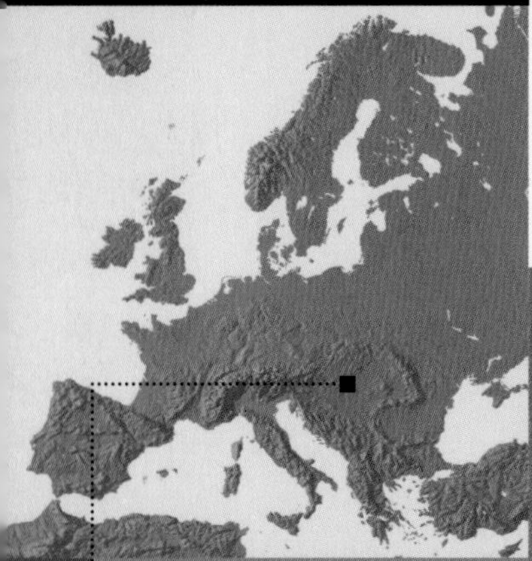

Budapest

Population: 1.8 million, around one-fifth of the population of Hungary

Area: Budapest has 23 districts, 16 on the Pest side of the River Danube, 6 on the Buda side, and 1 district on Csepel Island in the Danube

Mean annual temperature: 52.16°F (11.2°C)

Average waterflow of the Danube at Budapest: 70,628 cubic feet (2,000 cubic meters) per second

COUNT ISTVÁN SZÉCHENYI AND THE CHAIN BRIDGE

The great reformer, Count Széchenyi, was inspired to initiate Budapest's Chain Bridge across the Danube, after being unable to cross the treacherous winter river to attend his father's funeral in 1820. He called to Budapest an English architect, William Tierney Clark, and a Scottish engineer, Adam Clark, the latter presiding over the project until its completion in 1848. Not only was this the first Danube bridge in Hungary, it was also a symbol of modernization, whereby the traditionally tax-exempt nobles (to their indignation) were obliged to pay the toll for crossing it. Széchenyi's other major reforms included founding the Academy of Sciences, the National Theater, and the Danube Steamship Company.

RIGHT: *Traffic crossing the Chain Bridge, Budapest's first permanent stone bridge across the River Danube.*

The Danube, here flowing north-south, divides Budapest in half. The original three cities (Buda and Óbuda on the west bank, and Pest, gateway to the Great Hungarian Plain, on the east bank) were united in 1873. While the government bureaucracy lived and worked in Buda, Pest was the center of commerce. The huge Csepel Island stretching downstream to the south became a center of heavy industry during the 19th century. With numerous spas, Budapest's waters have been exploited down the ages by the Celts, Romans, Turks (some of whose baths still exist), and the Hungarians themselves.

The Treaty of Trianon after World War I greatly reduced the cosmopolitan look of the city (for instance, the large Serb population of the 19th century largely vanished). However, during World War II a large number of Budapest Jews survived and some returned, helping to shape Hungarian culture—particularly in the arts, law, and in business. Judaism is represented by the Nagyzsinagóga (Great Synagogue) in Dohány utca, while the Lutherans (about four percent of Hungarians) and the Calvinists (around 20 percent) have their own churches on Deák tér and Kálvin tér (Deák and Calvin Squares). The Serb and Greek Orthodox faiths are also present, while the noblest churches (the cathedral in Pest and the

BELOW RIGHT: *Budapest's Inner City Parish Church (Belvarosi) was rebuilt in Baroque style between 1725 and 1739.*
BELOW: *The neo-Romanesque Fisherman's Bastion illuminated at night.*

Matthias Church on Castle Hill) are Roman Catholic (about 65 percent of all Hungarians).

Buda's Castle Hill contains the reconstructed Royal Palace (now the National Gallery) and the old town with its Gothic and Baroque remnants. Pest is cut by 19th-century boulevards lined with grand neo-Renaissance apartment blocks and boasting some monuments in Ödön Lechner's (1845–1914) "National Style", influenced by art nouveau. Hösök tere (Heroes Square) at the end of the greatest boulevard (Andrássy út) is the patriotic focus of Pest, with its monumental equestrian statue of the seven leaders of the original Magyar tribes who occupied Hungary in AD896.

Changing Times

Since the fall of communism in 1989, Hungary's economy has made the switch from polluting heavy industries to high tech industries (such as software writing), services, and tourism. In May 2004 Hungary joined the EU, an alliance from which it is hoped that Budapest—and the country as a whole—will benefit greatly.

BELOW RIGHT: *Commuters crossing the sunken plaza, which leads into the neo-Renaissance Eastern Railway Station.*

BACKGROUND: *Statues at the Cemetery of Communist Monuments.*

THE STORY OF...

The Eraviscan Celtic tribe who lived at the spas of Buda and Pest called the place "abundant waters", a name Latinized to "Aquincum" under Roman rule until the fourth century AD. Magyars (Hungarians) settled at this strategic crossing point on the Danube around AD896. The native Árpád dynasty of kings founded by King Stephen, who converted the nation to Chistianity, died out in 1300. The succeeding Anjou rulers built up the palace on Buda Hill, but the city fell to the Turks in 1541. Around 145 years later, Buda and Pest were recaptured and repopulated by the Habsburgs.

Throughout the 18th and 19th centuries, Hungarian national consciousness increased, culminating in the War of Independence of 1848–49. Following the suppression of this revolution, the Habsburgs sought a "Compromise" with Hungary in 1867, to form the Austro-Hungarian Empire. Budapest grew into a great metropolis in the late 19th century, but two World Wars destroyed its prosperity. In 1948 it fell under communism, which was challenged by a failed uprising in 1956.

Only in 1989 did freedom return to Budapest, which is now a vibrant city with restored buildings and spas frequented by visitors from home and abroad.

1241
The first fortress is built on Buda Hill, after the Tartar hordes had laid waste Hungary

1485
Matthias I (Corvinus) establishes a glittering Renaissance court at Buda

1686
Christian armies reconquer Buda and Pest, which had been under Turkish rule since 1541

1872–73
The separate cities of Pest, Óbuda, and Buda are formally united to create the metropolis of Budapest

1956
The popular uprising against Stalinism in Budapest (and elsewhere in Hungary) is crushed by the Soviet Union, whose puppet government thereafter pursues its idiosyncratic version of "goulash" communism

Dublin

statistics

Population: 496,000

Phoenix Park: largest city park in Europe 1,728 acres (700 ha)

Glasses of Guinness consumed in 150 countries: an estimated 10 million

Oldest University in Ireland: Trinity College (1592)

ST. PATRICK'S FESTIVAL

Each year, for five days—usually from 16–20 March—the streets of Dublin are taken over by a world-class festival of carnival-style parades, fireworks, visual arts, and Ireland's largest outdoor dance event. Established by the Government of Ireland in 1995 as the St. Patrick's "Day" Festival and held for the first time in 1996, the event aims to reflect the talents and achievements of Irish people and acts as a showcase for the many skills of the people of Ireland, from every background. The Festival takes 18 months to prepare and attracts 1.2 million people.

apital and largest city of the Republic of Ireland, Dublin sits at the mouth of the River Liffey which empties into Dublin Bay and splits the city into a north/south divide. Traditionally, those who lived on the Northside were said to be more working class while the majority of Southsiders were wealthier, although now that term refers to anyone from either side who is considered middle class.

Dublin is the cultural center of Ireland and has a dual personality. It retains many of its Gaelic names and roots, whilst keeping up with the modern European world. Around 48 percent of the population are under 35 years of age. Migrants sweep in from the countryside and students from the city's three universities bolster a vibrant social scene which centers on the rejuvenated Temple Bar area. Dubliners are fiercely proud of their city and like to party. Irish dancing, which has seen a growth in popularity around the globe, flourishes here. Set dancing, that is stepping in tune with precision to the beat of a *céili* band, is taught in schools, while music inspired by the harp, fiddle, tin whistle, and *bodrán* (drum) is a spontaneous art form. This legacy of Irish music spawns innovation among modern-day musicians, from The Corrs to the rock band U2.

The historic heart of the city lies south of the River Liffey. Mainly Georgian in appearance, it has many important buildings. The University of Dublin dates from 1592 when Trinity College was established by Royal Charter under Elizabeth I, and protects the Book of Kells, written by Irish monks in the ninth century. Along the classical Georgian houses of Merrion Street is No 24, reputedly the birthplace of the First Duke of Wellington (1769–1852). In the Museum district are the National Gallery, Natural History Museum, and Leinster House, seat of the Irish National Parliament.

The Legacy of Guinness

Nothing distracts a Dublin bartender as he waits for a pint of Guinness to settle with a thick, creamy head. Ireland's national drink is brewed at the Guinness Storehouse in St. James' Gate. In 1759 Arthur Guinness opened a small brewery and began producing ale. Though one of the most technologically advanced breweries in the world, the Storehouse no longer delivers the amount of Guinness it used to. In the 1970s the headquarters moved to London and the several thousand-strong workforce was reduced to 600.

BELOW: *Ha'Penny Bridge across the River Liffey.*
BELOW RIGHT: *The Reading Room at the National Library*

THE STORY OF...

Vikings settled in the 10th century in this area known as Dyfflin which had two names, An Dubh Linn (Black Pool) and Ath Cliath (Hurdle Ford). Following a victory by the Celts, the settlement was invaded by Anglo-Normans, and Dublin Castle was built in 1207 as the seat of British rule. The English dominated under King Henry II and in the 17th century English statesman Oliver Cromwell (1599–1658) took possession. Britain's second city prospered and its architecture grew elegant and grand. However, by the 1800s the city was in decline as a result of peasants fleeing poverty in the countryside.

The potato blight of 1845–47, a disastrous famine, left many peasants starving or caused them to emigrate in their masses to America. Following the 1916 Uprising against the British, independence was won in 1922, which in turn was followed by civil war. Modernization began in the 1960s and in 1973 Dublin gained entry into the European Union. Since then it has been shaking off its colonial past to emerge culturally fashionable and independently Irish.

FAR LEFT: *Trinity College's Old Library.*
LEFT: *Kilmainham Gaol.*

key dates

10TH CENTURY
Vikings establish settlement of Dyfflin

1922
Irish Free State created

1949
Dublin becomes capital of the Republic of Ireland

1973
Republic of Ireland enters the European Union

1991
Dublin designated European City of Culture

Population: 55,638 on 118 separate islands

Foreign visitors to Dubrovnik in 2003: 308,757

Dubrovnik hosted its 55th annual summer festival (The Dubrovnik Summer Festival) in July and August 2004

70 percent of the city's buildings suffered direct hits during the 1991–92 siege

DUBROVNIK FESTIVAL

Known locally as *Libertas* (liberty) Dubrovnik's annual summer festival (held in July and August) is a celebration of the city's independence and freedom. The first festival was held in 1949, although it has its origins in the 16th century. Two constants have been the red Libertas flag that hangs proudly on Orlando's column during the festival and high quality performances by artists from around the world. Historic venues that are usually closed to tourists open their doors, while outdoor spaces are transformed into open-air venues. Amazingly, the festival went ahead during the 1990s siege with brave actors performing against the backdrop of war.

ABOVE: *Performers entertaining the crowds at the Dubrovnik Festival.*

Dubrovnik

ocated on the central Adriatic coast, Dubrovnik is one of Europe's most attractive cities and the pride and joy of many Croatians. This fortified city, whose medieval walls have never been breached by an invading army, flanked by limestone cliffs and the clear, warm, turquoise sea wins over visitors with its relaxed Mediterranean living. In addition, Dubrovnik's compact Old City is a living museum that illuminates the city's past, with the majority of Baroque-style buildings within the Old City dating from the 17th century when the city was painstakingly reconstructed after the devastating earthquake of 1667. Statues of the city's patron saint, St. Blaise, located throughout the old center serve as ever-present reminders of Dubrovnik's quest for liberty and freedom. Meanwhile the Rector's Palace (an 18th-century reconstruction) is symbolic of the principle of democracy upon which the Republic of Dubrovnik was founded. From the 16th to 18th centuries the palace was home to the republic's figurehead, the Rector, but in effect it became a virtual prison as he was prevented from contacting the outside world, unless on official business, during his month in office. This meant that the Rector could not even see his family.

Today the Old City is no staid museum piece, as it remains central to life in Dubrovnik. Within its solid stone walls there is a lively daily market, where organic produce is the norm and citizens hang their laundry over the street to dry. The plethora of buzzing sidewalk cafés and seafood restaurants that exist alongside this traditional way of life illustrates the careful balance that authorities have managed to maintain, ensuring that tourism does not eradicate real life from the city's historic heart.

BELOW: *Floodlit Minceta Tower.*

A City in Harmony

During its time as an independent republic (1526–1806), Dubrovnik spawned great artistic, literary, and scientific talent, and the city remains at the heart of Croatia's cultural identity, with *Libertas* being at the center of the events calendar. In Gundulic Square, the statue of Ivan Gundulic (1589–1638)—the Dubrovnik born bard heralded as one of Croatia's greatest poets—encapsulates the romantic spirit of the city's population and the Croatian nation as a whole. This passion is also evident in the name that many locals proudly apply to their city, affectionately calling her *skladna*. In Croatian the term refers to harmony, a perfect moniker for a city in total harmony with her surrounds.

THE STORY OF...

The "Pearl of the Adriatic" began life as Ragusa, founded by a small group of refugees who had fled from the Slavs invading nearby Epidaurum (present-day Cavtat). Until 1526 Dubrovnik was, at different times, a protectorate of the Byzantine Empire, the Venetian Republic, and Hungary. From the 16th to 18th centuries the independent Dubrovnik Republic developed a strong economy and a navy to contain the threat of Venice. French invasion in 1806 stripped the city of its independence and, in 1809, made it part of the Illyrian provinces.

In 1815 Dubrovnik fell under Austrian (later Austro-Hungarian) rule, and then became part of the Kingdom of the Serbs, Croats and Slovenes (later Yugoslavia) after World War I. World War II saw the city pass briefly into Italian and then German control before returning to Yugoslavia in 1945. The declaration of Croatian independence (June 1991) resulted in the brutal siege of Dubrovnik with the first Serbian and Montenegrin shells hitting the city in October 1991. Seven months later, a battered Dubrovnik emerged as part of the Republic of Croatia.

Dubrovnik

key dates

AD614
Settlement of Dubrovnik (then called Ragusa) is established

1205
Dubrovnik is ruled by the Venetian Republic

1815
Congress of Vienna assigns Dubrovnik to Vienna

1918
Becomes part of the Kingdom of Serbs, Croats and Slovenes

1991
Dubrovnik comes under siege as Serb and Montenegrin forces shell the city

Edinburgh

- Population: 455,000
- Highest hill: Arthur's Seat at 822ft (250m)
- Plants in the floral clock in Princes Street: 2,000
- More booksellers per head of population than any other city in Britain

Set on the east coast of Scotland on the south shore of the Firth of Forth, Edinburgh is built on a series of extinct volcanoes. The historic capital of Scotland, Edinburgh encompasses the beauty, humor and drama of Scotland. Its people thrive in a vibrant atmosphere, fuelled by students from four universities, a top financial center, arts, literature and a tourism industry which brings in £2 billion a year. The redevelopment of the old sea port at Leith Harbor has allowed cruise liners from Scandinavia and the Continent to bring in even more visitors, many stopping to see the Royal Yacht *Britannia* which is berthed in the new Ocean Terminal. Locals escape to Arthur's Seat, a crag of the main volcano which overlooks the city, and is a quiet place to think.

Edinburgh Castle, atop an extinct volcanic crag, dominates the skyline and is a former residence of kings and queens, and retainer of the crown jewels. From the Castle, the Old Town rambles along the spine of the volcanic ridge and is split into two by Princes Street Gardens. The Royal Mile, as it is known, ends at the Palace of Holyroodhouse, home of the monarchs, including Mary Queen of Scots (1542–87) whose bedchamber is one of the most famous rooms in the world. Spreading from this spine is a medieval labyrinth of tiny streets, or wynds, with high-rise houses and underground passageways. The New Town was built to the north of Princes Street, in neoclassical Georgian townhouses; many designed by the architect Robert Adam (1728–92).

BELOW: *The tower of the Balmoral Hotel.*
BELOW RIGHT: *Cavalry marching at the Military Tattoo on the Castle Esplanade.*

BELOW: *Edinburgh (also known as "Auld Reekie" and "the Athens of the north"), viewed from Calton Hill.*

EDINBURGH INTERNATIONAL FESTIVAL

Seen as a post-World War II remedy to reunite Europe through culture, the Edinburgh International Festival began in 1947. It is now an annual event and has been joined by others, including the Fringe, film, book and jazz Festivals, and the Edinurgh Military Tattoo. Each August and September, they transform the city into an arts extravaganza with performances in theaters, streets, churches, tents and galleries, for which many millions of tickets are sold. The Festival rightly claims to be the largest arts festival in the world.

ABOVE: *A juggler entertaining during the Edinburgh Fringe Festival.*

At the foot of the Royal Mile is the controversial Scottish Parliament Building. In 1998, following a competition to find a suitable architect, Barcelona architect Enric Miralles (1955–2000) was chosen to design the new building. Miralles died during through the project which was initially estimated to cost around £50 million, but in fact cost £431 million. A series of oval-shaped structures containing meeting rooms, galleries, and chambers, the parliament building was officially opened in August 2004 by Her Majesty the Queen, Elizabeth II (b. 1926).

Great Minds

Over the centuries, many great masters of prose and poetry were either born, studied, or spent time in Edinburgh, including Daniel Defoe (1661–1731), David Hume (1711-1776), Adam Smith (1723-1790), Robert Burns (1759–96), Sir Walter Scott (1771–1832), and more recently Muriel Spark (b. 1918), Irvine Welsh (b. 1961) and Ian Rankin (b. 1960). Robert Louis Stevenson (1850–94) based his character in *The Strange Case of Dr Jekyll and Mr Hyde* on local arch criminal Deacon Brodie, while Sir Arthur Conan Doyle (1859–1930) found inspiration for Sherlock Holmes in an Edinburgh university professor whose excellent powers of deduction helped police solve crimes.

ABOVE: *John Knox's House on the Royal Mile.*

THE STORY OF...

The city began with a hillfort of the Celtic tribe, Gododdin, on the volcanic crag of Castle Hill (or Rock). In AD638 Scotland was conquered by the Northumbrians who called the city Edinburgh. In the 11th century King Malcolm II defeated the Northumbrians and the Rock became Scottish. Holyrood Abbey was completed in 1141 and various religious orders began to arrive, building churches and abbeys.

In 1296 Edinburgh was besieged by English King Edward I's forces, but in 1313 the city was recaptured. In 1328 the Treaty of Edinburgh was signed, ending wars of independence with England. Meanwhile, the city had expanded from Castle Hill down the Royal Mile, branching out, yet becoming overcrowded and polluted. In the 18th century—the "Age of Improvement and Enlightenment"— the New Town was built to house noblemen and the learned.

During the Victorian era, the city suffered due to unemployment, riots, and epidemics of cholera. It has since regained its crown through its arts scene, its status as a major tourist destination and as the new home of democracy.

BEFORE SEVENTH CENTURY
Celtic tribe Goddodin establish a hillfort on Castle Hill

1296
English capture Castle Hill

1824
Great Fire devastates the densely-packed Old Town

1999
Scottish Parliament re-established

2004
Scottish Parliament Building opened by Her Majesty the Queen, Elizabeth II

LEFT: *The statue of the little dog, Greyfriar's Bobby.*

29

statistics

- Population: 475,337
- Tourist numbers (2003): 2.1 million
- Main industries: tourism, textile manufacture, leather goods, metalwork, pharmaceuticals, glass and ceramic production, jewelry and craftwork
- UNESCO calculates that 30 percent of the world's most important works of art are located in Florence

LORENZO DE' MEDICI, IL MAGNIFICO

Lorenzo de' Medici (1449–92) was a scion of the banking dynasty that controlled Florence from the 14th to 18th centuries. His lifetime coincided with the greatest achievements of the Renaissance, in great part due to the climate of intellectual freedom and tolerance that he encouraged. An accomplished poet and philosopher, he surrounded himself with the age's greatest intellectual and artistic talents, patronizing Sandro Botticelli (1447–1515) and the young Michelangelo Buonarroti (1475–1564). He was an accomplished diplomat, keeping the constantly quarrelling Italian states on a relatively even keel, and presenting himself as *primus inter pares* (first among equals), the extent of his domination of Florence kept relatively hidden.

RIGHT: *The cupola of the Basilica of Santa Maria del Fiore.*

Florence

lorence, the capital of the region of Tuscany, lies in a valley on either side of the River Arno, and attracts over 2 million visitors a year, drawn by the city's unique artistic legacy, synonymous with the flowering of the Italian Renaissance. Florence is among the most prosperous cities in Italy, and the *centro storico* (historic center) is surrounded by a sprawl of suburbs and industrial complexes, whose factories contribute to the occasional poor air quality. The superb architecture is severe and uncompromising, and the city's narrow streets are crowded, traffic-ridden, and noisy, making Florence less immediately pleasurable for many visitors than other major Italian art centers.

The heart of the old city lies on the north bank of the Arno, and is centered around the complex of the Duomo (cathedral), surmounted by Brunelleschi's (1377–1446) great dome. South from here lies the Piazza della Signoria, whose main building is the Palazzo Vecchio, once the seat of Florence's government, and still used by the city council. Just off the Piazza stretches the Uffizi, home to what is arguably the world's most famous art gallery, housing a staggering collection of great Renaissance paintings. Between and around these two focal points are great palaces, museums, and churches, all linked by some of Italy's most elegant shopping streets, home to big designer names. South of the river is the Palazzo Pitti, a huge Medici palace containing five museums and backed by the Giardini di Boboli, a wonderfully formal park rich in tree-lined alleys, topiary, and fountains. This southern area, the Oltrarno, has other fine churches and thriving artisan workshops of every kind, while the Piazzale Michelangelo, higher up the hill, gives superb views over the river, (which is spanned by bridges such as the famous Ponte Vecchio), to the whole city and its outlying hills.

Quality of Life

Florence has a thriving arts scene, patronized at the top end by its well-heeled citizens, who can enjoy a year-round cultural diet of art shows, opera, theater, and ballet, while the large student population ensures the full range of clubs and live-music venues. Restaurants, bars, and cafés are constantly packed, shopping is among the best in Italy, and Florentines and visitors can enjoy a wide range of spectator and participatory sports. These benefits have to be balanced against a constant, year-round tourist presence, placing immense burdens on the city council, which has to balance the 21st-century needs of its citizens against Florence's role as one of the world's most outstanding artistic treasure-houses, with all that that implies.

RIGHT: *Michelangelo's* David *statue at the Galleria dell'Accademia.*
BELOW RIGHT: *The* Ponte Vecchio *over the River Arno.*

THE STORY OF...

Founded in 59BC by Julius Caesar (100–44BC), Florence was a substantial walled settlement by the eighth century, when it became part of the Holy Roman Empire. In 1115 the city became a free *Comune* (city-state) run by a 100-strong assembly. Banking and trade flourished, and a powerful oligarchy of merchant princes emerged, pre-eminent among whom was the Medici family, which controlled the city from 1458.

Under the Medicis, the Renaissance blossomed, with architects, sculptors, and artists embellishing the city. With some interruptions, the Medicis ruled Florence and Tuscany until 1743, the city coming under French rule between 1799 and 1814. From 1865 to 1870, Florence was the capital of the newly united Italy, and afterward remained capital of Tuscany, one of the richest regions in Italy.

The 20th century saw tourist numbers rise and world attention focused on the city following the catastrophic floods of 1966 and again after the 1993 Uffizi bombing. Florence today has to balance her role as an art city of immense importance with that of a regional capital and industrial center.

59BC
Florentia is founded by Julius Caesar

1115
Formation of the first Comune; Florence emerges as city-state

1469–92
Rule of Lorenzo de' Medici "il Magnifico"; full flowering of Florentine Renaissance

1743
Last Medici, Anna Maria Luisa, dies; art collections bequeathed to city of Florence

1966
River Arno bursts its banks leading to catastrophic flooding of the city

Geneva

- Population: 187,758
- Over 44 percent of city's inhabitants are foreigners
- 22 international organizations have their headquarters in the city
- Lake Geneva, with a capacity of 23.5 trillion gal (89 trillion litres), is the largest freshwater lake in Western Europe

S witzerland's third largest city, after Zurich and Basel, is dramatically situated on the southwestern shores of Lac Léman (Lake Geneva) and flanked by the Alps. This flat, mainly French-speaking, and cosmopolitan city is home to a large number of non-government organizations (NGOs), such as the International Red Cross, the United Nations, and the World Health Organization, consulates and diplomatic missions, which are all attracted by the city's modern and efficient infrastructure. Swiss neutrality also makes Geneva a popular place for politically sensitive negotiations. A considerable number of international corporations have located the Swiss arm of their operations in Geneva, with commerce and industry (engineering, construction, pharmaceutical, chemical, jewellery manufacturing, electronics, IT, and telecommunications) all contributing to the city's thriving economy. Geneva is also important as an oasis of private banking and as the centre for the manufacturing of Swiss watches, renowned throughout the world as high-quality precision timepieces.

The eclectic range of businesses and international institutions located in the city are complemented by an equally diverse and multicultural population, with over 40 percent of Geneva's inhabitants being well-heeled expatriate workers. The prevalence of diplomats and wealthy individuals from around the globe means that luxury cars, large mansion houses, and private yachts are all part of the city's fabric, as are myriad high-quality international restaurants.

JET D'EAU

Since its construction in 1891, the Jet d'Eau (Water Fountain) has gradually become one of the city's icons. Spurting high over Lake Geneva the fountain projects a continuous stream of water, weighing 7 tonnes, 459ft (140m) into the air at a speed of 125mph (200kph). Spawned from a practical need to release unneeded water pressure at night, when Geneva's busy craft machines were sleeping, Europe's tallest water fountain replaced an earlier safety valve (which only produced spurts a few metres tall). Since 1930 it has been illuminated at night.

Natural and Cultural Attractions

When they are not working hard, Genevans like nothing better than to shed their supposed reserve and take advantage of the city's location and open green spaces. On warm sunny days the Parc des Bastions and the Jardin Anglais (English Garden) fill with people, as do the various cruises that ply the waters of Lake Geneva. Other favourite haunts of the locals, in both summer and winter, are the nearby Jura Mountains and the Alps.

In inclement weather Genevans turn to the city's cultural attractions, which include over 30 museums that champion everything from the history of art and science to the philosophies of Voltaire. Meanwhile the Cathédrale de St. Pierre is an austere reminder of the city's role as the birthplace of Calvinism—relics dating from the fourth century have also been excavated from beneath the church's foundations. The colossal Monument de la Réformation also pays tribute to the sermons of Calvin, Knox, and their followers. Inscribed on the memorial is the Latin phrase *Post Tenebras Lux*, meaning "After Darkness, Light" which Geneva has adopted as a symbol of the city and an eternal reminder of its democratic values.

LEFT: *Montreux Palace, Lake Geneva.*
BELOW RIGHT: *A flower clock design in the ornamental gardens.*

THE STORY OF...

Geneva's history dates back 5,000 years to when a settlement was first established on the shores of Lake Geneva. Down the centuries the city fell under Roman, Burgundian, Frankish, German, and French rule before joining the Swiss Confederation and becoming a Swiss Canton (region) in 1814. Geneva prospered during the 19th century, with the Swiss tradition of watch-making taking hold; financial and commercial institutions also flourished at this time.

A more unique aspect of Geneva's history is its role at the heart of the Protestant Reformation during the 16th century, with John Calvin (1509–64) and John Knox (1505–72), who both espoused the restrictive Calvinist doctrine, which forbade dancing and the wearing of jewellery, from the city's pulpits. During the Reformation, Geneva became a haven for French and Italian Protestants fleeing religious persecution. As the Calvinist dogma softened, Geneva spawned great intellectual talent, attracting the likes of Jean-Jacque Rosseau (1712–78) and Voltaire (1694–78), two 18th-century writers who championed democracy, reflecting the ethos of the city itself.

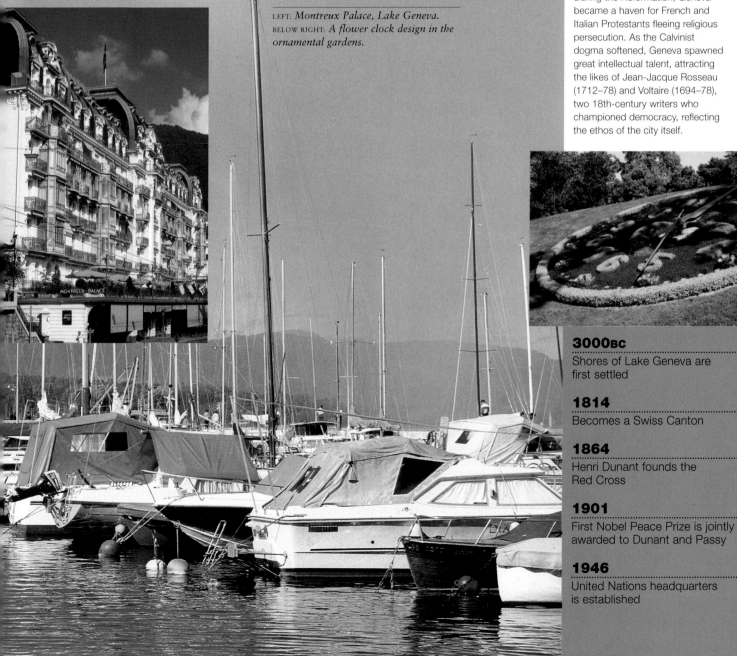

key dates

3000BC
Shores of Lake Geneva are first settled

1814
Becomes a Swiss Canton

1864
Henri Dunant founds the Red Cross

1901
First Nobel Peace Prize is jointly awarded to Dunant and Passy

1946
United Nations headquarters is established

Helsinki

- Population: 559,330
- 315 offshore islands
- Length of mainland shoreline: 61 miles (98km)
- Helsinki has a bigger sea area (193 sq miles/500 sq km) than it does land (71 sq miles/186 sq km)

ying out on a limb at the northeastern corner of Europe, Helsinki stares out toward the endless expanse of Russia and the Baltic Sea. Straddling a wide peninsula and a string of islands, the city looks far bigger than its population of just over half a million suggests. It had long been a forgotten city, ignored by travelers as much as European political leaders, but that began to change when Europe's northernmost capital took center stage as the European City of Culture in 2000. Slowly but surely visitors have been discovering one of Europe's last great secrets, a city often as much Russian in character as it is Scandinavian.

East Meets West

Helsinki is a modern and efficient city, with trams and buses nipping around wide streets, a wealth of stores, and all the usual fast-food outlets. Compared to her slick Scandinavian cousins Copenhagen and Stockholm, Helsinki is rougher around the edges. Nestling next

SUOMENLINNA

Suomenlinna (Sea Fortress) is the most famous of the islands that litter the bay in front of Helsinki. Home to 900 people, the island is dominated by a mighty fortress that traditionally guarded against invasion from the sea. Constructed by the Swedes (who called it Sveaborg) in 1748, the fortress houses the Ehrensvard Museum, which breathes life into Suomenlinna's colorful past including the 1808 Russian blockade, bombardment during the Crimean War, and its role as a naval defence for Russia during World War I. The fortress joined UNESCO's World Heritage List in 1991 and is symbolic of the Finnish resolve and desire for independence.

RIGHT: *Detail of the Sibelius monument, by Eila Hiltunen.*

to the big name stores are the stalls of Kauppatori (Market Square)—complete with a welter of fur rugs, hats, and coats—as well as the Hietalahti Flea Market and the Hakaniemi Market Hall. The city's most impressive attraction is the Senaatintori (Senate Square). Step into this central space and it could easily be Russia. The array of stunning 19th-century neoclassical buildings look like they are on loan from St. Petersburg—an illusion that is so strong that Hollywood producers often shoot scenes of "Russia" in Helsinki. The focal point of the square is Carl Ludwig Engel's (1778–1840) glaring white Tuomiokirkko (Lutheran Cathedral). Further east is Aleksei Gornostayev's impressive Uspensky Cathedral. This redbrick house of prayer constructed in a Byzantine-Slavic style clings to the city's waterfront. A relatively flat city, Helsinki is also blessed with a string of green parks and tree-lined boulevards, not to mention the archipelago of islands that lie temptingly just offshore.

ABOVE: *An organ grinder near Senaatintori (Senate Square).*
LEFT: *Orthodox Uspensky Cathedral behind 19th-century warehouses.*

THE STORY OF...

Given Helsinki's prime strategic location, it is unsurprising that the city's past reads like a who's who of European history. The first settlers in the area eked out a living in the unforgiving climate in the 16th century. As the town grew, the Swedish kings moved in and erected a fortress on the city island of Suomenlinna. Then it was the turn of the Russians, who had been eyeing Helsinki jealously during the Swedish period of power. The tsar's armies rolled into Helsinki in 1808 and stayed for a century, before being ousted at the end of World War I. The Russians returned to Finland during World War II.

During the Cold War, Finland shrewdly occupied the middle ground. Today Helsinki is the capital of the independent Finnish Republic and in 1995 the country solidified its position in Europe by joining the European Union. Martti Ahtisaari, Finland's president from 1994 to 2000, played a big part in raising the country's profile internationally.

BELOW: *A city suburb of Helsinki.*
LEFT: *The Helsinki waterfront.*

key dates

1550
Helsinki emerges as an important trading hub

1808
A great fire devastates much of the city

1909
City passes from Swedish to Russian hands

1917
Finns seize the opportunity to declare independence during the Russian Revolution

1990
US-Soviet summit takes place in Helsinki

Art and Culture

In addition to its world-class sights and dramatic Baltic Sea location, Helsinki is a haven of art and culture, with around 50 museums, including the world-class Kiasma (National Museum of Modern Art), an inherent part of the city's fabric. Contemporary design is also a prevalent feature in Helsinki, with everywhere from trendy bars and cafés to opulent restaurants that look as though they have just stepped out of the pages of a style magazine. The industry behind this vibrant and contemporary city is somewhat more traditional, with the manufacture of clothing and textiles, metal processing, printing, and food production all contributing to Helsinki's economy.

Istanbul

- Population: 11,000,000
- Number of blue and white tiles decorating the Imperial Sultanahmet Mosque (Blue Mosque): 25,000
- The only city that lies on two continents, Asia and Europe
- Number of mosques: over 500

CONSTANTINE THE GREAT (c274–337)

Flavius Valerius Aurelius Constantinus (Constantine I "the Great") ruled as Roman Emperor from AD306 to AD337 and became the first emperor to promote Christianity. His Edict of Milan brought tolerance and recognition to Christians throughout his empire and his new capital at Constantinople was a Christian city. Under Constantine Sunday was declared a holiday. He built a basilica on the site of the stable in Bethlehem believed to be the birthplace of Jesus Christ, and according to legend he is buried in a tomb in Jerusalem. On the Emperor's death his son, Constantine II, became ruler of Britain, Gaul, and Spain.

RIGHT: *View from the Galata Tower.*
FAR RIGHT: *Tiled ceiling in the Sultanahmet Mosque.*

The largest city and export port in Turkey, and the most populous, Istanbul straddles two continents, Europe and Asia. It is separated by the Bosphorus Strait, a channel of water so precious that vast empires have fought for it. Here is the heart of Istanbul's trade and commerce, a channel linking the Sea of Marmara to the Black Sea, the Bosphorus is busy from dusk until dawn with tankers plying their trade from Greece and Russia. One half of Turkey's manufacturing industry output and almost half of the income tax paid to the state comes from the city.

Istanbul itself is divided into two parts, the old city and the modern city. The legacies of Christian and Islamic empires are evident in its magnificent churches and mosques, its dusty backstreets where women cover their heads, and its trendy cafés populated with locals wearing the latest Western fashions. Described as a multicultural mosaic, Istanbul's population bears traces of 72 nations, including the Genoese, Arabs from Granada in Spain, Greeks, Armenians, Syrians and Kurds, Christians and Muslims. Such diversity means Istanbul has emerged as a cultural city to rival Western cultural centers such as Paris and Rome—not only in commerce and quality textiles, but also as a stage for cultural and art festivals. The International Culture and Arts Festival held annually hosts artists from around the world.

The old city is mainly in the southwest corner, in

BELOW AND RIGHT: *Silhouette of Yeni Mosque.*

Sultanahmet, and is busy with oxon carts and handcarts. Piercing the sky are the six minarets of the Imperial Sultanahmet Mosque (Blue Mosque) the biggest in the city with golden manuscripts of the Koran. The Aya Sofya Museum on the site of a basilica to Christianity built by Emperor Constantine, and the Topkapi Palace, seat of the Ottoman Empire for 400 years, protects the Spoonmaker's diamond—the seventh largest in the world. To the north is modern Istanbul, and a complete contrast with the trendy bars of Beyoglu and the smart cafés of Ortaköy.

The Business of Textiles

Carpets are synonymous with Turkey and shopping in Istanbul is a mesmerizing experience. Kapali Çarsi (Covered Bazaar) has 4,000 stores spread over 65 streets, its stalls and halls bursting with carpets and cashmere shawls, leatherwork, teas, spices, Turkish delight, and caviar. Many locals trade in high-quality textiles, which have become so sought after that Istanbul's Chamber of Commerce is among an organization that has launched an annual "Shopping Fest" between February and March, to promote Turkey's textile industry as a world brand.

RIGHT: *Grilled fish stall along the waterfront.*
FAR RIGHT: *Embroidered Turkish slippers in the Grand Bazaar.*
BELOW: *A vendor of salep (a winter drink) in Beyazit Square.*

Istanbul

THE STORY OF...

The city was originally settled by Greeks who named it Byzantium after their King Byzas. In the fourth century AD the Romans invaded and two years later Emperor Constantine I renamed the city Constantinople. Constantinople became a Christian city and the eastern capital of the Roman Empire until the Fall of Constantinople in 1453 when it became the capital of the Ottoman Empire headed by Mehmed II "the Conqueror." The Turks renamed the city Stamboul or Istanbul. During World War I, Turkey sided with the Germans, only to be defeated. Istanbul was then occupied by the Allies.

   After the War of Independence, when Turkish nationalists fought Greece, France, and Italy, the Republic of Turkey was recognized in 1923 and the Turkish city of Ankara succeeded as the capital. Istanbul was officially recognized in 1930 and has since expanded due to massive immigration and a boom in tourism. Istanbul is also becoming a cultural destination with the 2004 European Song Contest taking place in the city.

key dates

657BC
The city of Byzantium is founded by Greek colonists

AD330
Roman Emperor Constantine I ("the Great") renames Byzantium Constantinople, capital of the Eastern Roman Empire

1453
City falls to the Ottoman Turks and becomes capital of the Ottoman Empire

1930
City is officially renamed Istanbul

2005
City hosts its first Formula 1 race on a new purpose-built race track

Kiev

statistics

Official Population: 2,663,000

Subway stations: 40

Citizens killed in World War II: 657,000

Churches in AD1000: 400

MIKHAIL BULGAKOV (1891–1940)

The eldest son of a theology professor, Mikhail Bulgakov was born in Kiev and raised in the final years of Tsarist influence over the city. He attended Kiev's School of Medicine before serving in the Caucasus as a White Army medic for the Russian civil war. The experience inspired his first novel, *The White Guard*, which tells the story of a family in Kiev in the years following the Russian Revolution. The book was banned in 1929, despite rumors that the stage version was Stalin's favorite. *The Master and Margarita* remained unpublished until 25 years after Bulgakov's death because of its criticism of government bureaucracy and corruption; it is now considered his greatest work.

Kiev is a stately metropolis built upon the forested hillsides that rise up from the Dnepr River. Comprised of several distinct neighborhoods, long bridges connect the modern residential areas of the Left Bank with the more established quarters of Ukraine's ancient capital on the Right Bank. Kiev was built during distinct architectural periods, creating a diverse and eclectic architectural landscape: Byzantine ruins and baroque landmarks stand side by side with neoclassical Tsarist palaces, the opulent Opera House, and Stalinist tower blocks. Khreschatyk Boulevard runs through the city center, leading to the Maidan Nezalezhnosti (Square of Independence). The titanium Motherland statue and other Soviet War memorials feature prominently in public areas. Kiev is famous for its parks and green spaces, and in May the city is colored white with the blossoms of chestnut trees that line the city streets.

The majority of Kiev's inhabitants are ethnic Ukrainian or Russian, and both languages are used freely. While the official population is stated at just over 2.5 million, Kievans estimate their growing population—due to increased immigration from surrounding areas—is closer to 4 million. As the largest and most developed city in Ukraine, Kiev benefits from a strong and diverse manufacturing base that includes machine-building, pharmaceuticals, food processing, and agricultural commodities. The 450-seat *Rada*—or parliament—is based in Kiev and is home to Ukraine's national government, while next door stands the stadium of Dinamo Kiev, Ukraine's world-famous soccer team. The country's largest universities and most prestigious academies also attract a fair number of students to the capital.

City of Churches

Kievans have been building churches ever since the city embraced Christianity 1,000 years ago and Kiev's skyline now shines with the dozens of golden domes typical to Eastern Slavic architecture. The Byzantine basilica of St. Sophia is one of Kiev's oldest, constructed in 1051 by Prince Yaroslav the Wise. St. Vladimir's Cathedral was only completed a century ago and is known for its evocative murals. Kiev's most famous churches belong to the Caves Monastery complex, revered as the birthplace of Russian Orthodoxy and visited by thousands of pilgrims every year. White Baroque cathedrals topped with green roofs and golden domes guard the entrances to intricate underground passageways that lead to a series of catacombs and chapels. The monastery's bell tower is the tallest of any Orthodox church in the world at 300ft (96.5m). These important cultural monuments have come to represent Kiev's endurance through a millennium of hardship, and city inhabitants regularly attend in the spirit of remembrance and historical reverence.

RIGHT: *Traditional dolls at a market in the Square of Independence.*
FAR RIGHT: *Mural outside St. Michael's Monastery of the Golden Cupolas.*

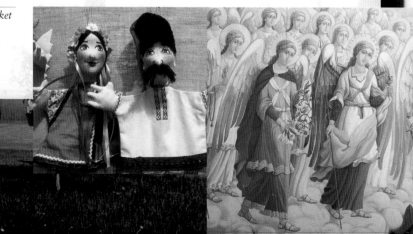

ABOVE: *Statue of Lenin.*

THE STORY OF...

Kiev was founded in AD560 by early Slavic tribes as a protective hill fortress nestled on the banks of the Dnepr River. The city swiftly evolved into a major center of trade between the Vikings in northern Scandinavia and the Byzantine Empire to the South. In AD988, Prince Vladimir the Great introduced Christianity to Kiev, unifying the empire of Kievan Rus. As Kiev was renowned for its commercial wealth, the Mongol's Golden Horde sacked it in 1240 and demanded tribute for over a century before Lithuania annexed the area in 1362.

In 1569, under the Union of Lublin, Poland was granted control of the city. The Ukrainian Cossacks fought successfully to free Kiev from Polish rule, only to have the Russians take over in the late 17th century. A thriving sugar industry attracted income and a working population—an important demographic in the Russian Revolution of 1917. In 1943, the Soviet Army liberated Kiev after two years of Nazi occupation, and in 1991, Kiev became the capital of an independent Ukraine.

LEFT: *St. Michael's Monastery of the Golden Cupolas.*

Kiev

key dates

AD560
Siblings Lybed, Schek, and Koriv found a city on the Dnepr River and name it after their older brother Kyi

988
Prince Vladimir the Great brings Christianity to Kiev, baptizing the city in the Dnepr River

1654
Cossack Bohdan Khmelnytsky signs the Peryaslav Agreement with the Russian Tsar, bringing Kiev under Russian jurisdiction

1921
After changing hands 18 times in three years, Kiev is finally conquered by the Bolsheviks, joining Ukraine to the Soviet Union

2004
Over one million Ukrainians converge on Kiev's main square to demonstrate for democratic presidential elections in the "Orange Revolution"

Copenhagen

Population: 1,700,000

Area covered by city's Tivoli Gardens: 3.23 sq miles (8.27 sq km)

Hans Christian Andersen wrote over 350 stories

Denmark has one of the highest per capita GDPs in Europe

THE LITTLE MERMAID

One of the most visited tourist sights in Copenhagen, and indeed all of Denmark, is Edward Eriksen's (1876–1959) statue of the Little Mermaid, a gift to the city from Carlsberg brewer Carl Jacobsen. The demure tiny mermaid, who has been looking wistfully across the Øresund Sound since her erection in 1913, was inspired by Hans Christian Andersen's (1805–75) *The Little Mermaid* and from local Danish folklore, which claims that the mermaids who once lived in the Øresund and lured sailors to their watery deaths (fortunately the fairytale incarnation was much friendlier) would sit on the banks of the channel.

RIGHT: *The Christianshavns Canal.*

It may be the largest city in Scandinavia, but Copenhagen manages to maintain an intimate small-town feel, with its warm and welcoming citizens adding to its appeal. One of the greenest cities in Europe, the center of Copenhagen comes complete with tranquil parks, gabled houses (half-timbered houses), narrow medieval streets, and bountiful church spires. In the summer months outdoor living comes to the city as the sidewalk cafés of the pedestrianized center spring to life and locals flock to the expanse of Tivoli Gardens with its myriad attractions, free events, and theme park.

At the helm of the oldest kingdom in Europe, Copenhagen's city center has not one, but four palaces— the 17th-century Frederiksberg and Rosenborg Palaces, the 18th-century Amalienborg, and the 20th-century Christiansborg Palace. The latter is the seat of the country's parliament. Denmark's political and cultural heart also keeps its citizens stimulated with a wealth of world-class museums, theaters, and a vibrant and avant-garde nightlife. Danish cinema is gradually making its mark on the film world, with award-winning productions and renowned directors coming out of the city. Danish furniture, jewellery, and new technologies are also at the forefront of design. Another key component of Copenhagen's makeup is water—the clean sea, lakes, and canals which serve as an ever-present reminder of the city's former role as a major port on the Baltic Sea. The opening of the Øresund Bridge, which provides a road link between Copenhagen and Malmø in Sweden, has also helped to elevate the city's importance within Scandinavia, the Baltic, and indeed the rest of Europe.

Stable Economy

Copenhagen's residents are, quite rightly, proud of their smart and attractive city and the high standard of living that they enjoy. An essential component of Copenhagen's good living is a strong and stable national economy, of which the city is the crux. Over 40 percent of the businesses registered in Denmark are located in or around the city, and between them they generate up to 50 percent of the country's GDP and export revenues. Design, pharmaceutical, biotechnology, and IT companies are amongst the firms attracted to the city by its highly educated workforce. Tourism is also becoming increasingly important to Copenhagen.

BELOW: *Radhusplatzen and Town Hall, Copenhagen.*

LEFT: *The statue of Hans Christian Anderson in Copenhagen's Town Hall Square.*

THE STORY OF...

This small village rose to prominence as an important trading port after Bishop Absalon fortified the island of Slotsholmen (the site of today's parliament) in the 12th century. In 1417 Copenhagen became the capital of the Danish Kingdom when the Pomeranian King Eric relocated here. The 17th century heralded an era of impressive construction. with Renaissance buildings such as the Rundetårn (Round Tower), Rosenborg Palace, and Børsen (Stock Exchange) dating from this period. The 18th century brought misery to the city in the form of a deadly plague that wiped out around 20,000 people in 1711, followed by two great fires in 1728 and 1795. Military attacks by the British in 1807, who feared that the Danes were about to take up Napoleon Bonaparte's (1769–1821) cause, inflicted further damage on Copenhagen.

After a period of reconstruction and industrialization, Copenhagen has re-emerged as an artistic hub and developed a reputation for cutting-edge design that has put it firmly on the map. The opening of a dazzling new Opera House at the beginning of 2005 put the seal on this renaissance.

LEFT: *The Black Diamond Building.*
BELOW: *The Danish Royal Guards.*

1167
Bishop Absalon builds a fortress on Slotsholmen

1940
Nazi troops occupy the city

1971
Squatters establish the Free State of Christiana

1996
Becomes a European City of Culture

2000
Øresund Bridge opens

key dates

Krakow

Population: 800,000
(1,500,000 metropolitan area)

At 678 miles (1,047km)
the Wisla, which runs
through the city, is Poland's
longest river

41 of Poland's 45 kings are
buried in Krakow

Krakow has more than 2
million precious works of art

S ituated in the south of Poland close to the country's borders with the Czech
Republic and Slovakia, Krakow is the nation's cultural heart. Spared from the
worst ravages of the retreating Nazi forces at the end of World War II (unlike
many of Poland's other cities), Krakow is blessed with over 2 million works
of art, 331 ancient houses, over 50 churches, and more than 30 museums. Today
Krakow is a cosmopolitan and successful city with the mainstays of its economy
being steel, commerce, services, and tourism. By the end of 2006 the city looks set
to have a new out of town office, apartment, entertainment and shopping complex,
the Nowe Miasto (New Town), which will create a wealth of retail jobs.

Life in Krakow revolves around the picture-perfect old town, which was
placed on UNESCO's World Heritage List in 1978, a bucolic haven brimming
with medieval and Renaissance buildings. At its historic heart is the Rynek
Główny (Market Square), the third largest civic square in Europe, which is
dominated by the Italianate Sukiennice (Cloth Hall). Once the heart of the
mercantile city, the hall buzzes today with a massive souvenir emporium.
Churches and medieval buildings rise from the cobbles around the square
while a solitary tower stands as a testament to the town hall that was torn
down in 1820. Around the Rynek Główny sidewalk cafés throng with
tourists, street entertainers, and students. Krakow's Jagiellionian University,

LEFT: *Statue of a dragon at the Dragon's Lair in the city.*

POPE JOHN PAUL II (1920-2005)

Born Karol Jozef Wojtyla, Pope John
Paul II became pontiff in 1978.
During his priesthood, Wojtyla
worked both in St. Florian's Church
in Krakow and as a professor at
Lublin University. In 1963 he became
the Archbishop of Krakow, and in
1967 was made a cardinal. Just over
a decade later he became pope,
partly—it is said—because the
cardinals were unable to agree on
a successor for John Paul I. After
his inauguration Pope John Paul II
travelled to over 100 countries
promoting world peace and
tolerance. He also worked tirelessly
and dedicated himself to restoring
people's faith in the Catholic Church.

LEFT: *Detail of the gate at the entrance to the Old Synagogue.*

one of the oldest in Europe, has spawned talents such as the astronomer Nicolaus Copernicus (1473–1543) and Pope John Paul II. Today 60,000 students contribute to the city's vibrancy.

Wawel Palace, one of the most splendid Renaissance royal residences in Europe, hovers omnipotent over the Old Town streets on one side and the Wisła River on the other. Its 71 chambers house a myriad of artifacts from 16th-century tapestries to an oriental collection. On the adjacent hill is Krakow's cathedral—the burial site of kings, poets, and national heroes.

Krakow's Jews

There is a darker side to Krakow's past that the local authorities are keen to play down. The Telpod electrical factory in the Jewish quarter was the place where former owner Oscar Schindler (1908–74) saved the lives of 1,000 local Jews, as the Nazis set about destroying Krakow's Jewish community. Another ever-present reminder of the genocide committed on Polish soil is Auschwitz-Birkenau; just 43 miles (70km) from Krakow. This was where the Nazis herded millions of Jews and "political undesirables" from all over Europe to their deaths in the gas chambers.

LEFT: *Krakow Cathedral.*

Krakow

THE STORY OF...

The eighth century AD brought Slav settlers to Krakow and within 200 years the city had become an important commercial hub under the Polish state. In the 13th century Krakow was obliterated by Tartar invaders, with Kazimierz overseeing much of the reconstruction during the 14th century. The Polish monarchy also established a university and allowed Jews to live in the city. King Sigismund III's relocation of the Polish capital to Warsaw in 1596 came as a blow, as did the Swedish invasion of 1655.

After various Russian, Austrian, and French occupations, Krakow was incorporated into the Austro-Hungarian Empire in 1846, under which Krakow flourished as a liberal center for writers, artists, and dissidents. The conclusion of World War I gave Poland a brief stint of independence, with World War II bringing Nazi occupation followed by subjugation under the USSR. Krakow's communist legacy is Europe's largest steelworks and the ensuing environmental pollution is an issue that came to the fore in the run up to Poland's accession to the EU in May 2004.

BELOW: *The Royal Castle overlooks the Vistula River.*

key dates

1364
Jagiellionian University is established

1380
Krakow becomes capital of Poland

1596
Warsaw becomes capital city

1815
Congress of Vienna creates the Independent Republic of Krakow

2005
The city mourns its one-time archbishop, Pope John Paul II

Lisbon

statistics

- Population: 960,000
- Unemployment: 6.2 percent, among the lowest in the EU
- Main industries: tourism, finance, insurance, telecommunications
- The population of Greater Lisbon accounts for 48 percent of Portugal's purchasing power

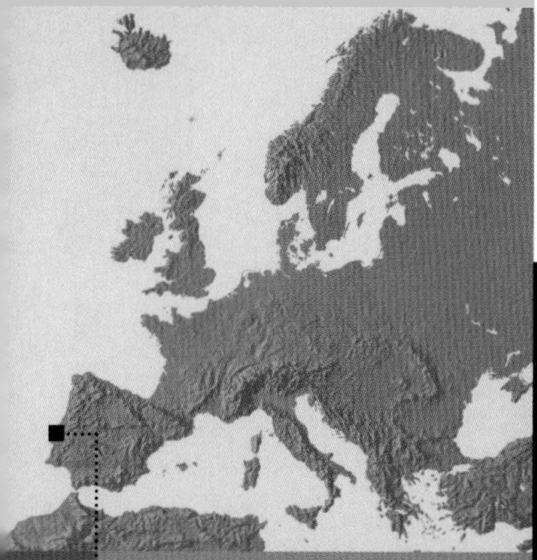

Beautifully set on the northern bank of the River Tagus estuary on Portugal's west coast, Lisbon is the country's capital and its largest city. Despite an ever-growing modern suburban sprawl, Lisbon has escaped the blandness of many similar-sized European cities, retaining an appearance and atmosphere all of its own. This is typified by the physical reality of the city center, laid out after the 1755 earthquake on an elegant grid plan, surrounded on three sides by hills and open to the water on the fourth. This Baixa area, centered around the main Rossio Square and the expensive stores of the Chiado district, contrasts with the older hillside neighborhoods; the Alfama, still a warren of Moorish alleys overlooked by a splendid castle, and the Bairro Alto, a beguiling area that is the heart of Lisbon's thriving party scene. Further away from the waterfront stretches the Avenida da Liberdade, a wide boulevard lined with grandiose 19th-century buildings that is backed by the Parque Eduardo VI, central Lisbon's largest park. West from the Baixa lies the suburb of Belém, home to the superb Manueline Mosteiros dos Jerónimos (Hieronymite Monastery), built in

BELOW: *The Monument to the Discoveries.*

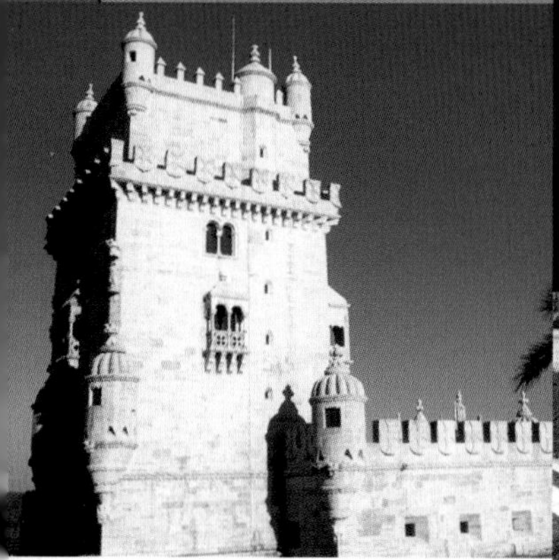

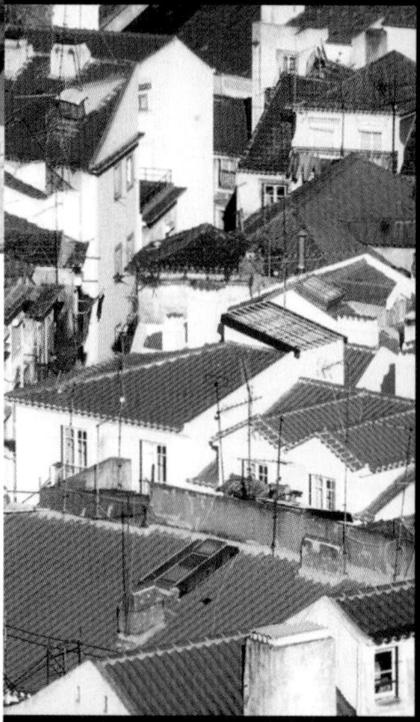

TORRE DE BELÉM

The Torre de Belém—a superb amalgam of the Portuguese Manueline style of architecture with Renaissance elements—stands on the waterfront of Belém, some 3 miles (5km) from the city center. Constructed between 1514 and 1520 as part of a group of forts providing a defensive bastion against invaders, it is one of Portugal's most potent national symbols and was declared a World Heritage Site in 1983. Adorned with towers, turrets, and battlements, it recalls Portugal's great maritime voyages of discovery and is decorated with motifs associated with these and symbols of the Order of Christ, the successors in Portugal to the Knights Templar.

ABOVE RIGHT: *Rooftops of Alfama, viewed from Largo das Portas do Sol.*

1502 in thanksgiving for the Portuguese Discoveries, and a clutch of monuments and museums in an unparalleled setting. *Lisboetas* flock here to relax, and are also blessed with the option of heading to the superb Atlantic beaches west of the outlying resorts of Estoril and Cascais, or northwest to the cool green hills around Sintra.

Lisbon's Catholic population has swelled in the last half-century, augmented by an influx of immigrants, many from the historical Portuguese colonies of Cape Verde, Angola, and Mozambique, whose labor was vital to the massive 1990s construction program which transformed a backward capital into one of Europe's most exciting cities.

New and Old

Modern Lisbon is seen at its best from the waterfront Parque das Nações, built to house Expo '98. This huge urban project transformed a run-down and polluted area into a showcase of modern architecture, overlooked by the soaring 10.5 miles (17km) sweep of the Ponte Vasco da Gama (Vasco da Gama Bridge). This gleaming, futuristic site contrasts splendidly with the old city center, where creaking trams and funiculars still operate, and the cobbled streets are lined with buildings lavishly decorated inside and out with beautiful *azulejos* (glazed tiles), one of Portugal's most characteristic products. First made in the 14th century, *azulejos* are either polychrome or blue and white and are used to decorate and weatherproof everything from church interiors and palaces to stores, markets, and metro stations.

Buildings in the Rossio area of the city.

TOP: Sun Man *sculpture by Jorge Viera (1998), Parque das Nações.*
ABOVE: *Blue tile detail.*
ABOVE RIGHT: *The cloisters of the Jerónimos Monastery in Belém.*

THE STORY OF...

The ancient settlement of Olissipo, modern Lisbon, became a Roman provincial capital in 138BC, falling to the Visigoths in AD469. From AD714 it was part of Moorish Iberia, emerging as the capital after being retaken by Afonso Henriques, first king of Portugal, in 1147. From here, mariners embarked on the great 15th-century voyages of discovery and by the 1500s Lisbon had become a prosperous city endowed with fine buildings.

The 1699 discovery of gold in Brazil produced a further surge of lavish construction, much of which was destroyed in the devastating earthquake of 1755. Lisbon was rebuilt, only to become embroiled in the Napoleonic Wars from 1807 to 1814. Decades of political turmoil followed, culminating in the Salazar years of virtual dictatorship. The 1974 Carnation Revolution ended the regime and in 1986 Portugal joined the European Union and Lisbon became European City of Culture in 1994. European funds poured in, and Lisbon boomed. The huge new waterfront area constructed for the 1998 Lisbon Expo marked Lisbon's new role as a mainstream European capital.

138BC
A Roman settlement, Olissipo, is founded on the site of modern Lisbon

714
The Moors occupy Lisbon and rule for over 400 years

1255
Lisbon becomes the capital of Portugal

1755
Two-thirds of Lisbon is destroyed in the Great Earthquake

2004
Lisbon hosts the opening match in the European Football (soccer) Championships

45

Ljubljana

JOŽE PLEČNIK

No one has exerted a greater influence on the physical appearance of Ljubljana than Jože Plečnik (1872–1957). The architect, who was born here, developed strong opinions about how his beloved hometown should look. After studying in Vienna and working in Prague, he returned to make his mark on the city. Plečnik's work is visible almost everywhere, from the bridges that cross the Ljubljanica River, the riverbanks, and the city's theaters, to the university library, Ljubljana's central market, Žale Cemetery, and the suburb of Trnovo where he lived.

ABOVE: *Robba Fountain and Town Hall.*

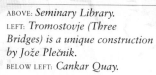

ABOVE: *Seminary Library.*
LEFT: *Tromostovje (Three Bridges) is a unique construction by Jože Plečnik.*
BELOW LEFT: *Cankar Quay.*

Slovenia's compact capital city straddles the Ljubljanica River, a narrow and peaceful stretch of water whose banks are lined with medieval houses and drooping willow trees. The oldest part of the city, the Old Town, lies on the right bank of the river and is complete with Baroque dwellings dating from the 16th and 17th centuries. Ljubljana Castle, which is perched on a hill overlooking the Old Town, remains central to city life serving as a venue for weddings and cultural performances. It also houses the Virtual Museum which recounts 2,000 years of the city's history. Ljubljana's daily market, a charming antidote to the supermarkets that reign supreme in much of Europe today, is also located on this side of the river. At the market everything is traded from fresh fruit and vegetables, cheese, and bread to fresh flowers, wooden kitchen utensils, and homemade honey.

The city's left bank is the center of business and cultural life and this is where the majority of offices, hotels, museums, restaurants, and theaters are found, as well as one of the oldest philharmonic concert halls in Europe. Key industries in Ljubljana include retail, finance, services, and tourism, with the Slovenian capital generating around 25 percent of the country's annual GDP. Ljubljana is proud of its scholarly tradition and the left bank is also home to impressive university buildings that house various academic faculties. With such a sizeable student population the streets and cafés on this side of the river can be as lively as those in the Old Town. Tivoli Park provides a tranquil retreat for Ljubljana's citizens who flock there to walk, cycle, and run.

City of Writers

Ljubljana is a vibrant city with a predominantly young population— around 20 percent of its residents are enrolled at the University of Ljubljana. The Slovene authors Primož Trubar (1508–86), Ivan Cankar (1876–1918), and France Prešeren (1800–49) have left an indelible mark on the city infusing its inhabitants with a sense of romance and appreciation of the arts. Many of the city's aspiring young poets put pen to paper in what has been lovingly described as a "national affliction." This is a country, after all, where 8 February, the day that Prešeren died, has been declared a national holiday dedicated to culture.

ABOVE RIGHT: *Painted exterior of the Cooperative Bank.*
ABOVE: *The monument to France Prešeren.*

THE STORY OF...

Ljubljana's early Copper Age inhabitants lived in stilt-houses built on marshland. They were followed by the Celts in the third century BC, the Romans in the first century BC (who called the city Emona) and the Slavs in the sixth century AD. From the 12th century until 1918, Ljubljana fell largely under the rule of the Austro-Hungarian Empire. During this time French forces, under Napoleon Bonaparte (1769–1821) briefly occupied the city between 1809 and 1813.

In 1918 Slovenia became part of the Kingdom of Serbs, Croats, and Slovenes (renamed Yugoslavia in 1929), where it remained, with the exception of World War II, until 1991. Almost 70 years of centralized, socialist rule from Belgrade in Serbia left Ljubljana's citizens, and Slovenes in general, feeling cheated and dissatisfied with the system that redistributed the wealth they generated to other parts of the federation. In 1990 most Slovenes voted for their own country and six months later, in June 1991, the Republic of Slovenia declared its independence. After a 10-day war the Yugoslav authorities accepted Slovenia's independence. In 2004 Slovenia joined the European Union and NATO.

key dates

1144
Ljubljana (then known as Laibach) gets its first written mention

1511
An earthquake destroys large sections of the city

1895
A second earthquake demolishes much of Ljubljana

1918
Joins the Kingdom of Serbs, Croats, and Slovenes

2004
Slovenia joins NATO and the EU

London

Population: 7,400,000
(metropolitan London)

Area of Greater London:
580 sq miles (1,500 sq km)

There are 37 immigrant
groups with more than
1,000 people

The underground train
system ("the tube") is the
oldest in the world

LONDON EYE

Soaring 444ft (135m) into the sky from London's Right Bank, the British Airways London Eye is literally an unmissable attraction. Also known as the Millenium Wheel, this huge observation wheel opens up sweeping views, which on a clear day stretch for 25 miles (40km) of the city, from glass capsules. Visitors experience one revolution of the wheel, which on its 30-minute journey takes in some of London's key attractions, including the Houses of Parliament, St. Paul's, and the Swiss Re Tower ("the gherkin"). The London Eye was conceived as a short-term project to celebrate the new millennium. However, its huge success has fuelled talk of extending its life indefinitely.

London is a city that people can identify with immediately, whether they have been there or not. All over the globe iconographic images of London abound, from the red buses and black cabs, through to the pageantry of Buckingham Palace and the clock chimes of Big Ben. Under the guidance of Ken Livingstone (b. 1945)—who became the city's first independently elected mayor in 2000—the focus of London today is moving back toward the River Thames, where life in the city began. New attractions along the riverbanks include the Tate Modern art gallery, giving a new lease of life to a defunct power station, the gleaming new Hungerford Bridge, and the vaulting Swiss Re Tower. Each of these monuments is a perfect example of London's urban regeneration and the development of old and decaying parts of the city. Elsewhere in the city, Lord Norman Foster's (b. 1935) avant-garde glass roof, which was added to the "Great Court" of the British Museum in 2000, is further evidence of London's determination to shrug off its stuffy old image and reinvent itself.

Steeped in history and culture, London is also well known for its open green spaces, which include the manicured gardens at St. James' Park, Regent's Park (home to London Zoo), and Hyde Park (home to Kensington Palace), which is brought to life by a raft of outdoor concerts during the summer months. At weekends the city's parks fill with Londoners keen to shake off the stresses of office life.

Multicultural City

Home to 37 distinct immigrant groups, London is truly multicultural. The ethnic diversity of the city's population is perhaps most obvious in an eclectic array of restaurants, with everything from French, Thai, Malaysian, Vietnamese, Indian, and the regional cuisines of a whole nation in Chinatown all part of the mix. Outside the city center this diversity is also reflected in the collection of "villages" that make up the Greater London area, with highlights including the leafy riverside suburb of Richmond in the west, the futuristic skyline of the Docklands in the east, and bohemian Soho right at the heart of the city.

LEFT: *Admiral Lord Nelson's statue tops the column in Trafalgar Square.*
RIGHT: *St. Paul's Cathedral.*

The diversity of the population and the city itself is also reflected in London's booming economy, with tourism, hospitality, business, and finance all vital ingredients. London's wealth of academic institutions, its large student population, and the creative arts industry also make a significant contribution to the city's economy.

LEFT: *Looking over the River Thames to the Swiss Re Tower, also known as "the gherkin."*

THE STORY OF...

London's first real inhabitants were Roman invaders in AD43 who established an important trading center in the city. When the Roman Empire collapsed, London fell into decline, but re-emerged as an important commercial center by the 17th century, securing the attention of Danish and Norwegian Vikings and the Anglo-Saxons, who fought over the city between the ninth and 11th centuries. When Edward the Confessor (1003–1066) took the throne in 1042, London was the largest city in Britain. However, it did not become capital until William the Conqueror came to power in 1066.

London continued to prosper through to the 17th century, emerging as an important financial center. Early Stuart rule saw London's fortunes change and in 1665 and 1666 the dual tragedies of the Great Plague and the Great Fire decimated the city, claiming up to 100,000 lives. Under Queen Victoria (1819–1901), who ruled from 1837, the city blossomed again. The 20th century gave London innumerable theaters and the Millennium Dome, as well as the scars inflicted by two World Wars and the General Strike of 1926.

key dates

AD43
Trading center established by Roman invaders

1665
Great Plague of London kills up to 100,000 people

1666
Great Fire of London destroys 80 percent of the city's buildings

1940
Over 30 percent of the city is destroyed by German bombs and over 30,000 people die during the Blitz

2000
British Airways London Eye ("the Milennium Wheel") opens

Madrid

PLAZA DE TOROS

The Spanish passion for bull-fighting may be incomprehensible to many foreigners, but the *corrida* (fight) is an integral part of Spanish life and Madrid's Plaza de Toros is the world's most important bullring. Officially opened in 1934, this vast edifice seating 22,000 spectators is built in the neo-Mudéjar style, an imitation of the Moorish-Christian architecture of the 13th and 14th centuries. Keynotes of its design are its ornamental brickwork, trefoil doors and windows, and brightly colored tile decoration, while the interior also contains a museum devoted to the complex art of bullfighting.

Madrid, the capital of Spain, lies at a height of over 2,000ft (650m) in the center of the Iberian peninsula's high central plateau, the *meseta*. Bitingly cold in winter and blisteringly hot in summer, the city encompasses everything from historic buildings, palaces, skyscrapers, shopping malls, and great museums to sprawling industrial estates and shanty towns of abject poverty. It is a city of extremes, a capital chosen by Philip II (1527–98) in 1561 as much for its geographical position as for political reasons, whose inhabitants include immigrants from all over Spain. For these reasons the spirit of Madrid is both diffused and elusive, and *madrileños* have far greater loyalty to their own *barrio* (neighborhood) than to the city as a whole.

Madrid is divided into 21 *barrios*, each completely individual, the most central being the *barrio popular*, whose hub is the bustling square of the Puerta del Sol. This is a stone's throw from the oldest, and most atmospheric part of Madrid, centered around the 17th-century Plaza Mayor, built as the administrative center of the Court by Philip II. Today's Royal Palace, along with the cathedral, lies to the west, overlooking the River Manzanares, on whose opposite bank stretches the vast, and surprisingly wild, park of the Casa de Campo, a popular place for all kinds of sport. West from Puerta del Sol, a series of wide and leafy 18th-century boulevards, punctuated by superb squares and

BELOW: *The cloisters beneath the Casa de la Panadeira in Madrid's Plaza Mayor.*

fountains, are home to Madrid's great museums, the Prado, the Thyssen-Bornemisza, and the Reina Sofia, all lying within an easy walk of the beautiful central park and gardens of the Retiro. North from here is the Salamanca *barrio*, a quiet, expensive neighborhood that is home to the city's wealthiest residents and chicest shopping. By contrast, *barrios* such as Lavapiés—home to the famous Rastro flea market—Chueca, and Malasaña are noisy, vibrant, and chaotic.

The City that Never Sleeps

Madrid has an intense culture of late night partying, and a word—*madrugada*—which refers to the hours between midnight and 6am. Traffic jams clog the streets at 4am as young people head home or move on to early morning discos and clubs, while, as summer temperatures soar, the whole scene moves outdoors to the open-air *terrazas* scattered all over the city. *Madrileños* don't usually dine much before 10 or 11pm, resulting in a population surviving on less and less sleep as siesta hours are curtailed to bring the business day in line with the rest of Europe.

RIGHT: *The external glass lift of Museo Nacional Centro de Arte Reina Sofía.*
BELOW: *Bear and tree statue in Puerta del Sol.*

THE STORY OF...

The area of modern Madrid was first inhabited around 1000BC by Iberian tribes and later became part of Roman, then Visigothic, and finally Muslim Spain. In AD854 Mohammed I founded the city proper, which was reconquered from the Moors by Alfonso VI in 1085. It was recognized as a city by Alfonso VII in 1202, housing the Cortes (Parliament) from 1301 and becoming the permanent home of the monarchy in the 15th century. It became the Hapsburg dynasty capital in 1561 and the 18th century saw much construction in the French style under the Bourbon monarchs. Madrid was occupied by the French from 1808 to 1812, and the 19th century saw further construction and modernization, which has been almost continuous. Post-Franco, Madrid has changed immeasurably, the renovations of the 1980s giving the impetus to the *movidad madrileña* ("happening" Madrid). The city was extensively refurbished for its 1992 role as European Capital of Culture, and work continues on urban rehabilitation and the transport infrastructure.

BELOW: *The Casa de la Panadeira on Plaza Mayor.*

Madrid

key dates

AD854
Mohammed I of Cordoba founds the city of Madrid

1561
Philip II establishes the Royal Court in Madrid, making it the capital city

1939
General Franco becomes head of state following the Spanish Civil War

1975
Death of Franco, succession of King Juan Carlos, and restoration of democracy

1992
Madrid designated European Capital of Culture

Monte Carlo

- Population: 29,972 (in the principality of Monaco)

- The principality of Monaco and the city of Monte Carlo have the highest concentration of police per square meter in the world

- Lack of space and a high population density mean that Monte Carlo has some of the most expensive real estate on the planet

- People of 108 different nationalities live in the city

MONTE CARLO CASINO

Monte Carlo is renowned for its exclusivity and ostentatious wealth; so perhaps it is no surprise that the city's most famous building is not the royal palace, but the casino. Tall tales abound about this lavish gambling palace, which opened in 1863. Legend has it that Mata Hari (1876–1917), a dancer accused of being a German spy, once shot a spy inside Monte Carlo Casino, and it was here that actor Richard Burton (1925–84) melted the heart of Elizabeth Taylor (b. 1932) with an enormous and extremely valuable diamond. The Casino has also taken a starring role in numerous films including the James Bond spoof *Casino Royale*.

The tiny principality—equivalent in size to London's Hyde Park—enjoys an exceptional location, sandwiched between the Mediterranean and the Southern Alps. Mention Monte Carlo to most people and they think of the ultra rich in fast cars, designer clothes, and private yachts; the city's famous casino; the glitzy world of Formula One racing—Monte Carlo has one of the world's premier street car-racing circuits—and the glamor of the Grimaldi royal family. The Grimaldis still preside over Monaco today, but if they were to die out, the principality would legally revert to France, though this is unlikely given the number of siblings in line to the throne. The political system works surprisingly well considering Prince Albert (b. 1958), having recently succeeded the throne from his father, Prince Rainier, is the only constitutional autocratic ruler left in Europe and his decisions and beliefs become law, despite the existence of a puppet parliament. Perhaps the reason so few complain is that the citizens of Monaco pay no income tax whilst enjoying an incredibly high standard of living with virtually no crime.

Monte Carlo's unique history, stunning location, compact size, and status as a tax haven make it attractive to tourists, many visiting the city simply out of curiosity, with tourism at the forefront of the principality's economy. In a state with no taxes, banking and finance are key sectors, as is real estate, with the rich and famous seeking homes in the city to prevent their vast fortunes ending up in the taxman's coffers.

Princess Grace of Monaco (1929–82)

Princess Grace (formerly Grace Kelly) led a fairytale life. Having begun life in a humble Philadelphia family, she achieved iconic status as a Hollywood actress before marrying Prince Rainier of Monaco (1923–2005) in 1956. Her impact on the city is undeniable. Before their marriage the Prince did not even live in Monaco, let alone Monte Carlo, and the clifftop castle, today's royal residence, was falling into disrepair. Today the Palais Princier, which hovers above the city, is a well polished tourist sight, complete with costumed guards, sidewalk cafés, and souvenir stores, and a daily changing of the guard at 11.55am. For Kelly fans the Cathèdrale de Monaco is a particularly poignant spot. The venue for the wedding ceremony in 1956, it is also where the Princess was buried after she was involved in a tragic car accident in 1982.

BELOW AND RIGHT: *Pleasure craft tied up in one of the sheltered marinas overlooked by the high-rise buildings of Monaco.* ABOVE RIGHT: *Outdoor dining in Monte Carlo.* FAR RIGHT: *The wealth of the city's residents is evident in their choice of sports car.*

THE STORY OF...

Monte Carlo's earliest inhabitants were Ligurian tribesmen, followed by the Romans in the 12th century BC and marauding barbarians from the fifth century AD. At the end of the 13th century the Grimaldi family slipped into town under the guise of an order of monks and seized power. The Grimaldi reign was cut short in 1301, only to be restored in 1331. Other key events include the recognition of both Monaco's sovereignty (1489) and independence (1512) by the French.

Until the end of the 18th century the principality fell under the protection, at different times, of France, Spain, and Sardinia. In 1793 Monaco became embroiled in the French Revolution and Joseph Grimaldi's wife was beheaded at the guillotine. The first Treaty of Paris (1814) restored Monaco's independence, however the monarchy had to surrender 80 percent of its territory in 1861.

The 20th century was more stable, with Monte Carlo celebrating the 700th Anniversary of the Grimaldi Royal Dynasty in 1997. Prince Rainier III, Prince Albert's father, celebrated over 50 years on the throne before his death in 2005.

key dates

1297
François Grimaldi takes the Rock of Monaco

1512
France recognizes Monaco's independence

1869
Direct taxes are abolished

1929
Monte Carlo hosts its first motor Grand Prix

2005
Prince Rainier III, head of the Grimaldi family, dies

Moscow

statistics

- Population: 8,600,000

- Moscow has the world's largest bell (200 tonnes) and the largest cannon (40 tonnes) in the world

- Temperatures below –40°F (–40°C) have been recorded

- On average, 174 days of the year have a daytime temperature below 32°F (0°C)

MOSCOW UNDERGROUND

One of Moscow's greatest attractions is its vast underground system. Dating from 1935, it is a one-off, putting the functionalism of the likes of New York and London to shame. Many of the Moscow underground stations are more like palaces than transport hubs, with chandeliers and stunning sculptures. The pick of the bunch are the art deco Mayakovskaya, the baroque beauty Komsomolskaya, and the outlandish Ploschad Revolutsii.

ABOVE: *The Komsomolskaya Metro, an interior with marble halls, mosaics, chandeliers, and statues.*

Russia's capital is located in the European part of this vast country, straddling the River Moskva. For some people anachronistic images of Moscow still linger of soldiers goose-stepping across Red Square, crusty old communist leaders hailing the Red Army as it clanked through the capital, and the food queues that became the symbol of communism's flaws. In reality, Moscow is a buzzing capitalist hub powered by manufacturing—metalwork and textiles are the city's biggest industries—and the results of economic reforms that have stimulated consumer spending. Today well-heeled Muscovites like nothing better than to hang out in glitzy restaurants, trendy nightspots, and designer stores. Problems remain with some elements of organized crime, and terrorist attacks arising from Russia's conflict with Chechnya.

Red Square is very much at the heart of the city and few fail to be impressed with this epic set piece; a vast expanse with the onion domes of St. Basil's Cathedral catching the eye and the voluminous walls of the Kremlin—the old seat of Soviet power—rearing up along one flank. Moscow's myriad church spires are also symbolic of the city, with the cathedrals of the Assumption, the Annunciation, and the Archangel Michael all located inside the walls of the Kremlin. The recently rebuilt Church of Christ the Saviour, was originally taken down at Stalin's bequest in 1931 as part of his attempts to suppress religion.

BELOW AND RIGHT: *The yellow walls of the Great Kremlin Palace, built for Nicholas I between 1838 and 1849.*

Embracing Capitalism

It is not only the politics that have changed in 21st-century Moscow. Stalin's "Seven Sisters" skyscrapers still cast an unmistakable presence on the skyline of this largely flat city, but joining them recently have been new symbols of capitalism: gleaming glass and steel towers for the multinational and domestic companies that have moved into a city that generates a quarter of Russia's tax revenue. Many of Moscow's streets have been spruced up and some of its older buildings have been resurrected with this new investment. The enormous GUM department store on Red Square is one of the biggest symbols of the changing face of Moscow. In communist times there was little to buy, but today this grand building is stuffed full of chic designer stores. Moscow's ambitious mayor, Yuri Luzhkov, is pushing the city's retail sector, rejuvenating the city with new and renovated stores including a sprawling multi-level shopping mall that spreads its tentacles under Red Square.

ABOVE: *Monument to the 17th-century liberators Prince Dmitry Pozharsky and Kozma Minin.*
RIGHT: *The Tomb of the Unknown Soldier in Alexander Gardens.*

ABOVE: *The red granite Lenin Mausoleum next to the wall of the Kremlin in Red Square.*

THE STORY OF...

Moscow emerged as a modest settlement in 1156 under Prince Yury Dolgoruky, only to be destroyed by the Tartars in 1237. Recovery was quick and Moscow developed strongly throughout the 14th and 15th centuries. During the 18th century Moscow's intellectual might came to the fore with the printing of the city's first newspaper in 1703 and the opening of its first university in 1775. Communism emerged as a dominant force in the 20th century and Russia became entrenched in the bitter Cold War with the West.

From the mid-1980s Gorbachev's *glasnost* (openness) and *perestroika* (reconstruction) liberalization schemes ignited a chain of events that saw the walls of the communist empire fall, ending the Cold War. Russia's darkest days followed, characterized by the failed anti-Yeltsin coup in 1991, when the country seemed on the point of collapse. Just over a decade later, under Vladimir Putin, the picture is brighter for Moscow as the country's currency has stabilized and its economy has started to recover.

key dates

1156
Prince Yury Dolgoruky, credited as founder of the city, fortifies Moscow with a moat and wooden walls

1812
Napoleon and his troops briefly occupy the city

1917
The Great October Revolution heralds the coming of communism to the city

1991
A political coup fails, triggering the end of communism

2004
President Vladimir Putin is re-elected in a landslide election

Munich

statistics

Population: 1,298,000

Average quantity of beer consumed per head: 42 gal (190 liters)

Germany's largest university: 102,000 students

One of the largest city parks in Europe: 3 miles (5km) long and 0.6 miles (1km) wide

RICHARD STRAUSS (1864–1949)

Munich's greatest composer, Richard Strauss, was born in 1864, and eventually became the city's *Kapellmeister* (musical director). The breathtaking Bavarian scenery held a magnetic attraction for him, influencing his compositions considerably, and was particularly evident in his *Alpensinfonie*. His operas are still among the world's most popular and a fountain, depicting scenes from *Salome*, stands in the city center as a memorial.

Straddling the River Isar in the south of Germany, 1,000-year-old Munich is the country's third largest city and its economic heart. Surveys show that it is also Germany's most popular city and that, given the choice, over half of the German population would choose to live in the Bavarian capital. This is probably due to the fact that Münchners, despite their reputation for working hard, love the outdoors and make their *Freizeit* (free time) a priority. A typical weekend for many involves heading to the nearby Alps for hiking or skiing, or to one of the Bavarian lakes such as Ammersee or Starnbergersee, for swimming or sailing. After work and at weekends, the city's vast park, the Englischer Garten, fills up with people walking, cycling, rollerblading, playing soccer and even surfing on the river that flows through the park.

Parts of the old city walls and gates, such as the Isartor, are still standing, and within them lies the geographical and social heart of Munich, the Altstadt (Old Town). The focus is Marienplatz, a large square dominated by the 19th-century neo-Gothic Neues Rathaus (New City Hall), where the brightly colored figures of the famous Glockenspiel move and chime three times a day. The elegant streets around the square, such as Maximilianstrasse and Theatinerstrasse, are full of designer stores, and south of here is the Viktualienmarkt, an open-air food market that has been held for centuries. No mention of Munich would be complete without reference to the Italian Renaissance "onion" domes of the twin towers of the city's cathedral, the Frauenkirche, which are the symbol of Munich.

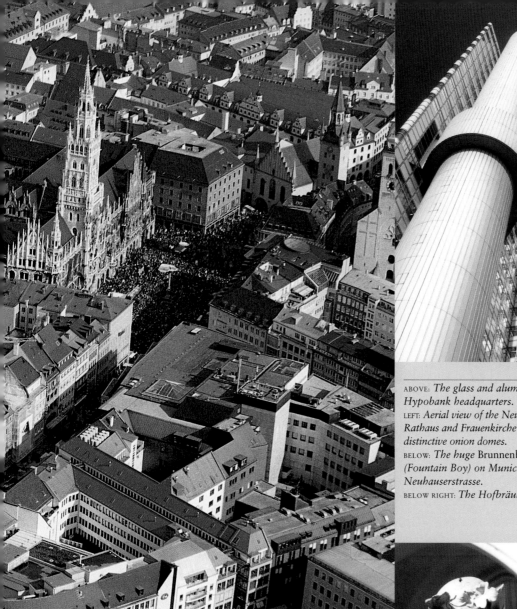

THE STORY OF...

In the 10th century, monks established a settlement on the banks of the River Isar, which became known as Munichen, before Henry the Lion took control of Bavaria in around 1158. A century later, Munich became the main residence of the Wittelsbach dynasty, which was to dominate Munich's history through its rule of Bavaria which lasted for 800 years. The dynasty commissioned many buildings which still stand today, such as the Residenz and the summer residence of the kings, Schloss Nymphenburg.

The November Revolution of 1919 led the last Wittelsbach ruler, Ludwig III and his family, to flee the city in the middle of the night, with Ludwig abdicating a few days later. Political unrest continued through the early 20th century, and in 1923, a young Adolf Hitler attempted to instigate a socialist revolution, but his revolt failed. After suffering heavy bomb damage during World War II, the city was rebuilt and continued to prosper, becoming the economic heart of Germany. Munich became the focus of sporting attention in 1972 when it hosted the Olympic Games, and again in 2006 with the World Cup.

ABOVE: *The glass and aluminium Hypobank headquarters.*
LEFT: *Aerial view of the Neues Rathaus and Frauenkirche with its distinctive onion domes.*
BELOW: *The huge* Brunnenbuberl *(Fountain Boy) on Munich's Neuhauserstrasse.*
BELOW RIGHT: *The Hofbräuhaus.*

The Business of Beer

Munich has the headquarters of Siemens, automotive giants BMW, and many insurance companies, as well as publishing and film production companies. However, the city is probably best-known internationally for the production, consumption, and celebration of beer. Munich's six main breweries play a significant economic role and the drink itself is an integral part of the culture, with beer halls and beer gardens all over the city. One of the largest of these, by the Chinese pagoda in the Englischer Garten, can seat 7,000 people.

The annual draw for many is the world's largest beer festival, the *Oktoberfest*, which begins on the third Saturday in September when the city's mayor opens the first barrel. This festival, which lasts just over two weeks, attracts 7 million visitors who, between them, consume over 1 million gal (more than 6 million liters) of beer, 400,000 sausages, and 600,000 chickens. Münchners dress up in traditional costume and, alongside the tourists, enjoy the huge funfair.

key dates

1158
Henry the Lion founds Munich

1327
The city suffers damage in a devastating fire

1505
Munich becomes the capital of Bavaria

1940
First air attack on Munich during World War II (another 70 follow before 1945)

2006
Hosts the opening match of the soccer World Cup

57

Oslo

- Population: 550,000
- Oslo has one of the highest Gross National Product (GNP) per capita levels in the world
- The Nobel Peace Prize has been presented in Oslo since 1901
- From November to February the average daily temperature is usually below 32°F (0°C)

AKERSHUS SLOTT

When it was constructed in 1300 Akershus Slott (Akershus Castle), one of Oslo's most historic buildings, was one of the most well built and impenetrable castles in Europe. The castle is situated within the protective confines of Akershus Festning (Akershus Fortress)—the dense stone and earth fortifications that still encircle the castle today—and served as both a royal residence and a protective bastion. In 1527 a large chunk of the complex was devastated by fire and again by 16th-century battles. Various reconstructions saw the medieval castle re-emerge as a comfortable Renaissance palace and today Akershus Slott is used for special events and state functions.

ocated at the tip of a dramatic 70 mile (110km) long fjord (the Oslofjorden) in southeast Norway, Oslo has a truly breathtaking setting. Despite its compact size Scandinavia's oldest capital has a rich and vibrant artistic and cultural scene. Bustling bars and cafés are joined by myriad museums, galleries, and theater houses, where the artistic offerings include works by Munch (1863–1944), Pablo Picasso (1881–1973), Paul Cézanne (1839–1906), and Hilaire Germain Edgar Degas (1834–1917). The city's fascinating Viking past and maritime history are brought to life in the museums of the Bygdøy peninsula.

Oslo is not generally renowned for the quality of its architecture, with many of the city's more imposing buildings dating from the 19th century, when the city emerged from the grip of its union with Denmark. Key sights include the Rådhus (Town Hall), a thoroughly 20th-century construction built to commemorate Oslo's 900th birthday in 1950, where the Nobel Peace Prize is awarded each December. In the same year that the Rådhus was constructed, one of the city's most historic buildings, the Domkirke (cathedral) dating from 1696, received a dramatic interior

RIGHT: *A statue outside the Rådhus.*

makeover that added impressive stained-glass windows and imaginatively painted ceiling frescos.

Oslo is the driving force behind Norway's economy, and is home to around 12 percent of the population who work in traditional industries such as shipping and forestry. Services, commerce, and oil are also important ingredients in an economy that allows the people of Oslo to enjoy one of the highest standards of living in Europe.

ABOVE: *The statue of Aker Brugge.*

Great Outdoors

The citizens of Oslo have a penchant for the great outdoors and, while others might curse the city's harsh winter days, many of the residents flock to the nearby ski slopes to help them fend off the winter blues. When the mercury rises and the city is blessed with seemingly endless sunny days, Oslo's residents like nothing better than to head back to the hills for long hikes. Others take a more sedate approach to their adventures, lapping up the sun on the beach on long days, chatting over coffee in the sidewalk cafés, relaxing in the park, or taking in the impressive artwork at the Vigeland Sculpture Park. In the warmer months the Aker Brugge waterfront area also springs into life, while another great outdoor pastime simply involves wandering around the city's old lanes, lapping up the vibrant street life and snatching views of the Oslofjorden from seemingly every corner.

RIGHT: *Ornamental pond with fountain jets and a bronze statuary group of bears in a tree-lined square in Oslo.*

THE STORY OF...

In the millennium since it was first settled, Oslo's fortunes have wavered. The construction of Akershus Slott in the 14th century boosted the city's military, political, and economic muscle. In 1350 two thirds of the population were wiped out by the plague, forcing Norway to join with Denmark—a coalition that moved the seat of power to Copenhagen and reduced Oslo to the status of a provincial town.

The city became Christiania in the 17th century (a name it kept until 1925) after King Christian IV who oversaw the city's post-fire reconstruction. In the 19th century Oslo established a university (1811), formed a more equal union with Sweden, became economically prosperous, and flourished as a center for art and literature, with painters such as Edvard Munch (1863–1944) and writer Knut Hamsun (1859–1952) amongst its residents. The 20th century brought two World Wars, the second accompanied by an occupying German army despite Norway's declaration of neutrality. The discovery of oil in 1970 led to the high standard of living that Oslo's inhabitants enjoy today.

key dates

1048
City is founded by King Harald Hårdråda

1350
Around two thirds of the population is wiped out by bubonic plague

1624
A great fire devastates the city

1814
Oslo's economy booms after Norway unites with Sweden and (later gains independence from Sweden in 1905)

1991
King Harald V comes to the throne

Paris

ocated in Northern France, Paris is split in two by the River Seine which loops northward before heading out toward the English Channel. It is the capital and largest city of France, the center of finance, and a world nucleus of style and the avant-garde. It is this that attracted great artists Pablo Picasso (1881–1973), Edouard Manet (1832–83), Henri de Toulouse-Lautrec (1864–1901), and great writers Ernest Hemingway (1899–1961) and James Joyce (1882–1941) to the city. Parisians are sociable—they love to go out, and enjoy sitting on the terraces of cafés watching the world go by or relaxing on Paris Plage, the man-made beach by the Seine. They also adore their arts, especially the cinema, theater, and the Palais Garnier, home to the Paris Opera and considered by Adolf Hitler (1889–1945) to be the most breathtaking building in the world. Students at the medieval Sorbonne congregate in the bookshops on the Left Bank. Paris is also at the forefront of fashion and shopping. Since Coco Chanel (1883–1971), a milliner who rose to become a premier fashion designer, replaced women's corsets with casual elegance, haute couture (high fashion) has become the city's trademark. The annual Paris Fashion Week is actually six hectic weeks of clamoring to see the following season's styles paraded extravagantly on the catwalk.

Many of Paris' landmarks stand on the riverbanks, which have been designated a World Heritage Site by UNESCO. On the Right Bank is the thoroughfare Avenue des Champs-Élysées (Elysian Fields) and the Arc de Triomphe (Arch of Triumph), commissioned in 1806 by Emperor Napoleon Bonaparte (1769–1821). On the Left Bank stands the Eiffel Tower, at 1,063ft (324m). Completed in 1889 for the Universal

ART NOUVEAU

A response to urban growth and the aftermath of the Industrial Revolution, the ornamental style known as art nouveau appeared in Paris in the early 1880s and lasted until the beginning of World War I in 1914. A style of architecture and design characterized by flowing lines, twining tendrils, and natural organic forms, this style took its name from "L'Art Nouveau", a gallery opened by art dealer Siegfried Bing in Paris in 1895. At the Exposition Universelle (world fair) in Paris in 1900, 51 million people viewed furniture, jewellery, ceramics, and metalwork. Examples of art nouveau survive in Paris, the best known being Hector Guimard's (1867–1942) Métro station entrances.

ABOVE: *Art Nouveau metro sign.*
ABOVE RIGHT: *Pont Neuf and the Eiffel Tower.*

Exhibition of the French Revolution, the metal tower draws thousands of visitors who climb the 1,665 steps for the finest view of the city. In 1996 the Bibliothéque Nationale François Mitterrand (National Library), one of the world's most spectacular libraries, opened as part of a grand development of the Left Bank. On Île-de-France is the Cathedral of Notre Dame, while to the north is Montmarte and the Basilica of Sacré Coeur. West of Paris is the Palace of Versailles, the former royal seat of Louis XIV (1638–1715) and later French kings.

Mona Lisa

Painted by Leonardo da Vinci (1479–1528) the oil-on-wood masterpiece that is the *Mona Lisa* attracts thousands of visitors to its home at the Palais du Louvre (the Louvre). Theory has it that the subject is a young Florentine woman called Mona. Whatever the truth about her identity, her gentle face is considered to be the prototype of the Renaissance portrait. In 1911, she was stolen from the Louvre, but two years later the painting was retrieved from a hotel in Florence.

BELOW: *The Louvre with its most recent addition, the 1989 glass pyramid entrance.*
BELOW RIGHT: *A museum visitor "paints a painting" in the Musée d'Orsay.*

THE STORY OF...

When the Romans arrived in 52BC a Celtic tribe, the Parisii, occupied the central island known today as Ile-de-France (Island of France). The Romans built a temple to worship Jupiter and renamed the settlement Lutétia, meaning "marshy place". The city spread north to the Rive Droite (Right Bank) and south to the Rive Gauche (Left Bank) of the Seine. Roman rule ended in the sixth century and the Franks moved in, followed by the Vikings. Feudal lords came to power and in AD987 the Count of Paris, Hugues Capet, became King of France and made Paris his capital.

King Louis XIV (1638–1715) later moved the royal residence from Paris to Versailles. On 14 July 1789 the people of Paris stormed the Bastille, the prison which was a symbol of absolute monarchy and power. The event marked the beginning of the French Revolution, a political upheaval which lasted until 1799. During World War II, the Nazis occupied Paris until the city was liberated by the Allies in 1944.

BELOW: *Historic Les Deux Magots café in St. Germain Des Prés.*

52BC
The Romans build Lutetia, later to become Paris

1789
The Bastille is stormed

1940
Paris is occupied by Nazi Germany and Allies liberate the city in 1944

1994
Channel Tunnel opens, shortening the journey time from Paris to London

1998
France wins the soccer World Cup at the Stade de France in Paris

Prague

DEFENESTRATION

When a band of Protestant noblemen threw the Emperor's Catholic councillors from the windows of Prague Castle in 1618, they were continuing what was already a well established tradition. Two centuries before, a riotous mob had invaded the upper floors of the Town Hall, freed the prisoners held there, and hurled the aldermen to their deaths on the cobbles below. The Imperial Councillors were luckier; landing on a dung-heap in the Castle moat, they suffered only minor injuries, and were able to escape. In 1948, the communists' last opponent, Foreign Minister Jan Masaryk, died after falling from the window of his Ministry. The controversy as to whether it was murder or suicide continues to this day.

ABOVE: *The window from which the Emperor's councillors fell.*

Strategically located astride the River Vltava in the middle of Bohemia, Prague is the natural capital of the Czech Republic and by far its largest city. Known as "Hundred-towered Prague", with a wealth of historic buildings of all periods, it is considered by many to be the most beautiful city in Europe. The broad but shallow Vltava is crossed by several bridges, the most striking being a marvel of medieval engineering, the 14th-century Charles Bridge. Overlooking the river and the ancient districts of Old Town and Malá Strana (Lesser Quarter) is the formidable Hradčany Castle, seat of the President. Much of the city's life is concentrated on the famous Wenceslas Square, the centrepiece of Charles IV's New Town. Beyond the historic districts are densely built-up 19th- and early 20th-century tenement suburbs, and beyond them vast multi-storey housing estates built during communist times.

Once a compact city of courtiers, tradespeople, entertainers (Wolfgang Amadeus Mozart, 1756–91, premiered his opera *Don Giovanni* here), and scholars, in the 20th century Prague grew into an important commercial and industrial centre. The heavy engineering of the communist era is now overshadowed by light industries and service establishments, and tourism—which has experienced spectacular growth since 1989—employs tens of thousands. The city and its surroundings have proved to be one of the most attractive areas in post-communist Europe for inward investment, and a significant expatriate community has settled here.

Leisure Time

A persistent housing shortage means that many Praguers marry late and even then continue to live in the family home (almost invariably an apartment). But fine countryside—hills, woods, rivers, lakes—is within easy reach, and possession of a weekend cottage is almost universal, helping to relieve the pressure on accommodation. On Friday afternoons, the exodus from city to countryside fills the roads, which are jammed again on Sunday evening. Some of those unable to escape in this way—men at least—find their way to the *hospoda* (pub); Czech beer enjoys a justifiably high reputation, and while the country's most famous brew comes from Plzeň (Pilsen), Prague has several breweries, each responsible for a distinctive product. The city's most characteristic drinking places are those dating back to medieval times, their cool cellars providing an ideal environment for keeping the beer in good condition. Drinkers sit at solid wooden tables beneath low vaulted ceilings, served by patrolling waiters who replace glasses as soon as they are empty.

FAR LEFT: *Malostranské Námesti (Lesser Town Square) in Malá Strana.*
LEFT: *Finely carved decoration on an old gravestone in Beth Chaim (the Old Jewish Cemetery).*

THE STORY OF...

Whether or not the tale of Princess Libuše is true, Prague owes its beginnings to the Přemyslid dynasty, whose most famous member was the "Good King" (actually a prince) Wenceslas, assassinated by his brother around AD930. Přemyslid rulers founded Hradčany Castle overlooking the ford over the River Vltava, and also fortified the Old Town on the far bank. Prague owes much of its character to 14th-century Emperor Charles IV (1316–78), who began the Gothic St. Vitus Cathedral, bridged the Vltava, and laid out the New Town, a stupendous example of medieval town planning.

After the Thirty Years War, Prague was beautified with a wealth of Baroque buildings, but its character became largely German. A Czech revival took place in the 19th century, and after the First World War an independent and democratic Czechoslovakia arose from the ruins of the Austrian Empire. A brutal occupation by Nazi Germany began in 1939, then hopes of postwar freedom and democracy were dashed by the communist coup d'etat in 1948. An attempt at democratization, the "Prague Spring" of 1968, was crushed by the Soviet Union, but in 1989 Prague was the chief seat of the Velvet Revolution that put an end to communism and restored western-style democracy.

ABOVE: *An art nouveau window, by Alphonse Mucha, decorating the Cathedral of St. Vitus.*

LEFT: *The Town Hall astronomical clock in Old Town Square.*

EARLY 9TH CENTURY

Legendary foundation of Prague by Princess Libuše and her ploughman husband Přemysl

1618

Defenestration of Catholic councillors unleashes the Thirty Years War

1918

Foundation of Czechoslovakia with Prague as its capital

1945

Liberation from Nazi rule by Soviet army

1989

End of communist regime

Reykjavik

Reykjavik is a small city on a peninsula at the habitable margin of the world. Across 170 sq miles (274.5 sq km) a jumble of concrete apartment blocks and low-rise modern offices is offset by the old wooden houses encased in corrugated iron, which give it its frontier feel and much of its charm. They are painted in dignified, earthy tones or bright modern shades to suit the city's latest rebirth as a destination for vibrant nightlife.

Looking Around

Reykjavik's dominant landmarks are the soaring spire of the Hallgrímskirkja church, built on Thingholt hill, and the space-age Perlan ("the Pearl") on Öskjuhlíð— a glass-domed restaurant atop the city's hot-water storage tanks. Both offer fabulous views, and it is easy to overlook the urban sprawl and admire the distant mound of Snæfellsjökull, or the nearer Mount Esja.

DISCOVERING NORTH AMERICA

A heroic statue stands in front of the Hallgrímskirkja. It portrays Leifur Eiríksson or "Leif the Lucky", eldest son of banished Icelander Erik the Red, who is widely credited with the earliest European discovery of North America. Leif sailed from Greenland around AD1000, and landed on Baffin Island ("Helluland") and at the tip of Newfoundland ("Vinland"), where the remains of a Viking farm have been uncovered. He was followed by Thorfinn Karlsefin, who spent three years exploring. There his wife Gudrid gave birth to their son Snorri—the first European baby born on the continent—before the family returned to Iceland to farm.

ABOVE RIGHT: *Hallgrímskirkja church on Thingholt hill.*

The city grew up around Aðalstræti, in the days before landfill when Hafnarstræti really did mark the line of the harbor. You can stroll around the old center in an hour or two, taking in the small grey Lutheran cathedral, the parliament building of 1881, the birdlife on Tjörnin pond, and the neighboring National Art Gallery—one of many excellent small museums. Pavement cafés spill out into pleasant squares. Between the buildings, bright flowerbeds tended by teenagers in the summer contrast with exposed patches of the black lava which underlies everything, reflecting back the moody skies.

The Gulf Stream keeps temperatures at a mild annual average of 40°F (4.8°C), with extremes of 27°F (−2.6°C) in winter and around 55°F (13°C) in summer. There's usually either a steady waft of clean, sharp sea air blowing through, or the smell of fish from the harbor. The modern harbor is home to a state-of-the-art trawler fleet which contributes to Iceland's most important product: fish and its processing accounts for three-quarters of national export income.

March of Progress

Prosperity may have come late to Reykjavik, but now, with one of the highest standards of living in the world, its population thrives on new technologies. Around 78 percent of citizens work in service industries. Biotech companies such as deCODE, a firm specializing in the study of genetics, are based here, and Iceland boasts the highest rate of computer use in the world.

Locals enjoy their endless hot water in open-air pools, or head down to the imported golden sands and warm lagoon of Nauthólsvík, in the shadow of the airport. The whole city is heated by naturally produced geothermal energy, and in the latest cutting-edge experiment, buses are being adapted to run on sustainable and eco-friendly hydrogen.

ABOVE: *A local dressed as a Viking.*

BELOW: *Taking the waters in one of Reykjavik's hot-water pools.*

THE STORY OF...

In the late 9th century Norwegian Ingólfur Arnarson established his farm where the gods washed his high seat pillars ashore, in a place he called Reykjavik, or "smoky bay", after the natural steam vents he saw. Iceland's geographical isolation and its lack of exploitable resources meant that it had a relatively quiet history. Norwegian and then Danish rulers treated the island as a far outpost. A trade monopoly imposed by Denmark (1602–1854), combined with a series of natural disasters, prevented growth, although unauthorized trade in fish continued with England, Holland, and Germany.

Reykjavik was a mere cluster of farmhouses when entrepreneur Skúli Magnússon (1711–94) started up factories for wool processing and rope-making. He went bankrupt, but Reykjavik was on the map, and the bishopric moved from Skálholt to the town's new cathedral in 1796. When the Althingi (parliament) was re-established in 1845, it was in Reykjavik rather than Thingvellir. The appointment of a city council in 1908 led to the introduction of utilities in the town, including fresh water in 1909 and electricity in 1921. In 1962, 18 years after Iceland became a republic, Reykjavik was declared a city.

key dates

AD874
Ingólfur Arnarson builds his homestead in Reykjavik and becomes Iceland's first settler

1786
With a population of just 167, Reykjavik gains its market town charter

1904
Reykjavik takes on the role of country in the throes of gaining independence from Denmark

1940
Wartime occupation by Britain and America brings income and infrastructure improvements, including the building of Reykjavik's airport

1986
Ronald Reagan and Mikhail Gorbachev hold a summit meeting at Höfði house, on Borgartún, that kick-starts the end of the Cold War

Rome

statistics

- Population: 3,800,458
- Population of Vatican City: 900
- Major industries: finance and banking, tourism, insurance, printing and publishing, fashion, film industry
- International organizations: Rome is the home of FAO (United Nations Food and Agricultural Organization) and WFP (World Food Program)

The ancient city of Rome, capital of Italy, stands on the River Tiber (Tevere) midway between the north and south of the country. Famously built across seven hills, its buildings span the centuries from the days of classical Rome to the 21st century, and the entire city is a treasure house of monuments, churches, palazzi, and superb Baroque fountains. West of the Tiber lies the Vatican, the Pope's separate city state, and the artisan neighborhood of Trastevere, now more noted for its nightlife and restaurants. The area east of the Tiber is roughly dissected by the Via del Corso, which runs through from the Piazza del Popolo to the Piazza Venezia, a spacious square dominated by the vast "wedding cake" of the Victor Emmanuel Monument. South from here are the Forum and the Colosseum—the heart of classical Rome. Between the Corso and the river lies the *centro storico* (historic center), an appealing mix of narrow medieval streets, Renaissance palaces, and fine squares. East of the Corso, there are more historic buildings and churches, while to the north the beautiful Villa Borghese gardens are an oasis of green containing some of Rome's best museums. There are shopping areas throughout the city, the smartest being clustered around the Piazza di Spagna, a beautiful square backed by the famous Spanish Steps. The city is also home to some of the country's best markets.

Capital City

The President of Italy has his official residence in the 16th-century Palazzo del Quirinale, while Italy's two houses of parliament meet in the Palazzo Madama and the Palazzo Montecitorio. The state employs over half a million office workers (more than six times Rome's industrial workforce), housed in ministries throughout the city, while the private and international business sectors concentrate their workforces either in the heart of the *centro storico* or 4 miles (6km) out in the EUR district, a Mussolini-inspired area built in

LEFT: *View from St. Peter's Basilica.*
BELOW RIGHT AND FAR RIGHT: *The Fontana dei Fiumi in Piazza Navona.*
BOTTOM RIGHT: *Flowers at the foot of the Spanish Steps.*

the 1940s and 1950s. EUR also provides venues for trade fairs and conventions, and is the site of the headquarters of the UN-run FAO (Food and Agriculture Organization).

Local government is in the hands of the mayor and city council, who have the task of maximizing the potential revenue from tourism and encouraging major companies to base themselves in Rome, while running a city under constant pressure from its physical past. The celebrations for the millennium provided a huge impetus for restoration all over Rome, and the benefits of a revamped transportation system, and renovated buildings, museums, and visitor facilities have benefited Romans and tourists alike.

VATICAN CITY

Founded in 1929 in order to ensure the independency of the Pope, the Vatican State is situated entirely within the city of Rome, covering an area of 0.17 sq miles (0.44 sq km) and with a population of around 900. Within it stands St. Peter's Basilica, the heart of Roman Catholicism, and the Vatican Palace and gardens, home to the Pope and the art collections that comprise the Vatican Museums. The Vatican issues its own stamps, publishes a daily newspaper, and runs a worldwide broadcasting service. Italian and Latin are the official languages and security is in the hands of the famous Swiss Guard, who first entered the Vatican in 1506.

ABOVE: *Ceiling detail in the Raphael Room at the Vatican Museum.*

BELOW: *The Via della Conciliazione leads to St. Peter's.*

THE STORY OF...

Legend has it that Rome was founded by Romulus and Remus, orphan twins suckled by a she-wolf. Dating from the eighth century BC, Rome became a Republic in 507BC. By 146BC it had become the dominant power in the Mediterranean and riches poured into the city. The Republic was overturned in 27BC and around 300 years of imperial power followed, the city falling to the northern barbarian tribes in the fifth century. Ruin followed, which was finally reversed by Pope Gregory I (c540–604), during and after whose pontificate the city became recognized as pre-eminent in the Christian world.

Under papal rule the city was transformed. Ancient monuments were restored and a series of major building projects, which drew artists of the highest calibre to Rome, were begun. The Pope remained in power until Italian Reunification in 1870, when the city became the new country's capital. Benito Mussolini (1883–1945) gained power in 1922, establishing Vatican City as a separate state in 1929. Since 1945, Rome has been the seat of numerous governments, and is a major tourist destination.

BELOW: *Monumental remains of the Foro Romano (Roman Forum).*

EIGHTH CENTURY BC
Foundation of Rome

507BC TO AD330
Roman Republic and Empire

AD590
Pope Gregory I establishes Rome as papal city and temporal power

1870
Rome becomes capital of united Italy, Pius IX becomes "Prisoner of the Vatican"

2000
Millennium celebrations mark end of immense restoration and refurbishment program

key dates

Salzburg

WOLFGANG AMADEUS MOZART

The composer Wolfgang Amadeus Mozart (1756–91) is Salzburg's most famous son. Even at the age of seven Mozart exhibited great talent, encouraging his father to include him on a journey that would see Mozart and his sister Maria Anna perform in venues throughout western Europe, playing to the courts of George III (1738–1820) in London and Louis XV (1710–74) in Versailles. In 1773 Mozart returned to Salzburg, where he worked tirelessly on his symphonies. He died penniless, the quality of his work never recognized even by the city of his birth. Today Mozart's birthplace and childhood home, as well as his adult residence, are amongst Salzburg's premier tourist attractions.

ABOVE: *The exterior of Mozart's Geburtshaus (birthplace).*

Those who have never visited Salzburg, but who have seen *The Sound of Music*, the 1965 musical staring Julie Andrews (b. 1935), will have an inkling of just how stunningly scenic it is. The city grew along the banks of the historic river, the Salzach, which neatly divides present-day Salzburg in two: the right and left banks. For residents and tourists the older left bank is the center of life in Salzburg. Here narrow pedestrianized lanes and regal squares crammed with an eclectic array of architectural styles that span the centuries—with buildings constructed in the Baroque, Romanesque and Renaissance eras, as well as the Middle Ages—mobilized UNESCO to place the Old City on its World Heritage List in 1997. Salzburg's chocolate-box beautiful old town, which many people compare favorably to Prague, has an enviable location encircled by the Mönchsberg (Monk Mountain), which itself is topped by the imposing 11th-century Hohensalzburg Fortress. Meanwhile the Kapuzinerberg (Capuchin Mountain) hangs omnipresent over the right bank of the river.

Salzburg, one of Austria's cultural centers, is blessed with a wealth of museums and churches, with the city's ecclesiastical life dominated by voluminous Salzburg Cathedral. It is also home to the opulent Mirabell and Hellbrunn Palaces and the grand performance venues of

LEFT: *Salzburg Cathedral dominates the skyline of the city.*

the Felsenreitschule (Rocky Riding School), the open-air theater that has been the home to the Salzburg Festival for around 80 years, and the Large and Small Festival Halls, both lavish 20th-century constructions.

A Successful Economy

Salzburg makes a fundamental contribution to Austria's economy, with just over five percent of the country's population generating almost 20 percent of its wealth, or net economic product. Administration and service industries are traditionally the biggest employers in Salzburg, employing over 60 percent of the workforce. Banking, financial services, and tourism—some four million people visit Salzburg each year—are also key contributors to its successful economy, with the city investing heavily in technological developments in recent years. A university city with a student population of some 17,000, Salzburg is also able to groom and keep some of Austria's top graduates. All these factors combined mean that, on average, those working in the country's administrative capital earn higher wages than those employed elsewhere in Austria, and many parts of the European Union.

THE STORY OF...

Celts and Romans were amongst Salzburg's early inhabitants, with the demise of the Roman Empire sparking a similar decline in the city's fortunes. Salzburg was resettled at the end of the seventh century by Bishop Rupert, with the clergy becoming increasingly powerful in the years to follow. During the 16th and 17th centuries Salzburg had Wolf Dietrich von Raitenau (1559–1617) at the helm, and this powerful archbishop engineered the Baroque reconstruction of the city. The city's religious leaders also had a negative influence on the city, banishing the Jewish population in the 15th century and persecuting its Protestant minority three centuries later.

By the 19th century, Salzburg's power had diminished and it came under the control of France (1809), Bavaria (1810), the Hapsburgs (1816), and Austria (1818). In 1938 the German Third Reich swallowed up Salzburg, with Nazi troops marching into the city virtually unchallenged. In 1955 Austria joined the United Nations, declaring its neutrality and regaining sovereignty.

BELOW LEFT: *The Octogon in Hellbrunn Palace.*
BELOW: *View from the River Salzach.*

SEVENTH CENTURY
Bishop Rupert founds present-day Salzburg

1167
The city is decimated by fire

1816
Salzburg joins the Hapsburg Empire

1818
Fire takes its toll on the city once again

1920
The first Salzburg Festival

St. Petersburg

ABOVE: *A chandelier in Trezzini's Baroque-style Cathedral of St. Peter and St. Paul.*
BELOW: *Equestrian statue of Medny Vsadnik (Peter the Great).*

St. Petersburg was built in the extreme north-western corner of Russia as Peter the Great's "Window on the West", his gateway to Europe, and is regarded by many as the most progressive, liberal, and westernized city in Russia to this day. Little of Peter's city remains—though the Summer Palace and the Peter and Paul Fortress are still there—and the image most people have is the grand neoclassical city, with its wide boulevards and huge palaces, and the bridges, canals, and rivers everywhere that can at times make it reminiscent of Venice.

The River Neva is at the very heart of the city and on its southern bank lies Palace Embankment, seemingly endless rows of grand palaces, imposing churches, tree-lined squares, and magnificent statues. It resonates with St. Petersburg's past grandeur, from the House of Fabergé (home of the bejewelled eggs that were the imperial family's favorite Christmas presents) to the gilded domes of St. Isaac's Cathedral to the Hermitage, one of the most celebrated museums in the world. In June, during the White Nights classical music festival, the river becomes a special focus, opening all of its bridges at 2am to celebrate the endless days when the sun barely sets.

St. Petersburg has always been a magnet for Russia's writers and artists. Alexander Pushkin (1799–1837), Nicholas Gogol (1809–52), and Fyodor Dostoevsky (1821–81) all lived and wrote here and composers such as Nicholas Rimsky-Korsakov (1844–1908), Modest Mussorgsky (1839–81), and Alexander Borodin (1834–87) had their work premiered at the Mariinskiy, while the Great Hall of the Philharmonia gave the first performances of works by Peter Tchaikovsky (1840–93) and Dmitri Shostakovich (1906–75).

statistics

- Population: 5,200,000
- The city's metro stations were planned by Stalin and completed in 1955 as "palaces for the people" using thousands of tonnes of marble, granite, and limestone, and decorated with statues and chandeliers
- Capital of Russia between 1712 and 1918, but was subsequently replaced by Moscow and is now Russia's second city
- Originally built on the banks of the River Neva, the city now spreads across more than 40 islands

THE WORLD CAPITAL OF BALLET

St. Petersburg is home to the most famous ballet company in the world, the Kirov. Its theater, the Mariinskiy, has seen many of the greatest dancers—from Anna Pavlova (1881–1931) to Mikhail Barishnikov (b. 1948)—on its stage, most of them taught at St. Petersburg's Imperial Ballet School. Dancers from the Kirov reintroduced ballet to western Europe in the early 20th century where it had become a forgotten art and their pure classical style became the yardstick for ballet companies worldwide.

ABOVE: *Aerial view of dancers at the Theater Mussorgsky.*

BELOW: *The classical frontage and dome of Kazan Cathedral.*

A Vibrant Prospect

The main artery of St. Petersburg has been Nevsky Prospekt since the early 18th century and it remains so today. It is probably Russia's most famous street. It is 3 miles (4.5km) long, runs from the Admiralty to Alexander Nevsky Monastery and is lined with many historic palaces, museums, theaters, and churches. The area around Nevsky Prospekt historically had most of the best shops in St. Petersburg and today, after decades of Soviet utilitarianism, a new wave of commercialism has returned the area to its earlier glory.

In this most cultural of cities, however, the arts are never far away and near Nevsky is the magnificent Arts Square, the gilded onion domes of the Church of Our Saviour on Spilled Blood, and the Mikhaylovsky Castle housing the Russian Museum, a superb collection of Russian painting and sculpture from early icons to Marc Chagall (1887–1985).

THE STORY OF...

Convinced after a trip to Europe that Russia must have a navy, Peter the Great (1672–1725) designed St. Petersburg as his northern port and the city's first buildings were the Peter and Paul Fortress and the shipyard. The site was not ideal—a marsh prone to flooding—but Peter's determination, and 40,000 prisoners of war and peasants, laid the first foundations. These were later built upon by Tsarina Elizabeth (1709–61) who built the Winter Palace and it was Catherine the Great (1729–96) who introduced neoclassical architecture to the city.

One of the earliest uprisings against the totalitarianism of the tsars took place in St. Petersburg on 14 December 1825 by a group of army officers, but hundreds were killed in what is now known as Decembrists' Square. In 1917 strikes broke out in the city, now called Petrograd; the tsar abdicated, and the Bolsheviks took over the government. After Lenin's (1870–1924) death, the city was renamed again, this time Leningrad. Post-Stalin (1879–1953) and the Cold War, the city was at the forefront of the progressive movement that led to the dissolution of the Soviet Union and the introduction of democracy.

LEFT: *The Rococo-style frontage of the Beloselskiy-Belozerskiy Palace on Nevsky Prospekt.*
FAR LEFT: *Bright domes on the Church of the Resurrection, also known as "Saviour on the Blood."*

1703
Foundation of St. Petersburg by Peter the Great

1712
St. Petersburg becomes capital of Russia

1917
Strikes break out in capital (now Petrograd) and tsar is forced to abdicate

1941
The Germans invade Russia and besiege the city (now Leningrad) for 900 days leaving 2 million people dead

1985
Mikhail Gorbachev introduces *glasnost* (openness) and *perestroika* (reconstruction)

Sofia

Despite Sofia's great age, most of the city dates from the time of its liberation from the Ottoman Empire, when it was redesigned on a grid system and with buildings heavily influenced by West European styles. These are generally small stuccoed palaces with ornamental features, though there are also mosques and orthodox churches that have a far more exotic air. Foremost among these is the Aleksandar Nevski Memorial Church, built to commemorate the country's Russian liberators, 200,000 of whom died fighting against the Ottoman Empire. It has glittering domes, vast frescoes, and 18 lb (8kg) of gold leaf donated by the Russians.

The vast majority of the people of Sofia are orthodox Christians but in recent years the small Muslim population has been allowed to reopen its remaining mosques. The Banya Bashi mosque was built during the Ottoman rule in 1576, and is a short walk from the synagogue built in 1909 and opened by Bulgaria's tsar, a testament to the religious tolerance of the city. Most of Sofia's Jews survived World War II— in spite of Nazi demands that they be

THE CHURCH OF SVETA SOFIA

The Tsurkva Sveta Sofia (Church of Sveta Sofia)—from which the city took its name in the 14th century— still stands at its center and is believed to date back to late Roman times, though much of it is far more recent. Nevertheless it still retains its original Byzantine shape—that of a symmetrical cross with a dome at the intersection—and much of the original brickwork. During the Ottoman rule, it was turned into a mosque and the minarets added, but it is now back in use in the orthodox tradition.

ABOVE RIGHT: *The Aleksandar Nevski Memorial Church.*

handed over—but most left to go to Palestine at the beginning of the Soviet era, when all religions were discouraged and the state proselytized in favor of atheism. Since the end of communism, there has been an enthusiastic re-embracing of all religions.

Mementoes of the Soviet Age

At the center of Sofia is Sveta Nedelya Square, once adorned with a massive statue of Lenin (1870–1924) but demolished in 1990. There are, though, still plenty of reminders of the Soviet period. The Party House dominates the Largo, one of Sofia's major squares. Built in the 1950s as the Communist Party headquarters, its solid grandeur reflected the totalitarian style of government and became a hated symbol, ultimately attacked by an angry mob in 1992. Also in the Largo is another reminder of a bygone age: the Tzum was a huge state-owned department store, but in Bulgaria's new capitalist era it now houses independent shops and cafés.

The Largo also has the oldest church in Sofia. In a small courtyard stands the Rotunda of Sveti Georgi, dating back to the fourth century. It has some remarkable frescoes from a variety of periods from the ninth to the 14th centuries, while outside there are some Roman remains.

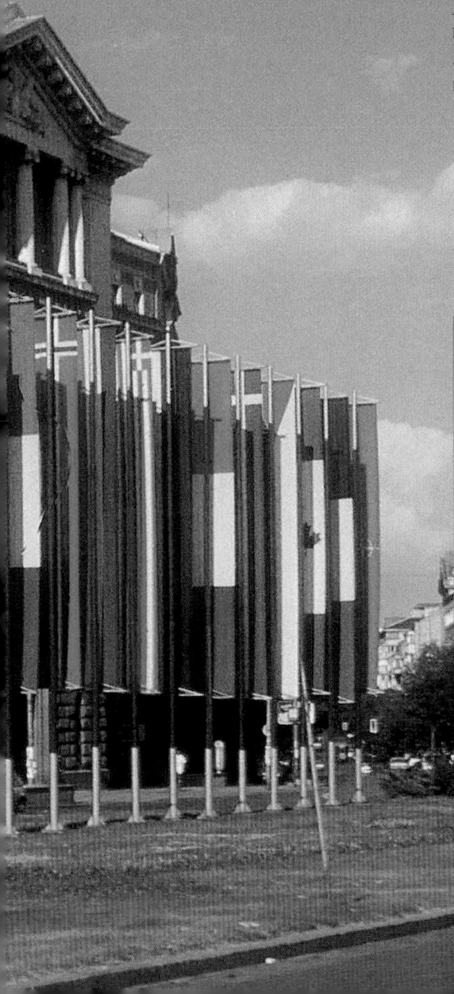

BELOW RIGHT: *The St. Nicholas Russian Orthodox Church.*
LEFT: *The Government Building.*

THE STORY OF...

The Romans called their early walled city Serdica after the Serdi tribe which lived there and the city became an important stop on the Roman road between Belgrade and Constantinople. It was captured by the Bulgar Khan Krum at the beginning of the ninth century and renamed Stredets. Sofia only arrived at its current name in the 14th century. It became part of the Ottoman Empire in 1382 and remained so for the next 500 years.

By the time Ottoman rule came to an end, Sofia was a mere provincial town but was nevertheless chosen as the capital of the newly independent Bulgaria. Most of Sofia's Turks left, the majority of the mosques were razed, and Sofia began to grow into a city with newly designed streets and public buildings. After World War II, Bulgaria became part of the Soviet bloc and grew rapidly during a period of industrialization. Since the Soviet era, the city has started on the path to democracy and economic renewal.

BELOW: *The Banya Bashi mosque is the only one remaining in the city.*

AD809

Sofia (then called Serdica) captured by Khan Krum

1382

Ottomans capture Sofia

1852

Earthquakes devastate the city

1878

Ottoman rule ends and Sofia becomes capital of Bulgaria

1946

Monarchy abolished and People's Republic declared with Sofia as capital

Stockholm

statistics

Population: 760,000

Rooms in the Kungliga Slottet (the Royal Palace): around 600

Number of museums: 70

Daily average number of cups of coffee consumed by each citizen: 4.4

The capital and Sweden's largest city, Stockholm is spread out on an archipelago of 14 islands, where Lake Mälaren meets the Baltic Sea. More airy than Venice, with wide-open spaces, it is one-third water.

Its other two-thirds combine arched bridges, jet fountains, and palatial buildings trimmed with gold. For Stockholmers, fans of the great outdoors, this is an amiable and graceful home and a healthy environment in which to live. Minutes from the city center are parks and woodlands for recreation, and clean water for swimming and fishing. In winter, everyone takes to ice-skating, on artificial rinks in the shadows of grand palaces, or on the frozen waters of the Djurgårdsbrunnsviken channel. Stockholm is also a city at the leading edge of fashion, design, and advanced technology. Fashion houses and IT companies use the city as a test market for their innovations, especially as Stockholmers are followers of technology, and many new ideas tried here take off globally.

Stockholm is the site of the government and parliament of Sweden. At its heart is Gamla Stan (Old Town) on Staden Island, the original settlement of Stockholm, and a labyrinth of medieval lanes and alleys and 17th- and 18th-century Renaissance buildings. Kungliga Slottet (the Royal Palace) is one of the largest in Europe and includes the Royal Treasury. Further north is the commercial shopping hub of Norrmalm and the elegant residential area of Östermalm. To the southeast is Djurgården, home to the 17th-century warship *Vasa* and Skansen, Europe's oldest open-air museum. Kungsträdgården Park (the king's gardens) is the city's meeting place and where many events such as festivals and street theaters are held.

TOP: *Stadshuset (City Hall).*
TOP RIGHT: *Mosaic in the Golden Hall of the Stadshuset.*
ABOVE: *One of the city's outdoor cafés.*

Stockholm's Water Festival

Stockholmers thrive on culture. At last count the city had 70 museums and attractions, the same number of cinemas, 100 art galleries, 70 stages for drama and music, and around 1,500 artists. Held over 10 days each August to mark Stockholm's strong affinity with water, the Water Festival takes over the city waterfronts and downtown area with open-air food stalls, fishing competitions, scuba diving, hydro bicycles, water-skiing, and live music. Celebrations culminate in a firework extravaganza, and the event attracts crowds from Sweden, Norway, Finland, and the rest of Europe. Ecology is emphasized: receptacles for grabage are everywhere, prizes are given for cleanliness, and litter pickers are out in force, while food vendors use paper plates and cups and wooden cutlery.

THE *VASA*

On first sight the *Vasa* takes the breath away. The sheer size of this 17th-century warship, 203ft (62m) long with gilded wood and massive canons, is as incredible as its history. It was built on the orders of King Gustav II Adolf (1594–1632) as a powerful warship, but sank in Stockholm harbor on its maiden voyage in 1628. There it lay in the mud for 300 years until in 1961 the ship was raised along with thousands of objects. Set in a massive supportive cradle, and slowly drying out, it is the centrepiece of its own museum called Vasamuseet.

THE STORY OF...

Because of its proximity to water, Stockholm grew in the 13th century as a strategic spot for the transport of iron from mines, as well as copper, fur, and tar. Soon what is known as the Old Town of mostly wooden buildings was established, and Stockholm was founded in 1252. In the 14th and 15th centuries the city was enlarged and many buildings reflect the influence of its inhabitants who were predominantly of north German descent. In 1634 Sweden was made an independent monarchy and Stockholm became its capital.

Throughout the 17th century palaces and castles were built for knights and rich merchants and by the 18th century the port was flourishing, with steamships and railways in operation. When Crown Prince Carl Gustaf Folke Hubertus (b. 1946) became King of Sweden in 1973, he adopted for his motto: "For Sweden – With the times", thereby declaring his intention of meeting the demands of society as a modern monarch and keeping the country at the forefront of global culture.

BELOW: *View of Strandvagen.*

key dates

1252
Stockholm serves as a post in the iron trade from mines in Bergslagen

1634
Sweden is made an independent monarchy, with Stockholm as its capital.

1912
City hosts Summer Olympics

1973
Carl XVI Gustaf Folke Hubertus is crowned King of Sweden

1998
Stockholm is designated a European City of Culture

Tallinn

statistics

- Population: 400,492
- Adult literacy: 99 percent
- 36 percent of the city's inhabitants belong to a Russian minority
- Over 65 percent of the city's residents own mobile phones

allinn is not somewhere that everyone can instantly place on a map. Tucked right up at the northeastern extremity of Europe, on the shores of the Baltic Sea, it is only a quick hop by ferry from Helsinki. Until 1991 Tallinn was clamped under the confines of Soviet rule, but since it broke free in a bloodless revolution it has made up for five decades of lost independence by switching seamlessly from communism to capitalism. Marx is out and mobile phones are in. The city is so switched on that the locals call their increasingly modern country "E-stonia", as it has one of the highest mobile phone ownership rates in the world and has internet cafés dotted all over Tallinn. On the fringes of the old core a new district is emerging with gleaming new hotels and offices as Estonia embraces its new role as a member of the European Union, which it joined in 2004.

Tallinn's divorce from the USSR saw the country's manufacturing market decline sharply and while traditional industries such as metal processing and machine construction still exist alongside emerging electronic markets, the capital's economy is driven more by the service and financial sectors, with around 70 percent of the workforce employed in the service industry. The thriving city is at the heart of Estonia's economic success and generates up to 60 percent of the country's GDP.

TALLINN TOWN HALL

The focal point of Tallinn's UNESCO World Heritage Old Town is Tallinna Raekoda (Tallinn Town Hall). Dating from 1404, Tallinna Raekoda is the only town hall built in a late Gothic style to be found in Northern Europe, and one of the oldest town halls on the continent. Alongside its Gothic façade the town hall boasts a 16th-century weather vane topped by the medieval guardian of the city, "Old Thomas". Not just a relic from the past, Tallinna Raekoda is still used today as a venue for various state functions, with pre-arranged tours of the building also permitted.

ABOVE: *Detail of Tallinn Town Hall.*
RIGHT: *View over the city's rooftops.*

A Medieval Beauty

Those harboring anachronistic images of Tallinn as an old Soviet Bloc city are pleasantly surprised by its chocolate-box medieval center, which is graced with lofty church spires, orange tiled rooftops, and narrow cobbled streets that have prompted comparisons to Prague. The epicenter of Tallinn life is the Old Town Square. This historic hub stretches out below Toompea Hill (the castle district) and is home to the city's tallest spire. In winter, snow ploughs work hard to shift the blizzards that breeze in from the Arctic, while in the warmer months outdoor cafés spill out on to the cobbles.

Tallinn also has a rich cultural scene and the capital is brimming with an eclectic array of museums, concert halls, theaters, and an opera house. In the summer, months the city's inhabitants readily swap these more cerebral attractions for the balmy seas of the nearby Baltic beaches, shaking off their characteristic reserve (which has sometimes earned them a reputation for being aloof) in the process.

ABOVE: *Medieval Market.*
BELOW LEFT: *St. Olav's Church and Fat Margaret's Tower.*
BELOW RIGHT: *Door of the House of the Blackheads, Old Town Square.*

THE STORY OF...

Estonia's capital city has a rich history, receiving its first written mention in 1154. In 1219 Danish troops fought for control of Tallinn and then ruled Estonia for much of the next 130 years, before selling the north of the country in 1346. In 1280 Tallinn joined the Hanseatic League (the most important trade organization in the region at the time), setting the scene for its metamorphosis into a thriving trading port between the 14th and the 16th centuries. In 1561 Sweden took the helm and while trade remained important, education also rose to the fore with the opening of the city's first secondary school and a printing house in the 17th century.

In 1710 Russia realized its ambitions for Tallinn, which it had unsuccessfully laid siege to in 1570 and 1577, and annexed Estonia. With the exception of a brief period of independence between 1920 and 1940, and occupation by German troops during the two World Wars, the country remained under Russian control until 1991 when Tallinn emerged as the capital of the newly independent Estonia.

BELOW: *The Defence Towers of Tallinn's City Wall.*

1219
Tallinn is ruled by the Danish monarchy

1561
Sweden takes control of Northern Estonia

1710
Estonia becomes part of Russia

1991
Tallinn becomes capital of an independent Estonia

2004
Estonia joins the EU

Population: 66,945 (1970: 111,500; 1950: 175,000)

Area of Venetian lagoon: 135,903 acres (54.4 ha)

Subsidence of urban areas of Venetian lagoon
since 1900: 9in (23cm)

Built on 118 separate islands with over 400 bridges
spanning 170 canals

Venice

The unique and historic city of Venice, once among the Mediterranean's most powerful states, lies in a salt-water lagoon at the head of the Adriatic Sea off the northeastern coast of Italy. Protected from the open sea by the islands of the Lido and Pellestrina, the lagoon is scoured by twice-daily tides and criss-crossed by navigable channels that provide water access to the outlying inhabited islands, such as Murano, Burano, and Sant'Erasmo. The city proper lies in the heart of the lagoon and, since 1846, has been linked to the mainland by a causeway carrying both trains and vehicles. Venice is built on more than 100 small islands, divided from one another by numerous canals that are spanned by over 400 bridges. The main canal is the Canale Grande (Grand Canal), a substantial waterway, lined with superb palaces, churches, and monuments, which snakes for 2.5 miles (4km) through the heart of Venice dividing the northern and southern city areas. To the north lie the three *sestiere* (city quarters) of San Marco, Castello, and Cannaregio; three more, Dorsoduro, San Polo, and Santa Croce are sited on the southern side of the Grand Canal.

Monuments of Venice

Venice's main monuments stand around the city's main square, the Piazza San Marco, where the Basilica di San Marco and the Palazzo Ducale (Doge's Palace) can be found. The Piazza is fronted by the expanse of the Bacino di San Marco (St. Mark's Basin), constantly busy with all types of shipping, including the trade-mark *gondole* and *vaporetti* (water buses) and dominated by Palladio's great church of San Giorgio Maggiore on the island of the same name. East from here, and linked to San Marco by the broad promenade of the Riva degli Schiavone, lies Castello and the Arsenale, the old ship-building yards that were once the city's economic power-house. To the west of the Piazza, the Grand Canal loops north to the Rialto area, home to Venice's superb food markets and spanned by one of the world's most instantly recognizable bridges, Ponte di Rialto. North again lies Cannaregio, a *sestiere* that is cut by three long, straight canals and scattered with Gothic palaces and treasure-packed churches. South of the

THE STORY OF...

The origins of Venice begin in the fourth century, when, in the final days of the Roman Empire, mainland refugees fled from the invading northern tribes into the lagoon. Settlements were built on the boggy islands and higher mudbanks, and in AD726 these communities elected the first documented Doge, the ducal ruler of the embryonic republic. By the ninth century, the majority of the lagoon's inhabitants were settling on the highest ground, the Rivus Altus (Rialto), and work started on the building of the Doge's Palace in AD814. The city acquired a powerful patron saint in AD828, when Venetians stole the relics of St. Mark from Alexandria, and work started on a basilica in his honor the following year.

In 1099, the city, now a powerful trading and ship-building maritime power, provided ships for the First Crusade, and in 1204 the Venetian-led Fourth Crusade sacked Constantinople, acquiring much of the former Byzantine Empire. The city continued to prosper as the supreme Mediterranean naval power. The discovery of sea routes to India and the Far East in 1498 marked the start of Venice's decline, and over the following three centuries the city gradually lost its wealth in a frenzy of spectacular consumption and revelry. In 1797 Napoleon Bonaparte (1769–1821) invaded and the last Doge abdicated. Handed to the Austrians by the triumphant allies in 1814, Venice became part of the newly united Italy in 1866.

The 20th century saw ever-increasing tourist numbers, structural decay caused by rising lagoon waters, population decline, and high pollution from the neighboring mainland industrial centers. In 2003 work started on the MOSE project, designed to control the destructively high waters which still enter the lagoon from the Adriatic.

LEFT: *Traffic on the Canale Grande (Grand Canal), the main waterway through the center of Venice.*
BELOW: *Gondoliers in traditional dress.*

Grand Canal, the three *sestiere* of Dorsoduro, San Polo, and Santa Croce are home to beguiling canals and *campi* and some of the city's greatest artistic treasures, in the shape of the Accademia art gallery, the churches of the Frari and Santa Maria della Salute, and the 20th-century Collezione Peggy Guggenheim—the most important museum in Italy for European and American art of the first half of the 20th century. Each *sestiere* has its own shopping street and market, with the best of international big-name stores in and around the Piazza di San Marco.

ABOVE: *Murano glassware.*
BELOW: *The Santa Maria della Salute viewed from San Marco.*

The Trouble with Venice

Modern Venice faces huge problems and challenges, chief of which are the effects of the ever-increasing high tides during the winter and a rapidly shrinking population. Modern technology and international aid are helping to tackle the rising water, with artificial barriers under construction at the lagoon's mouth to keep out dangerously high tides, and an on-going program of restoration

key dates

AD421
Venice is founded on 25 March, Feast of the Virgin Mary

THE NINTH CENTURY
Work begins on the Basilica of St. Mark and Doge's Palace

1498
Discovery of Cape Route to India marks start of Venice's economic and political decline

1797
Napoleon's invasion marks the end of the Venetian Republic

1966
Devastating floods throughout the city draw international attention to need for restoration

2003
Start of the MOSE protection project

throughout the city. Population decline is a harder problem; housing is expensive to buy and maintain, while the huge numbers of tourists (15 million annually), on which the economy is almost totally reliant, are driving away the young people that might stimulate alternative growth. Venice is in danger of becoming overwhelmed by the very visitors that provide 70 percent of the city's income and 50 percent of its employment. On the positive side, tourism ensures that the city remains firmly under international scrutiny in terms of restoration and pollution control against the heavily industrialized areas of Mestre and Porto Marghera on the edge of the lagoon, and has helped preserve the city's ancient tradition of glass manufacture.

ABOVE: *The five domes of the Basilica di San Marco, designed in the form of a Greek cross.*
BELOW: *The Palazzo Ducale (Doge's Palace).*

CARNEVALE

Between the 16th and 18th centuries, the Venice Carnival, (known locally as *carnevale*), was the most outrageous in Europe; a frenetic explosion of partying and carousing, when the fun lasted all week. During this time the city thronged with masked and costumed revelers, dancing and singing in the streets, watching free entertainments in the city's *campi* (squares), drinking, eating, gambling, and playing games. Behavior was outrageous, masks and disguises providing the anonymity that enabled the normally rigidly divided social classes to mingle freely. Dressed in a black hood, voluminous cape, and a mask, it was even difficult to tell men and women apart, and people could do as they pleased while remaining incognito.

The 1797 abolition of the Carnevale was a bitter blow, but all was not lost, for in the early 1980s the tourist board and city authorities re-instituted Carnevale as a means of attracting visitors at the quietest time of the year. Carnevale has been a resounding success, and in the 10 days leading up to Lent, there are once again masked and elaborately costumed figures in the streets. *Palazzi* are resplendently lit for balls and dinners and the celebrations culminate with the traditional burning of an effigy in the Piazza San Marco.

LEFT AND BELOW: *Typically elaborate masks and costumes worn at* Carnevale.

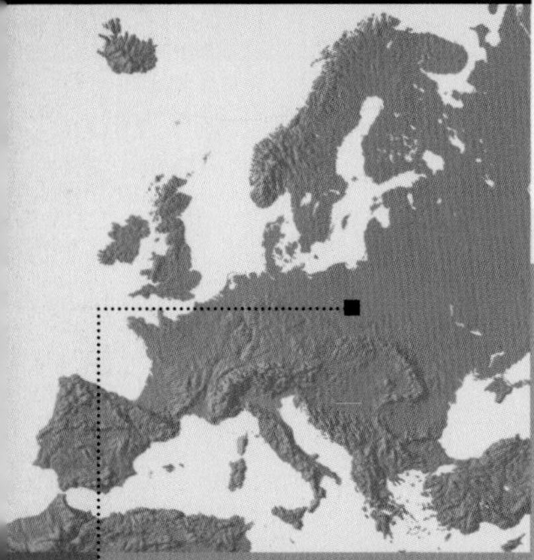

Warsaw

statistics

Population: 1,932,500

20 percent of the workforce is university educated

More than 60,000 Jews died in the Warsaw Ghetto Uprising in 1943

200,000 civilians died and 100,000 were injured in the 1944 Warsaw Uprising

Some people harbor out-of-date images of Warsaw as a grey wasteland of Soviet-era buildings, but there is far more to the Polish capital than its unappealing suburbs. The year 2004 brought EU membership, a move that has seen massive investment in the local infrastructure, with new shopping malls, conference centers, and a buzzing nightlife. Today Warsaw's economy is booming and is driven more by trade and the distribution of services than its more traditional manufacturing industries of steel production, food processing, and electronic components.

BELOW: *The statue of King Sigismund III on Castle Square with St. John's Cathedral behind.*

MONUMENT TO THE GHETTO HEROES

One of Warsaw's most poignant memorials, Rappaport and Suzin's Monument to the Ghetto Heroes, was erected in 1948 and stands as a stirring reminder of the city's Ghetto Uprising. The uprising began on 19 April 1943 when Nazi troops acted on Himmler's orders to exterminate Warsaw's Jews. The Jewish Fighting Organization (ZOB) held out against the Germans until 16 May 1943, but ultimately more than 60,000 of Poland's Jews died in the battle and the massacres that followed. The memorial features resistance fighters, as well as women and children being marched off to the concentration camps.

Tourism in Warsaw has greatly increased in recent years, and is more accessible with an increase in airlines flying into the city. The city's main attractions are located in the old center, and include the Royal Castle and St. John's Cathedral. Warsaw is a city that has many layers, but few visitors who amble across the cobbles of the Old Town delve into its darker days, such as the 1944 Warsaw Uprising when the city bravely rose up and fought against Nazi occupation. Visitors can learn about this asppect of the city's history at The Warsaw Uprising Museum, which pays homage to the many local heroes who stood up to the might of the German army.

Warsaw's bountiful green spaces offer an escape from the weight of its history. One of the highlights is Lazienki Park, a verdant oasis with walking trails, trees, and a boating lake. Locals flock here during summer weekends to listen to Frédéric Chopin (1810–49) recitals (the composer was born near Warsaw).

Post-War Reconstruction

Warsaw is a real survivor and the city's very existence is impressive in itself. By the end of World War II, roughly 85 percent of the city lay in ruins and much of the population had been killed, deported, or sent to the concentration camps. The majority of Warsaw's historic center was painstakingly recreated in the years after the war, in a move by the communist authorities that surprised the citizens of the city as much as it did the West. Some churlish critics have dismissed the "new" Old Town as being a "fake", but most visitors do not seem to mind and some scholars have suggested that the reconstructed buildings are far closer to the original structures than the pre-war incarnations were.

As a raft of construction projects rumble through the city center, a symbol of the past—the vaulting 758ft (231m) Palace of Culture that was a "present" to the city from Joseph Stalin (1879–1953)—casts an ever-watchful eye. Fittingly for Warsaw today, the Palace of Culture is now home to an eclectic range of business events, international fairs, and exhibitions.

BELOW RIGHT: *An organ grinder in the Old Town Square.*

THE STORY OF...

Warsaw's transition from a 13th-century fishing village into a prosperous member of the European Union has been turbulent. In 1596 King Sigismund III (1566–1632) relocated his capital to Warsaw. Less than a century later the city's fortunes took a turn for the worse, with the damage inflicted by both the Swedish-Prussian War (1655) and the Russian massacre of the city's inhabitants (1794). A year later Poland was wiped from the map and partitioned between Russia, Prussia, and Austria, where it remained until Napoleon "liberated" it in 1807.

In 1815 the Congress of Vienna divided Poland up again, with Warsaw an unwilling partner in the union with Russia, which violently suppressed the Poles in the 1830 November Uprising and the 1831 Polish-Russian conflict. 1918 saw Warsaw emerge as the head of an independent Poland, only to be dominated by Russia through the USSR and the Warsaw Pact after World War II. The tragic 1944 Warsaw Uprising, cost hundreds of thousands their lives as they struggled to oust Nazi troops. 2004 saw Poland join the EU, giving Poles more opportunities in Europe.

BELOW: *The Baroque Wilanow Palace which dates from 1675.*

key dates

1281
The name Warsaw first appears in written documents

1526
City is incorporated into the Polish Kingdom

1795
Poland split between Russia, Prussia and Austria

1918
Warsaw becomes capital of a reborn Polish state

1980
Reconstructed Old Town is added to UNESCO World Heritage List

Vienna

Vienna lies at the foot of an outlying spur of the Alps covered by the Wienerwald (Vienna Woods). Apart from a modern suburb including the huge UNIDO building, the city lies to the west of the Danube. It was the river that determined its early development, bringing both Christianity and trade downstream from the West.

Vienna has always been cosmopolitan. The mingling of races and cultures metamorphoses into a specifically Viennese culture; like the local cuisine, however, it shows Italian, Slav, Hungarian, and other influences. From the Middle Ages onwards Jews arrived, enjoying the uncertain protection of rulers, who periodically also found them useful scapegoats for economic or other disasters. Expelled in pogroms, they always drifted back, until the Nazis murdered or drove into exile the entire Jewish population in 1938.

Religion was always a determining factor of Viennese life. Apart from justifying pogroms with Catholic doctrine, it provoked the great struggle of the Reformation when Catholic Habsburgs resisted the will of their would-be Protestant subjects. Vienna was briefly 90 percent Protestant, but the dynasty summoned the Jesuits in 1551 and gave them control of the University in 1622. The city was flooded with Counter-Reformatory orders that set up monasteries and built Baroque churches. Persecution of non-Catholics only ended in 1781–82, when Joseph II (1741–90) issued a Patent of Tolerance for all faiths, including (with restrictions) Judaism.

WOLFGANG AMADEUS MOZART

Mozart (1756–91) spent the last 10 years of his life in Vienna constantly on the look-out for a job at Emperor Joseph II's (1830–1916) court. In the end he acquired a minor post: "too lowly for what I could do, and too elevated for what I'm obliged to do", as he commented. Indeed the Emperor famously complained of his opera *The Seraglio* that it contained too many notes. Of the composer's two greatest popular successes, *The Magic Flute* (1791) caught the fancy of the Viennese. Mozart represents the high point of the so-called *Wiener Klassik* that began with Franz Joseph Haydn (1732–1809) and influenced the early music of Ludwig van Beethoven (1770–1827), who lived in Vienna for 30 years.

RIGHT: *Silhouetted statue and the dome of the Hofburg, Vienna's imperial palace.*
LEFT: *Café in the Graben, one of the city's major shopping streets.*
BELOW: *Decorated roof belonging to the Stephansdom on the Stephansplatz.*

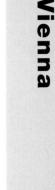

At the heart of Vienna is the Stephansdom (St. Stephen's Cathedral), a magnificent example of Romanesque and Gothic architecture. Elsewhere in the old city are the Baroque churches and palaces (such as the Karlskirche and the Belvedere) of Fischer von Erlach (1656–1723) and Johann Lucas von Hildebrandt (1663–1745). The 19th century saw historicist architecture built along the Ringstrasse and financed by the new and wealthy bourgeoisie: "neo-Gothic" for the city hall, "neo-Renaissance" for museums, luxury apartment blocks, and the university. Reaction against this sometimes pompous display came around 1900 with the decorative and symbolic style of the Vienna secession, to be followed by the puritanical functionalism of Adolf Loos (1870–1933). The ideological, religious, and political struggles of Vienna's past are all reflected in the styles of its buildings.

A European Crossroads

Today's arguments about skyscrapers spoiling the city skyline are an indication of Vienna's new wealth and prosperity. The economy still depends substantially on government bureaucracy, finance, light industry, transport, and tourism. In a good year, Vienna hosts six or seven times the population of the city itself as tourists, though many of these only stay a night or two. Mediating between the West and the newly democratized East, Vienna aims to be Central Europe's revived investment and trading hub.

BELOW: *A fountain in the grounds of the Art History Museum.*

THE STORY OF...

Originally Celtic, Vienna ("Vindobona") was Roman until the late fourth century. In the 10th century, Charlemagne's successors awarded his empire's eastern territories to the Bavarian Babenbergs, who ruled until the 13th century. As "Holy Roman Emperors", the Habsburgs made Vienna the center of their expanding dominions, which were split in 1521, with one line of Habsburgs ruling the east, and the other in the west. After surviving the Reformation, Counter-Reformation, and sieges by the Turks in the 16th and 17th centuries, the city flourished under Maria Theresa (1717–80) and Joseph II.

The Napoleonic Wars followed, ended in a period of repression which led to revolution (1848). Franz-Joseph (1830–1916) ruled from that year until 1916, as Vienna developed into a modern society. Economic turmoil led to annexation by Nazi Germany in 1938 with Vienna (and Austria) regaining freedom in 1955. Vienna is today a prosperous and ecologically aware city.

1156
The Margrave (later Duke) Heinrich IV of Babenberg establishes his residence in Vienna

1278
Rudolf of Habsburg takes over Vienna and the Austrian territories, beginning an empire that lasts 640 years until 1918

1683
The Turkish army fails in its second and last attempt to take Vienna, initiating 16 years of reconquest, resettlement, and a longer lasting Baroque building boom

1857
Emperor Franz-Joseph orders the bastions round the old city to be demolished, inaugurating both the Ringstrasse, with its monumental civic buildings in historicist style, and a new era of modern civil society

1955
The Austrian State Treaty is signed by the victorious powers in Vienna's Belvedere Palace, ending 10 years of post-World War II occupation by Russian, American, British, and French forces

Zurich

Population: 360,000

Lake Zurich is 25 miles (40km) by 2.5 miles (4km)

Average low temperature for January: 27°F (–3°C)

Over 75 percent of the population works in the service sector

Switzerland's largest city is located on the northern shores of Zürichsee (Lake Zurich). Renowned worldwide as *the* center for international banking, many aspects of the city are governed by finance, and the wealth of both the city and its residents is manifest. Opulent riverside houses line the banks of the lake, while the extensive Bahnhofstrasse is overflowing with banks, chic bars, trendy cafés, and boutiquesd selling designer goods. When they are not spending their money in the city's myriad shops and hostelries, Zurich's residents turn their attention to more cerebral pursuits—there are more than 30 museums in Zurich, as well as a wealth of galleries, theaters, concert halls, and an opera house. Offerings from Zurich's cultural scene range from contemporary art to pottery and Asian art. The highlight for many visitors and locals are the Kunsthaus Zürich (Zurich Art Gallery), which focuses on 19th- and 20th-century masterpieces, including works by Claude Monet (1840–1926) and Edvard Munch (1863–1944), and the Schweizerisches Landesmuseum (Swiss National Museum), which houses the treasures of the nation.

More than Banking

While finance and commerce are both vital to Zurich's prosperity, tourism, manufacturing (electrical equipment, electronics, printing, machinery production, and textiles), and education also play an important role. Within the realm of education Zurich's universities have eked out a reputation as centers of pioneering research, particularly within the field of design and technology.

Tourists are attracted by the city's dramatic natural setting, its proximity to the mountains, and the opportunities for getting to grips with the great outdoors. For many it is also about experiencing the high life that the city's residents enjoy and simply relaxing in the wealth of cafés, restaurants, and bars. Another popular pastime for visitors is

CARL GUSTAV JUNG (1875–1961)

The theories of Carl Gustav Jung (1875–1961), who was influenced by the teaching of Sigmund Freud (1856–1939), remain influential in modern psychology. Born in Kesswil, Switzerland, Jung's early career took him to Zurich's Burghoelzli Mental Hospital and he later established a private practice in the city and lectured at its university. Like Freud, Jung was driven by a desire to understand the human mind (conscious) and developed a theory of personality that has influenced not only psychology but philosophy and the arts. Jung believed that dreams, fantasies, visions, and artistic expression could all contribute to greater self-awareness. After traveling widely, Jung retired to Zurich where he died in 1961.

ABOVE: *Zurich and the River Limmat by night.*
RIGHT: *St. Peterskirche (St. Peter's Church) is the oldest church in Zurich.*

relaxing in the grassy parks that fringe the lake, which provide a tranquil oasis for picnicking families, joggers, and skaters, as well as local artists. For the sightseer, Zurich offers a compact and historic old center, the highlight being the Grossmünster and Fraumünster churches that gaze at each another from either side of the Limmat River. The former is actually a twin-towered cathedral that dates from the 11th century and is one of the most prominent symbols of the city. The main attractions of the ninth-century Fraumünster church are its graceful 18th-century spire and beautiful 20th-century stained-glass windows.

ABOVE: *View of the city and the River Limmat.*
LEFT: *The main railway station.*

THE STORY OF...

Evidence of human habitation in Zurich dates back to the third century BC, when temporary dwellings were established near the shores of the lake. In 500BC Celtic tribes settled in the area, with the Romans arriving in 15BC to establish Turicum as a place for collecting import duties. The demise of the Roman Empire in the fifth century AD saw the city pass into the control of the Alemanni, the Franks, and the Swabia (all Germanic tribes). In AD929 Switzerland's leading financial center became a town and by 1218 it had become a free town under the guardianship of the Holy Roman Empire.

In 1351 the city joined the Swiss Confederation (an association of independent states) and slowly developed a reputation as a center for intellectual thought, with Huldrych Zwingli pushing the city towards Protestantism during the early 16th century. In 1648 Zurich became part of the newly independent Switzerland and emerged as a financial, commercial, and transport hub in the 19th and 20th centuries.

BELOW: *A bar in the Letten district by the River Limmat.*

AD929
Zurich receives its first written mention

1351
Joins Swiss Confederation

1877
Swiss Stock Exchange opens in Zurich

1918
The army quashes the General Strike with civilian fatalities

1992
The Swiss people elect not to join the European Union

87

Asia, Australia, and New Zealand

The great cities of Asia include some of the most densely populated and mysterious places on earth, from the human bustle of Mumbai or Hong Kong to the remoteness of high Kathmandu or the Forbidden City at the heart of Beijing. Modern finance has been the spur for metropolises such as Tokyo and Singapore, where trade in money has become as important as trade in goods—and the market is flourishing. And while chaotic Bangkok must be a highlight of every backpacker's tour, many of these cities deserve to be better known to curious visitors, including Ho Chi Minh, Lahore and Phnom Penh. The influence of the Pacific Rim has spread to previously-isolated New Zealand and Australia, but by contrast their cities cultivate a laid-back image, where sports such as sailing, surfing and cricket are at least as important as making money.

Auckland

statistics

- Population: 1,300,000

- Near the city, the Auckland Peninsula is only 6 miles (10km) wide

- Average temperatures range from 51°F (10.6°C) in July to 80.2°F (24°C) in January

- At 1,076ft (328m), the city's Sky Tower is the tallest structure in the southern hemisphere

New Zealand's largest city is a thoroughly modern conurbation whose skyline would not be out of place in North America. Sandwiched between two harbors and home to the country's largest port, Auckland has the largest economy in New Zealand, accounting for around 35 percent of the national GDP. As the center of finance, business, manufacturing, retail, and tourism, many of the nation's top companies are located in the city and many of its residents enjoy a high standard of living. Not all Aucklanders share in the city's good fortunes, however, as was highlighted by Lee Tamahori's (b. 1950) 1994 film *Once Were Warriors*, which shows the problems that Maori people living in Auckland face today. Over 150 years of domination by the Pekaha (white population) left many Maori families in poverty.

Recent years have seen a reduction in ethnic tensions and have also witnessed a renaissance in Maori culture. One of the most important buildings in the city is the Auckland Museum, which houses an impressive collection of Maori art. Other tourist attractions include galleries, Kelly Tarlton's Antarctic Encounter, and Underwater World—complete with penguins, sharks, and stingrays—and the indigenous animals at the city's zoo. Meanwhile, Auckland's colonial past is brought to life in Parnell Village, where galleries and boutique stores have been reconstructed in Victorian style, and by the collection of 19th-century mansions dotted around the suburbs, including Kinder House and Ewelme Cottage.

SIR EDMUND HILLARY (B. 1919)

Sir Edmund Hillary, Auckland's most famous son, started out as a professional beekeeper and served in the country's air force during World War II. Hillary developed a passion for mountaineering as a teenager, his greatest achievement being the first person to reach the summit of Mount Everest 29,028ft (8,848m) above sea level on 29 May 1953 at 11.30am—quickly followed by Nepalese sherpa Tenzing Norgay (1914–86). For New Zealanders his charitable work, as much as his climbing prowess, has made him a national hero. Hillary's Himalayan Trust has constructed around 30 schools, as well as clinics and hospitals in Nepal.

ABOVE: *Sir Edmund Hillary and his sherpa guide, Tenzing Norgay.*

ABOVE LEFT: *Auckland Harbor from Bayswater North Shore.* ABOVE: *The Esplanade Hotel in Devonport.* ABOVE RIGHT: *Preparing for a sky jump from the top of the Sky Tower.*

A City of Volcanoes

Auckland's greatest attraction is its dramatic natural setting, sandwiched between the harbours of Waitemata to the east and Manukau to the west. The city and its surrounding areas are also constructed on more than 60 dormant volcanoes, with the hilly landscape giving exceptional vistas across the city to the sea from myriad vantage points. Prime viewing spots include Mount Eden, One Tree Hill, and the observation deck at the Sky Tower.

For those who really want to appreciate the great outdoors, the Coast-to-Coast walk, approximately 8 miles (13km), traverses the narrow isthmus, while locals like nothing better than to relax on the numerous beaches that surround the city. Milford Beach, Takapuna Beach, and Mairangi Bay in the north are amongst the favourites, and then there is the surfers' paradise of Muriwai Beach to the west, the popular suburb of Devonport across the Waitemata Harbor, and the Hauraki Gulf islands.

ABOVE: *Piha Beach*. LEFT AND BELOW: *Maori carving on the Auckland Waterfront*. BELOW RIGHT: *The Otara Polynesian Market*.

THE STORY OF...

Maori tribes settled in the Auckland region around 700 years ago. Conflict between the tribes grew over time and when the British arrived in 1839 the warring Maoris were not capable of stopping them. In 1840 tribal leaders signed the Treaty of Waitangi, which protected Maori rights in return for allegiance to Queen Victoria (1819–1901), and Governor William Hobson (1793–1842) located the capital in Auckland. The relocation of the capital to Wellington in 1864 saw Auckland's fortunes slump and the New Zealand Wars (1843–72) saw its young men conscripted to fight against the Maoris. The end of the decade heralded a short-lived Gold Rush (1867–72).

Auckland prospered during the 20th century, gaining self-rule in 1931 and independence in 1947, the biggest shadows being cast by the two World Wars, which claimed the lives of thousands of New Zealanders. In the 1980s the nation declared itself nuclear free, an assertion which led to the sinking, by the French, of the *Rainbow Warrior*, a Greenpeace ship that had been protesting against nuclear testing in the South Pacific, in Auckland Harbor in 1985.

key dates

1840
The Treaty of Waitangi, credited as the founding document of New Zealand, is signed

1864
Wellington takes over from Auckland as the capital of New Zealand

1947
Auckland becomes part of the newly independent New Zealand

1985
The Rainbow Warrior is sunk in Auckland harbor

2000
Auckland hosts the America's Cup

Bangkok

Population: 7,750,000

Bangkok's Thai name is the longest place name in the world comprising 164 letters

80 percent of Thailand's university graduates live in the city

Expected capacity for Bangkok's new Airport (Suvarnabhumi International): 100 million passengers per year

A PROGRESSIVE MONARCH

King Mongkut (1851–68), the fourth monarch of the ruling Chakri Dynasty, is perhaps best known in the West through the portrayal of him by Yul Brynner (1920–85) in the popular 1956 musical *The King and I*. However, this portrayal is misleading. Mongkut was in fact a progressive monarch who learned much from the West, including English and Latin, and corresponded with Queen Victoria (1819–1901). A keen scientist, he was also a gifted astronomer. Together with his son and successor, King Chulalongkorn (1868–1910), his erudition and far-sightedness succeeded in keeping Thailand, almost alone in Asia, independent throughout the colonial period.

When King Rama I made Bangkok his capital, he renamed it: *Krungthepmahanakhonamonrattanakosin mahintaraayutthayamahadilokpopnoppar atratchathaniburiromudomratchaniwetmahasathanamonpi manavatansathirsakkathatityavisnukamprasiti*. The longest place-name in the world, it may be translated: "Great City of Angels, City of Immortals, Magnificent Jeweled City of the God Indra, Seat of the King of Ayutthaya, City of Gleaming Temples, City of the King's Most Excellent Palace and Dominions, Home of Vishnu and All the Gods"—quite a tongue-twister, even for Thais, who generally shorten the name of their capital to "Krung Thep" or "City of Angels." Since its founding, Bangkok has prospered and grown into a megalopolis estimated to be around 40 times larger than any other city in Thailand. Bangkok has a reputation for traffic jams, though in recent years the situation has changed for the better and continues to improve. But it is also a city of culture, haute cuisine, and vibrant nightlife. What is more, it is both safe and very welcoming.

One feature of Bangkok soon apparent to the visitor is the absence of any single center. The old royal city on Ratanakosin Island is the cultural and historical heart of the city. Downtown Silom Road is Bangkok's Wall Street—with all the major banking and trading institutions, as well as, near Silom's eastern end, the world-famous entertainment area of Patpong, known for its night market and neon lights. Sukhumvit Road is a shopper's paradise, as well as a preferred residential area. In recent years Bangkok has also become a city of gleaming shopping malls, best exemplified by the Emporium, the MBK Center, the World Trade Center, and the region around Siam Square. Yet it remains a city of canals dominated by the great Chao Phraya River which cuts the Thai capital neatly in half on its way to the Gulf of Siam. Also on the river, Bangkok's Klong Toey district is the nation's major port, exporting huge amounts of rice and other agricultural produce, textiles and electronic goods, and importing oil and industrial machinery.

ABOVE: *Roses for sale at Chatuchak Market.*

ABOVE: *Yak Temple guardian, Grand Palace.*

ABOVE: *Sunset over the Chao Phraya River.*

The Grand Palace

The greatest monument in Bangkok and a definite "must" on any itinerary is the Grand Palace and Wat Phra Kaeo, the Temple of the Emerald Buddha. This tiny but elegant Buddha image, made of jasper and only 30in (75cm) high, stands at the center of the temple on a high pedestal, encased in glass. Regarded as the Palladium of the Kingdom, it cannot be photographed, and—perhaps partly because of this—is surrounded by an aura of mystery and respect.

RIGHT: *A low bridge spanning a pond at Wat Benchamabophit (the Marble Temple).*
BELOW: *A line of monks parades through the Grand Palace.*

THE STORY OF...

Bangkok began as a small fort and riverine trading center called Bang Makok, serving Ayutthaya the Thai capital, until it was sacked by Burma in 1767. A new capital was established at Thonburi on the west bank of the Chao Phraya River, before in 1782 King Rama I (1737–1809) built a palace on the east bank and made it his capital. The new royal city was centered on Koh Ratanakosin, an artificial "island" created when Rama I ordered three rings of concentric canals to be constructed as defences. A settlement of Chinese merchants, which had previously inhabited the area, was moved south and east, to form Yaowarat, Bangkok's thriving Chinatown.

In the 19th century the city was commonly known as the "Venice of the East" because of its many canals. During the 20th century this changed almost beyond recognition, as the "place of olive plums" became one of the great cities of Asia, criss-crossed by elevated superhighways and studded with high-rise towers.

key dates

1782
Chao Phraya Chakri (Rama I) establishes Bangkok as the new Siamese capital

1784
The dazzling Wat Phra Kaeo (Temple of the Emerald Buddha) is built to house Siam's most sacred image, the Emerald Buddha

1863
King Mongkut (Rama IV) builds Bangkok's first paved road, known to foreign merchants as "New Road"

1884
King Chulalongkorn (Rama V) introduces electric lighting and initiates work on an electric tram system

1998
The 13th Asian Games are held at various locations across the city

Beijing

The heart of modern Beijing remains the Forbidden City, which was closed to ordinary citizens until 1911, but now draws millions of visitors annually. Arranged according to the dictates of Chinese geomancy, the massive walled complex is aligned with the cardinal directions immediately south of Jingshan Hill, once the exclusive preserve of the imperial family, which offers magnificent views across the city. Outside the southern entrance to the Forbidden City is Tiananmen Square, the largest public square in the world. After the death of Mao Zedong (1893–1976), the authorities ordered that his body be embalmed. Within one year, the Mao Mausoleum was built at the southern end of Tiananmen Square, and Mao's body was placed in a crystal coffin draped with the red flag of the Communist Party. The Museum of the Chinese Revolution is located on the east side of Tiananmen. On exhibit are more than 3,300 photographs, documents, and items, from the Opium War in 1840, to the 1911 Revolution, the May Fourth Movement in 1919, the founding of the Communist Party in 1921, the anti-Japanese War of Resistance, and the civil war and liberation in 1949. The Museum of Chinese History, located in the same building as the Museum of the Chinese Revolution, houses many historical artifacts and works of art.

Beijing's wooden Drum Tower, just north of Jingshan Park, was built in 1424 during the Ming dynasty. During imperial times, 24 drums would announce the night watches. The Bell Tower, a 108ft (33m) tall structure just north of the Drum Tower, was erected in

BELOW: *Chinese acrobats performing in Beijing's Chaoyang Theater.*

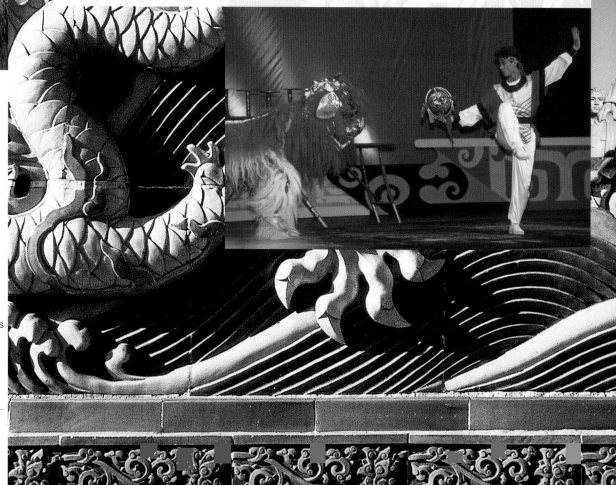

statistics

Population: 10,600,000

The Imperial Palace (the "Forbidden City") is the largest palace complex in the world: 3,152ft (961m) long and 2,470ft (753m) wide

200,000 Chinese Muslims live in the city

2 million registered vehicles navigate the streets; 64 percent are privately owned

THE ARCHITECT OF BEIJING

In 1402 Ming Emperor Yongle (Chengzu) (1360–1424) began rebuilding Beijing. To protect the city a massive wall, complete with watchtowers, was erected. Established by Yongle between 1406 and 1420, the Zijincheng or "Forbidden City" is the best preserved and most complete collection of imperial architecture in China. With 9,999 rooms and an outer courtyard designed to accommodate 90,000 people during imperial ceremonies, it remains the largest royal complex ever constructed. The Imperial Palace was the home of China's emperors from 1420 to 1911. Almost burned to the ground in 1644, the palace was rebuilt many times, but always retaining Yongle's original design.

ABOVE: *The multiple roofs of the Watchtower in the Imperial Palace.*

1747. The massive bronze bell was rung every evening until 1924, when the last emperor was forced to leave the Forbidden City. It is said that the bell could be heard for a distance of over 12.5 miles (20km). Southeast of the city center, the Temple of Heaven is one of the best examples of religious architecture in China. Construction began in 1406 during the reign of Yongle and took 14 years to complete. The complex contains three main buildings where the emperor, as the "Son of Heaven", went during the winter solstice to offer prayers and sacrifices for a good harvest.

Capital Communications

Beijing is one of four municipalities in the People's Republic of China (PRC), and is under the direct control of the central government. The city has been a municipality since the founding of the PRC and is the second largest city in China after Shanghai. It is also a major transportation hub, with dozens of railways, roads, and expressways connecting the capital city in all directions. It is served by Capital Airport.

THE STORY OF...

Although there have been settlements in the area of Beijing from at least 1000BC, it was not until the Yuan Dynasty (1279–1368) that Kublai Khan (1214–1294) made Beijing the capital of China for the first time. The imperial heart of Beijing, known as the "Forbidden City", was built by the Ming Dynasty between 1402 and 1416. After the Manchus overthrew the Ming in 1644, they expanded the Forbidden City and built several pleasure palaces on the outskirts. Beijing remained the imperial capital under the Qing, though the Nationalists set up their capital in Nanjing in the 1920s, where it remained until 1949, when they retreated to Taiwan. The Red Army marched into Beijing in the same year, and once again the city became China's capital.

Beijing changed dramatically over the subsequent five decades. The old city wall was torn down in the 1950s, but the city's real boom came after economic reforms were launched in the 1980s. Today Beijing is thriving and is regarded by many as one of the world's truly great cities.

LEFT: *Mao's Mausoleum in Tiananmen Square.*
FAR RIGHT: *Roof of the Imperial Palace.*
BELOW: *Detail of the Nine Dragon Screen in the Northern Sea Park.*
BELOW: *Tiananmen Gate.*

key dates

AD700
Mongols, Koreans and local Chinese first establish a frontier trading post

1267
Kublai Khan begins construction of Khanbaliq (present-day Beijing), completing the huge rebuilding project in 1293

1403
Emperor Yongle completes the Forbidden City and other major works in Beijing

1949
Mao Zedong announces the formation of the People's Republic of China from Tiananmen in central Beijing

2008
The city is due to host the Olympic Games

Delhi

Delhi stands at the western end of the Ganges Plain, bordered on the eastern side by the state of Uttar Pradesh and on the other three sides by the state of Haryana. Old Delhi, the capital of Muslim India between the mid-17th and late 19th centuries, is full of fine mosques, monuments, and forts. It is a lively area of colorful bazaars, narrow streets, and busy traffic. Its main thoroughfare is Chandni Chowk, named after the old silversmiths' bazaar. The red sandstone walls of the massive Red Fort rise 108ft (33m) above the bustling city as a reminder of the magnificent power and pomp of the Moghul emperors. The Red Fort's Lahore Gate is a symbolic focal point for modern India and attracts a major crowd each Independence Day.

By contrast, New Delhi, the imperial city created during the final years of the British Raj, consists of spacious, tree-lined avenues and imposing government buildings, and has a sense of order absent from other parts of the city. The hub of New Delhi is Connaught Place, where most of the airline offices, travel agents, and banks are located. Major landmarks include Rashtrapati Bhavan (once the Viceroy's House, but now the official residence of the President of India), Parliament House, and the Indian Parliament building, the Lok Sabha. A 131ft (40m) stone war memorial known as India Gate dominates a broad ceremonial boulevard called Rajpath, which is flanked with ornamental ponds and is the venue for important national parades.

Modern Economy

Delhi is the largest single market in the country despite being smaller in population than Mumbai. This is primarily because the per capita income in Delhi is higher than elsewhere. Since the 1990s it has become an important destination for foreign direct investment and numerous multinational companies have set up offices in Delhi and its suburbs. An extensive highway and rail network serve the city, placing it at the center of a national hub. Indira Gandhi International Airport links Delhi with Europe, North America, and the rest of Asia. In 2002 work started on a New Delhi Metro, which should help to alleviate the city's endemic traffic congestion. The Interstate Bus Terminal is located at Kashmir Gate, north of Old Delhi Railway Station. As the Indian capital, Delhi attracts students from all over the country. It has many government and private colleges offering higher education in the fields of science, engineering, medicine, arts, law, and management. The most prominent educational institutes are Delhi University, the Indian Institute of Technology, and the All India Institute of Medical Sciences.

DELHI'S JAMA MASJID

Delhi's great Friday Mosque is the largest in the country, with a courtyard capable of holding 25,000 worshippers. It was built in 1644, the last in a series of magnificent architectural achievements by Shah Jahan (1592–1666), the Moghul emperor who also built the Taj Mahal and the Red Fort. The elaborately decorated mosque has three great gateways, four towers, and two 131ft (40m) high minarets constructed of alternating bands of red sandstone and white marble. Non-Muslims are welcome to visit the mosque, but preferably not during prayer times.

ABOVE: *The elegant stonework at Jama Masjid.*

LEFT: *The Friday Mosque.*
RIGHT: *Preparing and cooking puris on the streets of New Delhi.*
CENTER RIGHT: *The ultra-modern glass frontage of a high-rise office block in Delhi's commercial area.*
FAR RIGHT: *The Lal Qila (Red Fort), is named after its sandstone walls.*
OPPOSITE: *Looking through red flowers toward Humayun's Tomb.*

THE STORY OF...

Delhi is said to be the site of Indraprastha, capital of the Pandavas of the Indian epic the *Mahabharata*. Excavations have unearthed shards of painted pottery dating from around 1000BC, though the earliest known architectural relics date from the Mauryan Period, about 2,300 years ago. Since that time the site has been continuously settled. The city was ruled by the Hindu Rajputs between about AD900 and 1206, when it became the capital of the Delhi Sultanate.

In the mid-17th century the Moghul emperor Shah Jahan established Old Delhi in its present location, including, most notably, the Red Fort or Lal Qila. The Old City served as the capital of the Moghul Empire from 1638 onward. Delhi passed under British control in 1857 and became the capital of British India in 1911. In large-scale rebuilding, parts of the Old City were demolished to provide room for a grand new city designed by Sir Edwin Lutyens (1869–1944). New Delhi became the capital of independent India in 1947.

BELOW: *Twin-domed pavilions on the road toward the India Gate.*

c1450BC
The Pandavas found Indraprastha (a site close to present-day Delhi)

1206
The slave general, Qutb-ud-Din, founds the Delhi Sultanate

1638
Emperor Shah Jahan starts building Shahjahanabad, commonly known now as Old Delhi

1911
The British shift the capital of India from Calcutta to Delhi

1947
Delhi becomes the capital of a newly independent and modern India

Ho Chi Minh City

statistics

Population: 4,800,000

Ethnic mix: Vietnamese 80 percent, Chinese 20 percent

Biggest port in Vietnam: handles more than 10 million tonnes per year

The gardens of the Artex Saigon Orchid Farm contain over 1,000 species of orchid and a total of 50,000 plants

Saigon, the largest city in Vietnam, was officially renamed Ho Chi Minh City after reunification in 1975, though most southerners continue to refer to downtown Ho Chi Minh City as "Saigon", while the traditional Chinatown area further to the west is generally known as "Cholon." Ho Chi Minh City is newer, larger, and brasher than Hanoi. Downtown Saigon is as much a creation of France as of Vietnam, but the city's rather distinguished colonial style acquired something of a glitzy veneer between 1954 and 1975 when Saigon served as the capital of the US-backed Republic of Vietnam.

Ho Chi Minh City lies on the south bank of the Saigon River and is the main port for the fertile Mekong Delta and most of southern Vietnam. It is served by nearby Tan Son Nhat International Airport and has road links with the Delta, the Central Highlands, nearby Cambodia, and more distant Hanoi. It is also linked with Hanoi by a single-track railway line and a rail service called the "Reunification Express." Ho Chi Minh City's main exports are agricultural produce, especially rice, as well as rubber, coal, minerals,

"UNCLE HO", FATHER OF MODERN VIETNAM

Nguyen Sinh Cung (1890–1969) was born near Vinh, in north Vietnam. He traveled to France and joined the French Communist Party in 1920, and in 1924 he became an agent of the Comintern in Moscow. In 1930 he formed the Indochinese Communist Party in Hong Kong before taking the name Ho Chi Minh ("He who Enlightens"), and returned to Vietnam to launch the struggle for independence in 1941. In 1945 he proclaimed Vietnamese independence in Hanoi, then defeated the French at Dien Bien Phu in 1952. He became the first Prime Minister, and then President, of North Vietnam in 1954. He died in 1969 before having seen Vietnamese reunification.

ABOVE: *A statue of Ho Chi Minh with the Hotel de Ville beyond.*

crude petroleum, ores, and seafood. Local industries include food processing, textiles, machine parts, mining, cement and fertilizer production, glass, tyres, oil, and fishing. Electronic and high-tech industries are increasingly important. The population is predominantly Viet (Kinh), with a substantial percentage of ethnic Chinese (Hoa).

A City of Culture and Commerce

Running north-west from the Saigon River, busy Dong Khoi is the heart of the old French Quarter and leads directly to Notre Dame Cathedral, a towering redbrick structure that was erected in 1883. Other colonial buildings in the vicinity are the General Post Office, the Municipal Theater on Lam Son Square, and the magnificent former Town Hall at the north end of Nguyen Hue Boulevard. Most of Saigon's Museums are located in the central area. These include the War Remnants Museum, the Revolutionary Museum, the Military Museum, and the Ho Chi Minh Museum. The History Museum and Art Museum both have excellent collections. Right in the heart of Saigon, Ben Thanh Market is packed to overflowing with stalls selling all manner of wares and thousands of busy, haggling shoppers. Most locals will be shopping for fresh food or clothing, but there are also souvenirs for sale—conical *non la* hats, silk *ao dai* costumes, silk-screened T-shirts, coffee from Dalat, and a range of imitation antiquities.

THE STORY OF...

Ho Chi Minh City is larger than Vietnam's capital Hanoi, yet less cohesive and with a far shorter history. Until the late 17th century it was no more than a small Khmer fishing settlement called Prey Nokor, a name still widely applied by Cambodian nationalists to the city today. When a group of Chinese refugees from the Qing Empire arrived in the region, the Cambodian governor turned for advice and help to the Nguyen Lords of Hue. The price of settling the Chinese and restoring order was Vietnamese suzerainty. Later, the town—named Saigon by the Vietnamese—expanded to join the nearby Chinese settlement of Cholon. In 1859 the city was seized by France and soon became the capital of the French colony of Cochinchina.

Briefly, between 1956 and 1975, Saigon functioned as the capital of the Republic of Vietnam. After the communist seizure of power in 1975, Hanoi once again overshadowed Saigon—a development symbolized by the change of name to Ho Chi Minh City in 1976.

BACKGROUND: *A circular doorway in the Phung Son Tu Pagoda, Cholon.*

ABOVE: *Colonial Saigon and modern Ho Chi Minh City.*
FAR LEFT: *A Cyclo driver.*
CENTER LEFT: *This Post Office in Ho Chi Minh City was designed by Gustave Eiffel.*
LEFT: *A water feature and sculpture outside the Ho Chi Minh City Opera House.*
BELOW: *A performance with traditional Vietnamese musical instruments.*

1698
The Lords of Hue establish a customs post on the site of the ancient Khmer town of Prey Nokor, present-day Saigon

1859
French forces seize Saigon; in 1862 the city becomes the capital of Cochinchina under the Treaty of Saigon

1956
Prime Minister Ngo Dinh Diem declares Saigon the capital of the anti-communist Republic of Vietnam

1975
NVA (North Vietnamese Army) captures Saigon and Vietnam is finally reunited

1976
Saigon becomes Ho Chi Minh City; communist authorities rename the city after the great nationalist leader and founder of modern Vietnam

Hong Kong

statistics

Population: 7,250,000

Victoria Peak is home to the world's steepest railway: it takes 8 minutes for carriages to reach the summit

Hong Kong International Airport's cargo terminal is the largest in the world with a handling capacity of 3 million tonnes

Hong Kong's film industry produces over 600 films a year

JARDINE MATHESON

Jardine Matheson & Co was formed in China in 1832 by William Jardine (1784–1843) and James Matheson (1796–1874), both British citizens from Scotland. Both men began as smugglers of narcotics, making a fortune as ruthless importers of opium into China. Following the seizure of Hong Kong in 1842, their company played a central role in the founding and development of the colony, acquiring both respectability and massive wealth. Now one of the largest corporations in the world, Jardine Matheson have fired a cannon at noon by Hong Kong's Causeway Bay for many years; a tradition that continues today.

ABOVE RIGHT: *Views of Hong Kong by day and by night.*
RIGHT: *The Peak Tower.*

Hong Kong is a classic example of East meets West. It is a busy city of contrasts, where glistening skyscrapers dwarf small temples and fresh food markets. Hong Kong is divided into four main areas—Kowloon, Hong Kong Island, the New Territories, and the Outlying Islands. Kowloon and the New Territories are on a peninsula attached to the Chinese mainland, Hong Kong Island is on the southern side of the harbor facing Kowloon, and the Outlying Islands refers to the remaining islands, 234 in total. The New Territories has a border of 12.5-miles (20km) with China. The city itself is centered around Victoria Harbor. The main business district is Central, on Hong Kong Island. East of Central lies the Admiralty commercial district, Wan Chai, known for its restaurants and clubs, and Causeway Bay, a major shopping area. Towering above it all is the Peak, Hong Kong's best viewpoint and premier residential district.

Cantonese—the form of Chinese used in Hong Kong government matters—is spoken by most of the local Chinese population at home and in the office, while English is widely understood by more than one-third of the population. Although every major religion is freely practised in Hong Kong, Ancestor Worship is predominant due to the strong Confucian influence. Christianity is practised by 10 percent of the population.

THE STORY OF...

Occupied by Britain during the First Opium War in 1841, Hong Kong Island was formally ceded by China in 1842 under the Treaty of Nanking. Part of the adjacent Kowloon Peninsula was also ceded to Britain in 1860, while the whole of the New Territories was leased for 99 years in 1898. Although initially no more than a barren rock, Hong Kong prospered and became one of the world's great port cities by the end of the 19th century.

During the 20th century, despite four years of Japanese occupation between 1941 and 1945, the city continued to prosper. By the late 20th century, however, Hong Kong's colonial status had become increasingly anachronistic. In December 1984, by the Sino-British Joint Declaration, it was agreed that the whole territory of Hong Kong, both leased and ceded, would become the Hong Kong Special Administrative Region of the People's Republic of China (PRC) on 1 July 1997. Under the "one country, two systems" policy of Deng Xiaoping (1904–97), it was also agreed that Hong Kong would enjoy a high degree of autonomy in all matters except foreign affairs and defence until 2047.

FAR LEFT: *Cable cars climbing to the Peak Tower.*
CENTER LEFT: *City tram on Johnston Road, Wan Chai.*
LEFT: *Busy street life in Sai Yeung Choi Street, Mongkok, Kowloon.*
RIGHT: *Sightseeing boat in the Tsim Sha Tsui area of Kowloon.*

1841
British marines under the captaincy of Charles Elliot land on Hong Kong Island and plant the Union Jack

1888
Hong Kong's first tramway line to the Peak is built

1898
Britain signs a 99-year lease with China for Hong Kong Island and the New Territories

1941
The Japanese capture Hong Kong and begin four years of occupation

1997
Celebrations held on the night of 30 June mark the handover of Hong Kong to China

A City of Bustling Commerce

By population the fourth largest city in China, Hong Kong is one of the most densely populated areas in the world. Most people live in apartments in high-rise towers. Away from the city, much of the open spaces are covered with parks and woods. About 60 percent of the land is designated as Country Parks and Nature Reserves. The irregular and long coastline of Hong Kong also provides many bays and beaches for its inhabitants. Environmental concern and awareness is growing, however, as Hong Kong ranks as one of the most air-polluted cities in the world.

Hong Kong has a bustling economy that is heavily dependent on international trade. It is one of the world's freest economies, as well as the world's 10th largest trading entity and 11th largest banking center. Natural resources are limited, and food and raw materials must be imported. Hong Kong had extensive trade and investment ties with the PRC, even before its reunification with China in 1997. The service industry represented 86.5 percent of the GDP in 2001, and the territory, with a highly sophisticated banking sector, houses the Asian headquarters of many multinational corporations.

Jakarta

statistics

Population: 16,650,000

Ragunan Zoo is home to more than 3,000 animals indigenous to the Indonesian archipelago, including the famous Komodo dragon— the world's biggest lizard

Jakarta's population grows by more than 200,000 each year

The Monas National Monument in Jakarta's Merdeka Square is topped by a 45ft (14m) bronze flame covered in 73lb (33kg) of gold

THE FATHER OF MODERN INDONESIA

Sukarno (1901–70) was the first President of Indonesia. The son of a Javanese aristocrat and his Balinese wife, Sukarno was born in Surabaya. Like many Javanese, he had just one name. He became a leader of the Indonesian movement when it was founded in 1927. He was arrested in 1929 by Dutch colonial authorities and sentenced to two years in prison. By the time he was released, he had become a popular hero. He became president on independence in 1945 and remained in power until deposed by General Mohammed Suharto (b. 1921) in 1967. Megawati Sukarnoputri, President of Indonesia from 2001–2004, is his daughter.

ABOVE: *President Sukarno making a speech c1946.*

Jakarta is a vast, modern metropolis with little in the way of historic buildings but some very fine high-rise architecture. The city is centered around Medan Merdeka or "Freedom Square." Here may be found the Monas National Monument, the huge Istiqlal Mosque, the ultra-modern headquarters of Pertamina, the state-owned oil monopoly that supplies nearly 10 percent of OPEC's oil output, and the National Museum with its fine collections of Indonesian art and antiquities. Jalan Thamrin dominates South Jakarta, a broad street lined with yet more high-rise blocks and glittering shopping malls. Little remains of the Javanese *kampung* or "villages" of old Jakarta, and Glodok District, once the city's Chinatown, has largely disappeared beneath millions of tonnes of steel and concrete. The nearest the visitor can come to "Old Batavia" is Sunda Kelapa, the old harbor, where the mile-long wharf is lined with dozens of two-masted traditional schooners that still ply the waters of the archipelago.

As the capital of Indonesia and the center of government, politics, and economics, Jakarta attracts many immigrants, both foreign and domestic. As a result, the city has a decidedly cosmopolitan flavor and a diverse culture. Many of the immigrants are from other parts of Indonesia, speaking a mixture of dialects and bringing traditional cuisines and customs from their ancestral homes. Jakarta has several art centers, notably the Senyan Center, where traditional music and shadow puppet performances are staged. As the largest city in Indonesia, it attracts artists from all over the archipelago who hope to find a wider audience and more opportunities for their arts and crafts.

ABOVE: *The statue of Prince Diponegoro in Liberty Square.*
LEFT: *The city of Jakarta at night.*
BELOW: *A bajaj (three-wheel motor-scooter driver) in Java.*

A Major Port City

Despite the presence of many wide boulevards, Jakarta suffers from heavy traffic congestion, especially in the central business district. To reduce traffic jams, some major roads in Jakarta have a "three in one" rule during rush hours, prohibiting vehicles carrying fewer than three passengers on certain roads. There are railways throughout Jakarta; however, they are inadequate in providing transportation for everyone. The railway connects Jakarta to its neighboring cities, and Jakarta's port is the most important hub in the archipelago's huge and vital shipping network. Jakarta Airport provides frequent international links with Asia, Europe, and North America.

Economically, Jakarta can be identified as the center for the national economy, as an administrative center in its own right, and also as a major industrial base. Its location as a port also makes it an important center for regional and international trade.

THE STORY OF...

The first recorded settlement at what is now Jakarta was the port of Kelapa, near the mouth of the Ciliwung River. By the 12th century it was a major port for the Hindu Kingdom of Sunda. In the early 16th century the Portuguese were granted permission to build a fort at Kelapa. The port of Jakarta is still called Sunda Kelapa today, after this early settlement. In 1527 Fatahillah conquered the city and changed its name to Jayakarta, from which Jakarta is derived. In 1619 Dutch forces conquered the city and renamed it Batavia. With direct rule by The Netherlands expanding to more parts of the archipelago during the 19th and early 20th centuries, the importance of Batavia increased.

Imperial Japanese forces seized the city in 1942, renaming it Jakarta, in order to gain local favor. Following Japan's defeat in 1945, the Dutch reoccupied the city despite the declaration of independence by the Indonesians on 17 August 1945. Jakarta became the capital of the Republic of Indonesia on formal independence in 1949.

1527
Fatahillah, a Sumatran Malay warrior, attacks the city of Kelapa and renames it Jayakarta (Jakarta)

1619
After attacking Jayakarta, the Dutch East India Company takes control of the city and renames it Batavia

1807
Dutch Governor Herman Daendels relocates Batavia a few kilometers south, building a new sector around the present-day Merdeka Square area

1945
Future president, Sukarno, proclaims Indonesian independence from his home in Jakarta. The City officially changes its name back to Jakarta

2004
Susilo Bambang Yudhoyono becomes Indonesia's first democratically elected president in an elaborate ceremony in Jakarta

RIGHT (TOP): *Wooden puppets for puppet theaters (wayang golek) in the Wayang Museum.*
ABOVE RIGHT: *Boats at anchor in Sunda Kelapa harbor.*
RIGHT: *Indonesian silver-gilt figure of Majusri from the Jakarta National Museum.*

Kathmandu

Kathmandu is an enigma, medieval in appearance and yet plagued by seething traffic. First-class hotels compete with an array of small guesthouses in the popular tourist district of Thamel—yet a walk of just five minutes in any direction leads to another city, rich in the smell of spices and old in time. This is the real Kathmandu, an unexpected and extravagant mixture of peoples and religions, child-goddesses, bare-foot porters padding in back alleys, and sacred cows. The Kathmandu most people come to see is the Old City, a tangled network of narrow alleys, stores, and temples located around central Durbar Square. The rambling old Hanuman Dhoka, or royal palace, takes up most of the eastern side of the square. Built four centuries ago by Nepal's Malla kings, only a small part of the complex is open to the general public. At the left of the entrance stands a statue of Hanuman, the monkey god of Hindu mythology, after which the palace is named. Within the main courtyard is a likeness of Narasimha, the half-man, half-lion incarnation of Vishnu, disemboweling a demon. Directly in front of the gates stands a large, tiered pagoda dedicated to Jagannath, a manifestation of Vishnu as Lord of the Universe, bearing an inscription dated 1563. There can be no doubt that these are the royal precincts of a Hindu kingdom.

THE GREAT STUPA OF BODHNATH

Some 3 miles (5km) north of Kathmandu stands the impressive form of Bodhnath, the center of Tibetan Buddhism and of Tibetans-in-exile in Nepal. Many small stalls selling Tibetan handicrafts surround the temple, and there are numerous monasteries in the area, some named after Tibetan retreats destroyed by the Red Guards at the height of China's destructive "Cultural Revolution." A stroll around Bodhnath provides the visitor with some cultural insight into the world of Tibetan spiritualism, as well as the opportunity to taste *chang*—Tibetan corn beer—and, should the inclination strike, a cup of salted yak-butter tea.

ABOVE RIGHT: *Durbar Square.*
RIGHT: *The temple of Swayambhunath.*

Nepal's Living Goddess

On the southern side of Durbar Square is the ornate doorway to the Kumari Bahal. This entranceway leads to one of the loveliest and most elegant courtyards in the capital. All four sides are lavishly decorated with wooden fretwork windows, ornamental brackets, and carved doorways. This is the home of Nepal's living goddess, the Kumari. According to tradition, a virgin female child of the Shakya community, carrying appropriate auspicious signs, is chosen to become the Kumari and carried in state to her new home, the Kumari Bahal. Here she remains as a living goddess, appearing in state to bless the people of Kathmandu and the royal family on festive occasions or at important religious ceremonies. As soon as she reaches puberty, she ceases to be considered divine, and is returned to normal life. Meanwhile, another little girl will have been chosen to become Kumari, extending continuing protection and blessing over the Kingdom of Nepal to keep it, and its people, from harm.

The city's communications with the outside world are limited to flights through Kathmandu's Tribhuvan International Airport and poor road links with Tibet (China) to the north and India to the south.

BELOW RIGHT: *Rani Pokhari Pond (Queen's Pond).*

THE STORY OF...

According to legend, the Kathmandu Valley was once a holy lake encircled by mountains. To this body of sacred water, inhabited by giant serpents, came the first Buddha who threw the seed of a lotus into the lake. The seed burst into a thousand-petaled lotus. When the Buddha saw the beauty of the flower, he caused the hills to part, draining the lake and forming a valley, so that a rim of mountains would always protect the lotus.

Many years later a Buddhist monk came to settle in the valley, where he built a tall pagoda with a gilded spire. This became known as the temple of Swayambhunath, which stands on a hill just west of Kathmandu. To this day the people of Kathmandu believe the gilded spire of Swayambhunath radiates a sacred light that protects the whole valley. Swayambhunath, magnificently set on a conical hill, provides a fine vantage point for visitors to the Nepalese capital. From its sacred steps, looking east and south, broad vistas of the city are apparent, from the snaking Bagmati River to the pagodas of distant Bhaktapur.

key dates

AD400
Early settlement in the area of present-day Kathmandu during the Licchavi dynasty

AD980
King Gunakamadeva I commences work on a new city, then called Kantipur

1482
Under King Ratna, Malla Kathmandu becomes a city state

1769
King Prithvi Narayan Shah conquers the Kathmandu Valley and proceeds to renovate many of Kathmandu's finest buildings

2001
Crown Prince Dipendra massacres 11 members of the Nepalese royal family, including the king and queen, in the royal palace

Kolkata

statistics

Population: 15,200,000

Literacy rate: 81.3 percent

Largest cricket stadium in the world: Eden Gardens with a capacity of 90,000

Howrah Bridge: 2 million people cross it daily

RABINDRANATH TAGORE (1861–1941)

Rabindranath Tagore was a poet, novelist, philosopher, and nationalist who was awarded the Nobel Prize for Literature in 1913, becoming the first Asian to be awarded a Nobel Prize. Born into the third generation of an educated and intellectually gifted Calcutta Brahmin family, Tagore devoted much of his time to promoting educational reform in Bengal. Although best known as a poet, he also composed novels, essays, short stories, travelogues, and drama. No less notable among his works are over 2,000 songs that are considered Bengali cultural treasures both in India and in neighboring Bangladesh. Tagore also penned the words for India's national anthem.

ABOVE: *A bust commemorating the life of Rabindranath Tagore.*

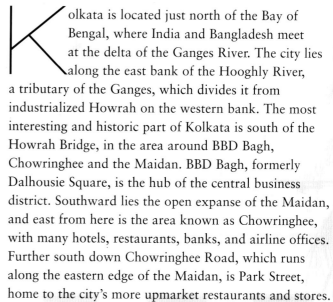

TOP: *A statue of Queen Victoria stands as a remnant of colonial times in Kolkata.*
ABOVE: *The elegant Raj Bhavan in Udhagamandalam, Kolkata.*
BELOW: *India faces the constant threat of flooding.*

Kolkata is located just north of the Bay of Bengal, where India and Bangladesh meet at the delta of the Ganges River. The city lies along the east bank of the Hooghly River, a tributary of the Ganges, which divides it from industrialized Howrah on the western bank. The most interesting and historic part of Kolkata is south of the Howrah Bridge, in the area around BBD Bagh, Chowringhee and the Maidan. BBD Bagh, formerly Dalhousie Square, is the hub of the central business district. Southward lies the open expanse of the Maidan, and east from here is the area known as Chowringhee, with many hotels, restaurants, banks, and airline offices. Further south down Chowringhee Road, which runs along the eastern edge of the Maidan, is Park Street, home to the city's more upmarket restaurants and stores.

At the southern end of the Maidan stands Fort William, dating in its present form to 1758. The fort is still in official use and is off-limits to visitors. Next door is the Victoria Memorial, a museum filled with remnants from the British Raj, including a piano that was played by Queen Victoria (1819–1901) as a young girl. It also includes the Calcutta Gallery and National Leaders Gallery, with exhibits on the city's history, the Raj, and its various political and social leaders. Just to the east, Birla Planetarium is one of the largest in the world, while south of the Maidan is the well established zoo and beyond that the peaceful Horticultural Gardens. Continuing about 1.2 miles (2km) further south, the Kali Temple, also known as Kalighat, was built in 1809 on the site of an earlier temple from which the city probably took its name. Nearby is Mother Teresa's (1910–97) Hospital for the Dying and Destitute.

Trade and Transport

Kolkata's position as one of India's pre-eminent economic centers is rooted in its industrial, financial, and trade activities, and role as a major port. It is also a major center for printing, publishing, and newspaper production, as well as for recreation and entertainment. The products of the city's hinterland include coal, iron, manganese, mica, petroleum, and tea. The city is the world's largest processor of jute, a locally grown plant that is used to make burlap. Engineering is another major industry, however in the late 20th century, large-scale manufacturing began to give way to high-tech industries, with the production of electronics and computer software. Road, rail, and air links with the rest of India are good, though the port continues to suffer from silting problems.

BELOW: *The Victoria Memorial was built in 1906; now it is a reminder of the city's colonial past.*

THE STORY OF...

The tax records of Moghul Emperor Akbar (1584–1598) and the work of Bipradaas, a 15th-century Bengali poet, both mention a settlement named Kalikata—in homage to the Hindu goddess Kali—from which the name Kolkata derives. Job Charnock, an agent of the East India Company, founded the first modern settlement in this location in 1690, and eight years later the company purchased the three villages of Sutanuti, Kolikata, and Gobindapur. In 1727 the Calcutta Municipal Corporation was formed and the city's first mayor appointed.

The Nawab of Bengal, Siraj ud-Daulah, seized Calcutta and renamed it Alinagar in 1756, but lost control within a year. The city was returned to the British and in 1772 became the capital of British India. In 1912 the capital was transferred to New Delhi, while Calcutta remained the capital of Bengal. Since independence and partition it has remained the capital and chief city of Indian West Bengal.

BELOW: *A coolie hauls a huge weight around the streets.*

key dates

1690
Job Charnock, of the East India Company, establishes a new British trading post on the Hooghly River

1722
Calcutta becomes capital of British India

1864
Cyclone hits the city, leaving 70,000 dead

1947
Calcutta becomes the capital city of the new state of West Bengal

2001
The city is officially renamed Kolkata

Kuala Lumpur

statistics

- Population: 4,100,000
- Ethnic mix: Malay 58 percent, Chinese 31 percent, Indian 8 percent, others 3 percent
- World's tallest flagpole: 328ft (100m)
- Menara Kuala Lumpur, the world's fourth highest telecommunications tower at 1,380ft (421m) contains the world's highest McDonald's restaurant

THE PETRONAS TWIN TOWERS

The Petronas Twin Towers are the tallest twin towers in the world. Completed in 1998 by architect Cesar Pelli (b. 1926), these tapering towers connected by a sky bridge were also known as the world's tallest building only surpassed, in 2003, by the height of Taiwan's Taipei 101. In a statement of Malaysia's primarily Muslim heritage, the 88-floor stainless steel and glass structure was designed to reflect designs found in traditional Islamic architecture. In 1997 French "spiderman" Alain Robert scaled the building with no safety devices, and using only his bare hands and feet. Below the twin towers is the popular Suria KLCC shopping mall.

Much of central Kuala Lumpur developed without central planning, so the streets in the older parts of town are narrow, winding, and congested. The architecture here is of an attractive colonial type, in a distinctively hybrid European and Chinese tradition. The stretch of Jalan Raja facing Dataran Merdeka, or Independence Square, is the elegant heart of downtown Kuala Lumpur. The Federal Court building with its distinctive copper domes and Moorish architecture stands here, as does the central Railway Station, also elaborately Moorish in design. The nearby Padang is an immaculate green park often used by cricketers; to complete the scene, an old clubhouse from British colonial times stands by the green.

Most of the city has developed in a modern, high-rise fashion, featuring steel, glass, and concrete. Because of this, architects have been encouraged to incorporate traditional Islamic design elements into their work. Notable examples of this fusion are the Dayabumi Building—Kuala Lumpur's first skyscraper—the Tabung Haji Building and Menara Telekom—both designed by local architect Hijjas Kasturi—and the well-known Petronas Twin Towers. Kuala Lumpur is the largest city in Malaysia and the capital of the Federation. Within Malaysia, the name is almost always abbreviated to "KL." The executive branch of government was moved to a new administrative capital called Putrajaya in the mid-1990s, but the legislature, parliament, and judiciary remain based in Kuala Lumpur.

A City Built on a Boom

Kuala Lumpur has advanced by leaps and bounds since the Asian Economic Boom of the 1990s when Malaysia was averaging 10 percent economic growth. Skyscrapers dominate the skyline and the city, formerly a rather languid colonial outpost, has become one of the most lively, advanced, and vibrant cities in Southeast Asia. The infrastructure has struggled to keep up with this rapid growth, although a new Rapid Transit System was built in 1992. Traffic jams are a scourge commuters endure daily, despite the construction of elevated six-lane highways. In 2002, a high-speed rail link called KLIA Transit was opened between the city center and Kuala Lumpur International Airport at Sepang. Nearby is the ultra-modern "cyber city" of Cyberjaya, located within Malaysia's Multimedia Super Corridor. Links with the rest of peninsular Malaysia by road, rail, and air are excellent, as are air links with Sabah and Sarawak, the eastern part of the Malaysian Federation. The main port for Kuala Lumpur is Klang, located on the nearby Straits of Malacca.

RIGHT: *The Sri Maga Mahamariamman Temple.* BELOW: *One of the railway station towers with a high-rise building behind.*

THE STORY OF...

Kuala Lumpur was founded in 1857 at the confluence of the Gombak and Kelang Rivers. The name means "muddy river mouth" in Malay. The settlement started when Raja Abdullah, a member of the royal family of Selangor, opened the Klang Valley to Chinese prospectors. A tin mine was established, encouraging traders to move in. As the settlement grew, the British rulers of Malaya appointed a headman, called "Kapitan Cina", to administer the settlement and ensure law and order; at this time Kuala Lumpur was a rough frontier town and gang warfare was common. The growing town was made capital of Selangor in 1880, and when the Federated Malay States were established in 1896, Kuala Lumpur became capital.

During World War II Japanese forces occupied Kuala Lumpur between 1942 and 1945. After independence in 1957, the city was made the capital of the Federation of Malaya, then of the Federation of Malaysia in 1963. In 1974 Kuala Lumpur was made a Federal Territory.

BELOW: *Sign identifying the Jalan Petaling Market.*

JALAN PETALING
街 麻 茨
PETALING STREET

1857
A band of Chinese tin prospectors found the small settlement of Kuala Lumpur

1896
The rapidly expanding city becomes the capital of the newly formed Federated Malay States

1942
Japanese troops capture Kuala Lumpur; the start of three years of occupation

1957
Independence from Britain is declared in the city's Dataran Merdeka (Independence Square)

1998
Kuala Lumpur becomes the first Asian city to host the Commonwealth Games

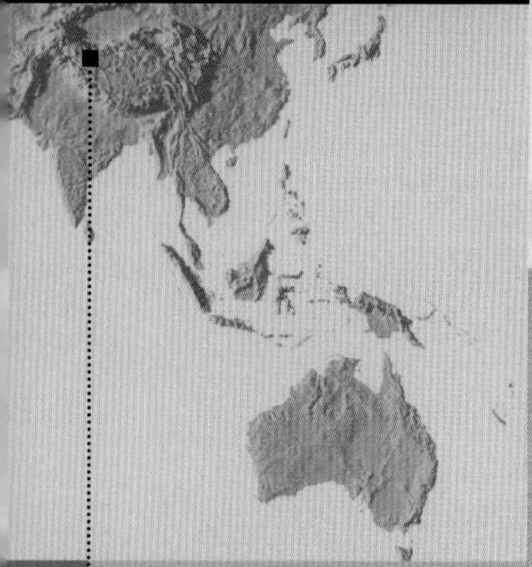

Lahore

statistics

- Population: 7,200,000
- Pakistan's largest university: 12,000 students
- Lahore's multi-use, all-seater Punjab Stadium holds 90,000
- Lahore museum, Pakistan's oldest, contains more than 40,000 coins and 2,500 miniature paintings

ahore is Pakistan's second largest city (after Karachi) and is the cultural and historic heart both of Sind Province and of the nation, though it has never served as the nation's capital, perhaps because of its proximity to the Indian frontier a mere 10 miles (16km) to the east. While Karachi was chosen as the capital of Pakistan on independence in 1947, and Islamabad became capital in 1962, Lahore remains the country's cultural, educational, and artistic center, and easily the most interesting city in the country. It is also Pakistan's movie capital, known affectionately as "Lollywood."

Lahore has long been a major trading center and city of commerce. It stands astride the old "Grand Trunk Road" linking Peshawar and the North-West Frontier with Delhi, Varanasi, and Kolkata in India. A motorway was completed in 2000, linking Lahore to Islamabad. Nearby Allama Iqbal International Airport is one of the largest in South Asia and provides frequent links with Europe, North America, and the Far East. A good railway service runs between Lahore and Karachi, as well as (when political relations are good) linking the city directly to the huge Indian rail network via Amritsar and Delhi. Lahore's major industries are metalworking, engineering, chemicals, textiles, and leather production.

THE EMPEROR JAHANGIR

Jahangir (1569–1627) was born at Fatehpur Sikri in India, the son of the great Moghul emperor Akbar (1542–1605). On Akbar's death, Jahangir assumed the throne. In 1611 he married his favorite wife, whom he gave the name Nur Jahan, or "Light of the World." Jahangir consolidated the Moghul Empire and assumed the title "World Conqueror", but is perhaps best known for his tolerance toward Hindus, Christians, and Jews, as well as for his patronage of painting, literature, and culture. Under his rule Lahore became a great center of the arts. Both Jahangir and Nur Jahan are buried in the city's Shahdara area.

RIGHT: *The Data Durbar Shrine.*
BACKGROUND: *Lahore Fort.*

A Major Tourist Destination

Lahore is Pakistan's primary tourist attraction, drawing more visitors than any other city in the country. With its shady parks and gardens, its attractive mix of Moghul and colonial architecture, and the exotic appeal of its congested streets and bazaars, it is not hard to see why. Major sites are The Mall, an area of parks and buildings with a distinctly British colonial flavor; Lahore Fort, filled with stately palaces, halls, and gardens; and the Old City, where a procession of rickshaws, pony carts, and hawkers fill the narrow lanes. Other attractions include Lahore Museum—the best and biggest in the country—Kim's Gun, the cannon immortalized in Rudyard Kipling's (1865–1936) 1901 classic *Kim*, Aitchison College, an elegant public school that boasts the cricketer and politician Imran Khan (b. 1952) as a former pupil, and the Shalimar Gardens, established by Shah Jahan (1592–1666) in 1637.

The Badshahi Masjid, one of the world's largest mosques, is located just outside the northeast corner of the Walled City. Nearby is a park called Hazuri Bagh where Maharaja Ranjit Singh (1780–1839) built a decorated marble pavilion. Every Sunday afternoon story-tellers, poets, and singers gather in the park to continue the city's oral tradition, reciting Punjabi, Urdu, and Persian classics aloud.

THE STORY OF...

According to legend, Lahore was founded by Loh, son of Rama, the hero of the Hindu epic story the *Ramayana*. In historic times, the city came under Muslim rule following the conquest of Mahmud of Ghazni (AD971–1030). Qutub-ud-din Aibak (r. 1206–10) was crowned in the city in 1206 and became the first Muslim ruler of the South Asian subcontinent. From 1524 to 1752 Lahore was an important part of the Moghul Empire, and during the reign of Akbar (1542–1605). During this period Lahore Fort was built on the foundations of an older fort dating from the 1560s. It was later extended by the Moghul emperors Jahangir (1569–1627), and Shah Jahan (1592–1666).

The last of the great Moghuls, Aurangzeb (1618–1707) who ruled from 1658, built the city's most famous monuments, including the Badshahi Mosque and the Alamgiri Gate. In 1947 Lahore became part of Pakistan following partition from India.

AD630
Chinese traveler Hsuan Tsang makes the first reliable reference to the city in his writings

1021
Mahmud of Ghazni, the city's first Muslim ruler, conquers the city

1157
Lahore becomes capital of the Ghaznavid Empire under the ruler Khusraw Shah

1584
Akbar, the third Moghul emperor, establishes Lahore as a center of learning and the arts

1999
Lahore Declaration, with the intent to promote peace and understanding between the countries

Melbourne

statistics

- Population: 3,200,000
- Melbourne's oldest building, the Mitre Tavern, dates from 1837
- Melbourne has the third largest tram network in the world
- Over 100 million trips are made on the Yarra Trams each year

ocated on the northern bank of the River Yarra and fanning out to Port Phillip Bay just 3 miles (5km) from the Central Business District (CBD), Australia's second largest city is an orderly creation. The extravagant 19th-century buildings that take center stage on Melbourne's grid-like streets and recount its history are an ever-present reminder of the city's past and present prosperity.

Despite losing its status as the country's leading financial center to Sydney in the 1970s, Melbourne's economy is flourishing, with the focus shifting to new technologies and multimedia ventures. A high standard of living and competitive costs have seen a number of companies from the Asia Pacific region relocate to the city.

Imposing European Architecture

Melbourne's CBD is divided into 10 distinct precincts which are showcased in the "Golden Mile Heritage Trail." This tourist route takes in Melbourne's most significant historical buildings and tells the story of the city's evolution. It encompasses everything from the Immigration Museum and the mock Venetian façades of the Winfield Building, to the Gothic-style Stock Exchange

MELBOURNE CRICKET GROUND

Colloquially known as the MCG, the current stadium of the Melbourne Cricket Ground dates from 1853, when Australia's first steam train was routed through the Melbourne Cricket Club's (MCC) previous ground. In 1861 England's national team first traveled to the stadium to take part in an inter-colonial competition. Since its inception the MCG has undergone a series of revamps, bringing new stands and a new pavilion. The stadium is currently undergoing a A$430 million reconstruction which, when completed in time for the 2006 Commonwealth Games, will have a seating capacity exceeding 100,000.

ABOVE RIGHT: *Victorian Arts Center.*
RIGHT: *Luna Park.*

and the colonial architecture of Como House. Other highlights include Collins Street, complete with its elegant and classically styled shopping arcades, ornate tearooms, and attractive churches, and the Old Treasury, widely regarded as one of the most striking public buildings in Australia, a pseudo Italian palazzo structure.

Melbourne is much more than a city of grand buildings. Victoria's capital is an energetic city with an exciting nightlife and a world-class eating and drinking scene, with fresh produce and the state's wines all close at hand. Melbourne also has a diverse population with their own ethnic neighborhoods, including a Chinatown. Home to myriad museums and galleries, the city's arts are thriving, with theater, ballet, opera, and aboriginal art part of the eclectic mix.

Australians are renowned throughout the world for their sporting passion, a national stereotype that applies to the citizens of Melbourne. In addition to a passion for cricket, the city's residents flock to events that include the Australian Rules Football Grand Final, a Formula One Grand Prix, and the Australian Tennis Open. Another popular pastime for locals who love the great outdoors is to head to the sandy shores of the nearby suburbs, with St. Kilda, just a 4-mile (6km) tram ride away, being one of the state's most popular beaches. This idyllic seaside district with its fine restaurants is also home to a small penguin colony.

TOP: *Restored barque at Melbourne Maritime Museum.*
ABOVE: *Yarra River footbridge in Southgate.*
RIGHT: *Doubles action in the 2003 Australian Open at the National Tennis Center, Melbourne Park.*

THE STORY OF...

Australia's indigenous people, the Aborigines, have inhabited the shore of Port Phillip Bay for over 40,000 years. However, Melbourne's foundation is most commonly associated with John Batman (1801–39) and John Pascoe Fawkner (1792–1869), who settled in the city in 1835. Melbourne began its early colonial existence as part of New South Wales, and then became the capital of the newly created state of Victoria in 1851. In the same year gold was discovered, with the ensuing gold rush seeing thousands descend upon the city each day. As its population swelled, urban development projects forged ahead at lightning speed, including the opening of Melbourne's first gas works and reservoir, the construction of its university and town hall, and the arrival of the telegraph, as well as the opening of Victoria's state library and Australia's first steam railway.

Melbourne continued to prosper throughout the 19th and 20th centuries, with the 1956 Olympic Games firmly putting the city on the world map. The Commonwealth Games in 2006 are set to bring Melbourne to the forefront of world attention once again.

Melbourne

key dates

1835
Melbourne becomes part of the colony of New South Wales

1851
The city becomes capital of the state of Victoria; the gold rush sees thousands flock to Melbourne

1880
Melbourne hosts the International Exhibition

1956
The city hosts the Olympic Games

2004
The Royal Exhibition Building and Carlton Gardens join UNESCO's World Heritage List

Mumbai

Population: 19,200,000

Mumbai's religious mix: 68 percent Hindu, 17 percent Muslim, 6 percent Buddhist, 4 percent Christian, 4 percent Jain, 1 percent Sikh, and others

The city's per capita income (48,954 rupees) is more than three times that of the rest of India

Biggest movie industry in the world: Bollywood makes around 400 films a year

BOLLYWOOD, INDIA'S FILM CAPITAL

India is a movie-mad nation. About 3.5 million people daily flock to the country's 13,000 cinemas, watching movies in 52 local languages and dialects—many seeing their favorite movies over and over again, sometimes a dozen times or more. The vast majority of movies are home-made products, the most well-known being Hindi-language films produced in "Bollywood", as Mumbai or Bombay has come to be known. Each year India produces about eight times Hollywood's annual movie output. At present, Indian films gross US$3 billion annually and the popularity of "Bollywood" is increasing internationally.

ABOVE: *Poster publicizing a Bollywood movie.*

Ostentatious wealth and poverty, alongside squalor and splendor, or tradition and modernity—Mumbai thrives on contrasts. One of the most visible contrasts lies in the city's architecture. While large areas consist of crumbling, shabby housing blocks, the southern part of Mumbai still boasts an array of stunning colonial buildings. Foremost is Victoria Terminus. Built between 1878 and 1887 and modeled on London's St. Pancras Station, it exhibits a plethora of filigree ornamentation. The roof has church-like little spires and an imposing, neo-Gothic middle dome. Every day some 2.5 million commuters are said to pass through its arched portals. Across the street is another unique architectural monument, the Municipal Corporation Building. Built in 1893, its Moorish middle dome is 234ft (71.5m) high, and this is surrounded by other smaller domes.

Other examples of elaborate Victorian elegance are clustered around the Oval Maidan, a giant open space, often playing host to amateur cricketers. Here the massive, 558ft (170m) long High Court, built in 1879, is an eclectic mixture of Venetian and neo-Gothic styles. To its south side stands the more subtle University of Mumbai, with its 262ft (80m) high landmark Rajabai Tower, a copy of Big Ben. In British times, the clock tower used to play "God Save the Queen" four times a day. North of the Oval Maidan, across the road from Churchgate Station, stands the Railway Administration Building. Built in exuberant Moorish style, it looks rather like a Moghul ruler's summer palace. Framing the Arabian Sea, Marine Drive is Mumbai's major promenade, sometimes called "The Queen's Necklace." The city's most famous landmark is the Gateway of India, an 85ft (26m) high archway erected on the spot where King George V (1865–1936), then Emperor of India, first set foot on Indian soil in 1911.

ABOVE RIGHT: *Marine Drive.* RIGHT: *Railway Administration Building.* TOP RIGHT: *Taxis outside the Chatrapati Shivaji Terminus (formerly Victoria Terminus).*

THE STORY OF...

After Vasco da Gama (c1469–1524) discovered the sea route to India in 1498, the Portuguese won control over the area around Mumbai in 1509. In 1534, the Sultan of Gujarat ceded to the Portuguese seven islands, which were later to become Mumbai. When, in 1661, Catherine of Braganza (1638–1705) married Charles II (1630–85), the islands were given as a dowry. Seven years later, Charles, finding no better use for the swampy, malaria-infested islands, leased them to the East India Company for a modest £10 per year. The EIC connected the seven islands through land reclamation; a fort, a mint, and docks were built.

Mumbai harbor soon attracted rich merchants. Immigrants poured in from all over the subcontinent, and also Arabs and Jews from the Middle East. Today, Mumbai—the "City of Gold"—has a staggering 19 million inhabitants, providing India with one-third of the country's overall income tax, while 50 percent of the country's exports pass through its harbor.

BELOW: *Fruit and vegetable market in Mumbai.*

Economy and Transport

As the country's commercial capital, Mumbai houses the headquarters of the majority of India's major companies. The Reserve Bank of India and the Stock Exchange are situated in the south of the city. Most of the inhabitants rely on public transport to travel to their workplace. Public buses and trains handle most of this traffic, though the Mumbai Suburban Railway runs around 1,000 trains daily. Mumbai is the headquarters of India's Western Railway and Central Railway, providing links with the entire subcontinent. The main stations are Mumbai Central and Chatrapati Shivaji Terminus (formerly Victoria Terminus). Domestic flights leave from Santa Cruz Airport, while international services use Chatrapati Shivaji International Airport. The port of Mumbai is the busiest in India.

key dates

1534
The Sultan of Gujarat cedes the area around Mumbai to the Portuguese

1661
Catherine of Braganza marries Charles II of England who receives Mumbai as part of the dowry

1853
First train in India runs from Mumbai to Thana, a distance of 21 miles (33km)

1915
Mahatma Gandhi lands in Mumbai arriving from South Africa

1995
Mumbai is officially taken as the new name for the city, formerly Bombay

Osaka

- Population: 2,600,000
- Kansei International Airport in Osaka Bay is constructed on the largest man-made island in the world. Over half a million passengers pass through each week
- Osaka is one of the wealthiest cities in the world with a GDP equal to that of Australia
- Osaka Aquarium (Kaiyukan) is the world's largest. It encompasses 286,000 sq ft (26,570 sq m) and contains 2.9 million gallons (13.2 million liters) of water

OSAKA CASTLE (OSAKA-JO)

Toyotomi Hideyoshi (1536–98), the warlord who unified Japan, built Osaka Castle in 1583. It is famed for its magnificent scale and the immense granite stones originally used to construct the walls. In 1665 it was struck by lightning and severely damaged. Further damage took place in the fighting that led to the Meiji Restoration in 1868. The present castle is a copy of the original, which was rebuilt in 1931, though the main gate and several towers are original. Inside the castle is a museum with displays and exhibits relating to Osaka and the Toyotomi clan, and at night the entire castle is illuminated.

ABOVE: *The tiered roof of Osaka Castle (Osaka-Jo).*

Osaka, Japan's third largest city, is 342 miles (550km) west of Tokyo and located on a delta plain formed by the Yodo and Yamato rivers. To the west it is bounded by Osaka Bay, but spreads out to the east across the Osaka Plain. Other rivers also flow through the city and it was once known as "The Water Capital" for its numerous waterways, canals, and bridges. Osaka developed as an Imperial capital, and then as a temple and castle town. However, under the Tokugawa Shogunate it became the political, cultural, and economic hub of Western Japan. After Tokyo, it remains the most important financial and commercial center in Japan.

Osaka's Citizens

Historically, Tokyo was primarily a political, Samurai class city, while Osaka was a commercial town run by the merchant class. Their respective citizens led different daily lives and even today, their ways of thinking, behavior, speech, culture, and cuisine are very different from one another. Osakans describe themselves as Shiminteki (people with no time for pretensions), as easy-going with a taste for the good things in life, and as people who know how to enjoy themselves.

Osaka is the spiritual home of the Japanese traditional arts of Kabukki, Noh, and Buraku (puppet theater). The city is also famous for its culinary gusto and creativity and its citizens are known to the rest of Japan as "Kuidore", or those who love food so much they will eat to physical and financial ruin!

City Architecture and Sights

Osaka has a unique energy, charm, and pride of its own, but it is not an architecturally beautiful city. Crowded and busy, and with no obvious town planning, the city is choked with traffic. Buddhist temples, grey commercial buildings, chrome skyscrapers, gaudy neon signs, huge open-air video screens, and Shinto shrines all exist side by side, vying for space and attention. For the visitor it is a place to wander, shop, eat, and sightsee. The area around Dotonbori Street in the Namba Railway Station district is the oldest and most popular quarter for shopping, restaurants, and nightlife. Osaka Castle is well worth a visit, as are Shitenno-ji Temple, Japan's first Buddhist temple, and its smaller neighbor, Isshinji Temple, some 1.2 miles (2km) southwest of Namba Station.

ABOVE: *The Tsutenkaku Tower, a well-known symbol of Osaka.*
RIGHT: *The city of Osaka, the commercial hub of western Japan.*
BELOW: *Dotonbori, Osaka's famous "food-lover's heaven."*

ABOVE: *Osaka Aquarium.*

THE STORY OF...

The site where Osaka now stands was founded in the fifth century AD as the port town of Naniwa, a trading post for Korea and China. Emperors of the era had palaces in Naniwa where they entertained envoys from their richer neighbors, and for a short period in the seventh century the town served as Japan's capital. It was in the 16th century, under the leadership of Toyotomi Hideyoshi, that Osaka began to grow as a great commercial city and a successful and upwardly mobile merchant class developed. Compared to the Samurai class, they were free-thinkers who supported the creation of a rich tradition of popular culture. Even today the city remains the spiritual home of the traditional performing arts of Noh, Kabuki, and Bunraku.

The population of Osaka had reached over 3 million by the outbreak of World War II, but by the end of the war much of the city was destroyed. During the post-war years, Osaka quickly re-established its position as the commercial center of Japan, as well as a hub of culture, entertainment, shopping, and eating.

BELOW: *A crab restaurant in the Dotonbori area of central Osaka.*

key dates

AD593
The first state Buddhist temple, founded by Prince Shotoku, is built and named Shitennoji Temple

AD604
Osaka, then called Naniwa, becomes Japan's first official capital city

1583
Toyotomi Hideyoshi orders the construction of Osaka Castle—today one of Japan's most visited attractions

1970
Osaka hosts the first World's Fair to be held in an Asian country

1994
The futuristic Kansei International Airport opens

Perth

statistics

Population: 1,430,000

Perth is the sunniest state capital in Australia

The average winter daytime temperature in Perth is 64.4°F (18°C)

The average summer daytime temperature is 84.2°F (29°C)

FREMANTLE

Established in 1829 as the port for the Swan Colony, Fremantle, just south of Perth, gradually became the "Gateway to Australia," as more and more passenger ships docked there; ships whose customers evolved over time from the convicts of 1850–68, to free settlers, and then tourists. Today Fremantle functions as a busy port, is home to a large fishing fleet and welcomes cruise ships. It also offers visitors alfresco living, street entertainment, museums, galleries, and historic buildings (including Western Australia's oldest public building, the Round House). A vibrant nightlife, the sidewalk cafés on South Terrace, markets, trams, and scenic cruises all contribute to Fremantle's relaxed ambience.

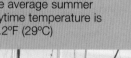

ABOVE: *Yachts moored at Success Harbor in Fremantle.*

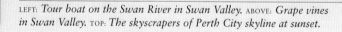

LEFT: *Tour boat on the Swan River in Swan Valley.* ABOVE: *Grape vines in Swan Valley.* TOP: *The skyscrapers of Perth City skyline at sunset.*

Australia's fourth largest city (in terms of population) enjoys an idyllic location on the banks of the Swan River, with a metropolitan area that spans out to the western shores of the Indian Ocean. While Perth has a bustling and attractive inner city, complete with designer stores, first-rate restaurants, and the gleaming skyscrapers of the CBD (Central Business District), its real appeal lies in its weather, stunning location, and the high quality of life enjoyed by its residents.

Substantial resources of gold and minerals propelled the development of Perth into a wealthy city and made it home to a significant number of millionaires. While the business climate in the city may have been tempered by the scandals of the 1980s, which saw key figures imprisoned for corporate fraud and an inquiry into corruption within the government, the 1990s saw entrepreneurs dabble in the dotcom industry with some lasting successes. Tourism is also an increasingly important part of the city's economy, with Perth welcoming over 3 million tourists each year. As the capital of Western Australia, Perth remains the driving force of a state that generates around a quarter of the country's total exports.

THE STORY OF...

Aborigines have lived in Australia for up to 150,000 years; with the nomadic Nyoongar tribes who first inhabited Perth and Western Australia believed to have been in the area for at least 40,000 years. The modern history of the city, though, dates back to 1828 when the British first arrived on the Swan River. A year later Captain James Stirling (1791–1865) had secured permission to colonize Western Australia and returned to establish the Swan Colony and the city of Perth. Unlike Sydney, Perth began its colonial history as a city populated by free settlers. However, a growing need for labor resulted in the first convict ships landing in Fremantle in 1850, transforming the settlement into a penal colony.

The discovery of gold in the late 19th century and the later excavation of minerals were two of the defining events in Perth's history, placing it at the helm of one of Australia's wealthiest and most economically productive states. Loyalty to the British Crown has seen the city's inhabitants embroiled in wars far from home, including the second Boer War (1889–1902) and both World Wars.

BELOW: *Kings Park, Mount Eliza.*

ABOVE RIGHT: *The Old Mill.*
RIGHT: *A surfer at sunset on Scarborough Beach.*

Alfresco Living

When they are not working, Perth's residents indulge in myriad outdoor pursuits, from jet skiing on and cycling along the Swan River, to parasailing or hiking in the Perth Hills. The quintessential local pastime, though, is going to the beach, with surfers and swimmers catching the waves at Trigg Beach and sun worshippers soaking up the rays on the trendy Cottesloe Beach. The white sands between Fremantle, to the south, and Yanchep, to the north of the city, are especially popular and have been collectively dubbed as the Sunset Coast, due to their spectacular vistas of the setting sun. However, there is more to Perth's suburbs than pristine beaches, with fine restaurants and first-class shopping opportunities at Scarborough Market or Sorrento Quay.

More sedate retreats include Kings Park and Gardens, a 988-acre (400 ha) green space located on Mount Eliza with stunning views over downtown and the Swan River. In the Swan Valley Wine Region, horse-drawn wagons take tourists from vineyard to vineyard, just 8 miles (13km) from the city center. Meanwhile Yanchep National Park, 31 miles (50km) out of town, is home to one of the state's biggest Koala populations.

key dates

1829
Captain James Stirling founds Perth

1850
Convicts from Britain are transported to Perth

1886
A gold rush sees the city's population swell

1970
The Indian Pacific railway arrives from Sydney, 2,704 miles (4,352km) away, for the first time

1987
America's Cup Challenge sailing is held in Fremantle

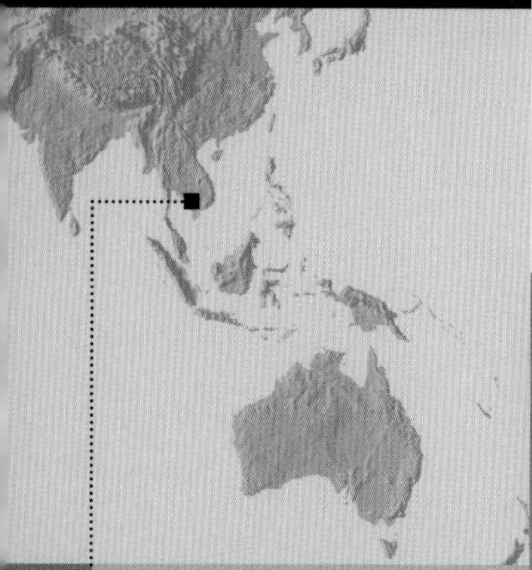

Phnom Penh

statistics

Population: 1,300,000

The Silver Pagoda's floor is lined with 5,000 silver tiles, each weighing 2.2lb (1kg): total weight 5 tonnes

The city's oldest temple dates back to 1373

Phnom Penh's National Library holds around 100,000 volumes—an amazing number considering the Khmer Rouge attempted to destroy all its books

P hnom Penh, the Cambodian capital, is an attractive riverside city of broad boulevards with numerous sights to please the visitor. It is still a rather shabby and run-down place due to the long years of war, and four years of Khmer Rouge abandonment, but improvements are well underway.

THE CITY FOUNDER

According to legend, around six centuries ago a wealthy Khmer woman called Daun Penh discovered five Buddha figures, four bronze and one stone, by the bank of the Sap River. Being pious, she had a temple constructed to house them on a nearby hill—in fact a mound just 88ft (27m) high, but the highest natural point in the vicinity—hence "Phnom Penh" or "Hill of Penh." Wat Phnom, the temple built to house the figures, has been rebuilt several times, most recently in 1926, and is still used as a place of worship. There is a small pavilion honoring Penh, the founder of the city, in the temple grounds.

ABOVE: *Figure of Penh.*

All of the more important attractions are located beside, or within walking distance of, the Phnom Penh riverside—an area which also has many of the best restaurants and cafés in town. Immediately to the south of the National Museum lie the extensive grounds of the Royal Palace, built in Khmer-style with French assistance in 1866. The palace has functioned as the official residence of King Norodom Sihamoni (b. 1953) since his coronation in 2004. North of the Royal Palace is the National Museum, housed in a red pavilion built in 1918, with a wonderful collection of Khmer art including some of the finest pieces in existence. It is also home to more than 2 million bats, which explains the sharp, acrid smell and the constant, day-long squeaking and twittering from above the strengthened ceiling.

Phnom Penh is also Cambodia's main center of commerce. The longest-established market in Phnom Penh is the *psar char*, or "old market", located near the riverfront, offering a wide selection of clothing, jewelry, dry goods, and fresh vegetables. A short distance to the south-west, in the commercial heart of Phnom Penh, is the magnificent *psar thmay* or "new market", built in 1937 during the French colonial period, in art deco style. The design is cruciform, with four wings dominated by a central dome. In and around the four wings, almost anything is for sale, including electronic equipment, tapes, videos, clothing, watches, bags and suitcases, and a wide variety of dried and fresh foodstuffs.

A Riverine Port

Phnom Penh is Cambodia's second most important port after Sihanoukville, on the Gulf of Thailand. Large ships can sail up the Mekong to offload fuel oil, manufactured goods, machinery, and processed food, while taking on rice, rubber, and other agricultural goods for export. The rivers around Phnom Penh, especially the Sap and its huge lake, Tonle Sap, are an important source of fish. Phnom Penh is linked with Thailand to the west by two highways, which are gradually being upgraded, and with Vietnam to the east by a new highway to Ho Chi Minh City, across the recently constructed Mekong Bridge at Kompong Cham. The inhabitants of the city are predominantly Khmer, with substantial and economically influential Vietnamese and Chinese communities.

TOP: *Passenger boats on the Mekong River.*
ABOVE: *Detail at Wat Phnom.*
LEFT: *The Royal Palace.*

ABOVE RIGHT: *Fabric for sale in Phnom Penh.* LEFT: *Traders selling goods in Phnom Penh.*

Phnom Penh

THE STORY OF...

Phnom Penh lies on the western side of the Mekong River, at the point where it is joined by the Sap River and divides into the Bassac River, making a meet place of four great waterways known in Cambodian as *Chatomuk* or "Four Faces." It has been central to Cambodian life since soon after the abandonment of Angkor in the mid-14th century and has been the capital since 1866. An elegant Franco-Cambodian city of broad boulevards and Buddhist temples, it was considered one of the jewels of Southeast Asia until Cambodia became involved in the Second Indochina War in 1965.

Ten years later, victorious Khmer Rouge forces captured the city. Led by the secretive Pol Pot (1925–98), these extreme left-wing communists ordered the immediate evacuation of Phnom Penh (and all other urban areas in Cambodia), causing up to 2 million deaths during the period 1975–79. During this time the city was abandoned and fell into ruin. Since the defeat of the Khmer Rouge in 1979 it has been gradually recovering, but still bears the scars of its terrible past.

key dates

1432
Khmer King Ponhea Yat abandons Angkor and moves his capital to the Phnom Penh region

1866
The Royal Palace is built with the assistance of the French and Phnom Penh is established as the new capital

1975
Phnom Penh falls to the ruthless Khmer Rouge; Pol Pot orders the city to be emptied of its population

1991
Ex-king Prince Norodom Sihanouk returns to Phnom Penh after 13 years in exile and in 1993 is re-crowned king

2004
King Norodom Sihamoni is crowned king within Phnom Penh's Royal Palace

Shanghai

- Population: 13,250,000
- Shanghai's tax contribution to China's central government is almost 25 percent of the total national bill
- The world's fastest Maglev (magnetic levitation) train: 188mph (300kph) in 2 minutes; 8 minutes to travel 18.5 miles (30km) to and from Pudong International Airport
- Tallest building in China: the Jin Mao Tower, 1,381ft (421m), supports the world's highest hotel, the Grand Hyatt Shanghai

SOONG CHING-LING

Soong Ching-ling (1893–1981) was born in Shanghai to a well educated, Christian family. She went to the United States to study before marrying Sun Yat-sen, the founder of the Chinese Republic, in 1915. Together they worked to bring social and economic order to the chaos of post-Imperial China. Soong Ching-ling spoke out against the condition of women in China in a manner that expressed her ideals of liberty and equality. For the next seven decades she remained an active participant in both the political and social arenas of Chinese life. She came to be known as "the Mother of China." Her former home is now a museum.

ABOVE: *A bust of the Chinese revolutionary Soong Ching-ling.*

A s recently as 1980 the Park Hotel, at the junction of Nanjing Road and the Shanghai Bund, was China's tallest building. A visitor gazing across the Huangpu River would have seen little but rice fields. Turning south, toward Shanghai Old Town—a depressing vista of run-down tenement buildings— would have met the eye. The neon lights of the International Settlement and the French Concession had been dimmed, and the city rang harshly to the shrill political slogans of the Cultural Revolution. Today, all this has changed almost beyond belief. Shanghai's waterfront, The Bund, has been restored to its former splendor, while Nanjing Road East is a pedestrian area thronging with shoppers. Further east, Pudong now rises like an Oriental Manhattan, featuring some of the tallest and most architecturally innovative buildings in the world. A network of new tunnels, massive suspension bridges, and elevated highways carry the city's ever-increasing traffic across or under the Huangpu, through Pudong Xinqu, a new extension larger than Shanghai itself, to brand new Pudong International Airport by the shores of the Yellow Sea.

Old Shanghai, the original settlement still defined by a roughly circular road delimiting the former city walls, is rapidly being restored and redeveloped. The area centered on the famous Huxingting Tea House and Yu Yuan Garden has been rebuilt in "Old Shanghai" style and is busy with shoppers and sightseers, both local and foreign. Nearby, Fangbang Zhonglu has also been restored and is lined with traditional-style Shanghai dumpling houses, bric-à-brac stores, and art galleries. Here you can stand beneath red Chinese lanterns casting their glow on an intriguing mix of reproduction 1930s cigarette-girl posters, Chairman Mao memorabilia, and other souvenirs. It could almost be the Shanghai of yesteryear, only much richer and much cleaner. Yet a glance north-east, toward Pudong, reveals a skyscraper skyline dominated by the Jin Mao Tower, at 1,381ft (421m) the fourth highest building in the world, confirming that Shanghai is indeed leading China into the 21st century.

BELOW RIGHT: *Lakes and fish in the Yu Yuan Gardens (Yu Gardens).*

A Regional Powerhouse

Grimy smokestacks no longer dominate the suburbs of Shanghai. Instead electronic and high-tech industries, textile factories, and food-processing plants stretch to the horizon. Links between Shanghai and Beijing, as with the rest of coastal China and broader East Asia, are excellent and constantly improving. Shanghai's current success is such that it poses a serious challenge not just to developed economies such as Japan, but also to the Southeast Asian "Tiger Economies" of Singapore, Malaysia, and Thailand.

ABOVE: *Lighting candles in the courtyard of the Chenxiangge Temple.*
BACKGROUND: *Nightscape in Pudong.*
BELOW RIGHT: *The Nanjing Road at night.*

THE STORY OF...

From the time of the Song Dynasty (AD960–1279), Shanghai—which means "on sea" in Chinese—gradually developed as a busy seaport. A city wall was built in 1553, but before the 19th century Shanghai was not a major city, and there are few ancient landmarks. The role of Shanghai changed radically in the 19th century, as the city's strategic position at the mouth of the Yangtze River made it an ideal location for trade with the West. After the First Opium War in 1842, Shanghai was forced to open to international settlement and trade. In 1863 the British and American settlements were merged to make the International Settlement. A separate French and, from 1895, a Japanese Settlement, were also established.

Between 1937 and 1945 Shanghai—by now the largest city in China—was occupied by the Japanese. In 1949 it passed under communist control. Although it became a center for the Cultural Revolution between 1966 and 1976, the city remained an important industrial center and was relatively prosperous. Reforms initiated in 1991 have ensured Shanghai's continuing economic primacy within China.

1074
The Song dynasty provincial bureaucracy promotes Shanghai from fishing village status to a commercial town

1842
The British force China to open several port cities including Shanghai

1945
Japanese occupying forces surrender, sparking a rush to rebuild and reinvigorate the city

1993
The Oriental Pearl Tower opens, nowadays the symbol of ultra-modern Shanghai

2010
Shanghai holds World Expo

Singapore

statistics

- Population: 4,500,000
- After Hong Kong, Singapore has the highest population density in the world: 16,786 people per sq mile (6,481 per sq km)
- Southeast Asia's largest bird park: 8,000 birds, 600 species
- The world's busiest port by shipping tonnage: 135,386 vessels in 2003

THE FOUNDER OF SINGAPORE

Sir Thomas Stamford Raffles (1781–1826) was the founder of the city of Singapore as well as being one of the British Empire's most celebrated statesmen. At 14 he started working as a clerk in London for the British East India Company, and in 1805 he was sent to Penang, where he worked his way up to become Lieutenant Governor of Java in 1811. Raffles declared the foundation of what was to become modern Singapore in 1819. He was also a founder and first president of the Zoological Society of London, being remembered in the name of the largest flower in the world, the *Rafflesia*. He was knighted in 1817.

ABOVE: *Statue of Sir Stamford Raffles.*

Singapore, once a city of opium dens and rickshaws, bum-boats, and godowns, is now a bustling business capital dominated by the steel and concrete towers of high finance. Yet the visitor can experience echoes of the colonial past while sipping a "Singapore Sling" cocktail beneath the ceiling fans of the Raffles Hotel. Singapore is affluent, safe, squeaky-clean, and—at least at first sight—disappointingly sterile. Yet it is still a very Asian city, with distinct areas associated with the different ethnic communities, Chinese and Indian, Malay, Arab, and European, which make up the city's population. It is also a gourmet's paradise, with a fantastic choice of cuisines available in settings ranging from air-conditioned high-rise restaurants to hole-in-the-wall cafés and extensive street markets. In the crowded streets of Chinatown, temple fortune-tellers, calligraphers, and traditional medicine stores are still a part of everyday life. In the boutiques and carpet stores of Arab Street, the call of the *muezzin* can be heard from the nearby Sultan Mosque, while in Little India you can still buy the finest silk saris, while the smell of freshly ground spices fills the air.

The city's commercial heart is beside the restored, highly-fashionable quays of Singapore Harbor and in the affluent shopping malls and finance centers along Orchard Road. Chinatown is Singapore's cultural heart and still provides glimpses of the old ways with its numerous temples, stucco terraces, and hectic commerce. In the area around Arab Street are the city's main mosques and bazaars selling all manner of goods from Indonesia, Malaysia, and the Middle East. Besides gleaming glass towers, downtown Singapore has many fine colonial buildings including St. Andrew's Cathedral

BELOW RIGHT: *An ornate 1920s building on the Serangoon Road.*
BELOW: *A young woman at the Thian Hock Keng Temple.*
RIGHT: *Sackloads of rice and spices fill a market store.*

THE STORY OF...

The island of Singapore served as an outpost of the Srivijaya Empire and was originally given the Malay name Temasek. The present name derives from the Sanskrit *Singapura* or Lion City, a name current by the late 14th century. Portuguese soldiers burned Singapura in 1617, after which the settlement was abandoned but remained a haunt of fishermen and pirates. In 1819 Sir Thomas Stamford Raffles, an official of the East India Company, made a treaty with the Sultan of Johore to establish a trading post on the island. Singapore prospered as a trading port and in 1867 was made a Crown Colony. During World War II the Japanese occupied Singapore which they renamed Syonanto or "Light of the South."

In 1959 Singapore became a self-governing Crown Colony and in 1963 it joined the Federation of Malaysia, but withdrew in 1965 to become the sovereign Republic of Singapore. The city-state has prospered and is today the second richest country in Asia.

BELOW FAR LEFT: *Colorful figures in the Sri Veeramakaliamman Temple, Little India.*
BELOW LEFT: *Doorman outside The Raffles Hotel*

1390
Iskandar Shah, a young Palembang ruler, establishes a small settlement called Temasek on the island of Singapore

1819
Convinced that the island will make a good trading post, Sir Thomas Stamford Raffles founds Singapore

1965
Singapore breaks from the newly formed Malaysian Federation and the independent Republic of Singapore is born

1987
The first section of the Singapore Mass Rapid Transit (MRT) system opens; now one of the world's most efficient

2004
Lee Hsien Loong, son of former Prime Minister and independence leader Lee Kuan Yew, is sworn in as new prime minister

and the Cathedral of the Good Shepherd, the Raffles Hotel, and Empress Palace Building. Further afield, Sentosa is an island park with museums, aquariums, beaches, sporting facilities, walks, and food centers. Bukit Timah Nature Reserve is a protected area of primary rainforest with over 800 species of native plants including giant rain trees, ferns, and native wild flowers.

An International Center of Finance

Singapore is the archetypal city of commerce. The busiest port in the world, it is also a major international stock exchange dealing in everything from oil futures and diamonds to coffee and cement. Communications with East Asia, Europe, and America are state of the art, as are the city's MRT, bus, and taxi systems. The city-state is linked to nearby Malaysia by a causeway, and ferry services serve various ports in Indonesia across the Straits of Singapore.

statistics

Population: 3,900,000

Over 70 percent of the city's population come from two different ethnic backgrounds

On a hot sunny day more than 50,000 people visit Bondi Beach

Sydney's Centrepoint Tower, the tallest structure in Australia, stands 1,000ft (305m) high

Sydney

Dramatically located on one of the world's largest natural harbors and fringed by the Pacific Ocean, Sydney is undoubtedly Australia's best-known city—blessed with a culture as vibrant and eclectic as New York, as tolerant and easy-going as San Francisco, and with a setting as spectacular as Rio de Janeiro. And then, of course, there is the weather: even in the depths of winter the temperature rarely dips below 53.6°F (12°C). A city replete with all the trappings of the 21st century, where seemingly anything goes, Sydney somehow manages to retain the relaxed ambience of a small town.

A Liberal and Multi-Cultural Society

Captain Cook in 1770 believed the harbor to be a "safe anchorage", and so it has proved for the waves of immigrants who have turned the ethnic mix on its head since World War II. The diversity of its population is reflected in its languages and cuisine, which includes virtually every type of food imaginable. A society where myriad cultures co-exist in harmony is also at the cornerstone of Sydney's famed "no worries" mentality, the catchphrase of a liberal people intent on enjoying each day rather than dwelling on the past or worrying about the future. In all levels of society the ubiquitous phrase is the response to most requests and everyone is welcomed with the universal appellation "mate."

Not just a refuge for immigrants, Sydney is increasingly becoming a haven for tourists as it cements its position as one of the world's premier destinations, with the iconic Harbor Bridge and Opera House the flagships of a city full of tourist sights. Sydney's twin signature attractions seem to be a microcosm for the city's attitude to life. Few other cities would have the sheer audacity and self-confidence to erect such architecturally adventurous structures on the country's most prominent patch of real estate.

Canberra may be Australia's capital, but Sydney is the place that drives the country's economy. Over the last decade manufacturing has declined, with business, finance, and property services generating the most revenue followed by retail. Tourism is also an important component in a city whose regional government reported, in 2004, that its economy was outperforming those of New Zealand and Singapore.

THE STORY OF...

Australia's indigenous people have inhabited the area around Sydney for over 40,000 years. The first tribes that passed through the region called the city Warran, which roughly translates as "this place." Sydney's written history, however, is far more recent, dating from 1770 when Captain James Cook (1728–79) traveled to present-day NSW, declaring it a British territory belonging to King George III (1738–1820). Almost two decades later, in 1788, Captain Arthur Phillip (1738–1814) landed at Botany Bay to establish a new penal colony. The convicted criminals and Phillip's small crew numbered around 1,000; 12 years later, as more criminals were transported to Sydney, this had swollen to 10,000. Conditions in the colony were harsh until Lachlan Macquarie's appointment as governor in 1810 began to turn its fortunes around, abolishing the trade in rum and replacing it with money. Three years later the fertile hinterland on the other side of the Blue Mountains was discovered, something that would help fuel Sydney's future prosperity. From 1840 no more convicts were sent to Australia and in 1842 Sydney became a city.

The discovery of gold in 1850 and the influx of immigrants that followed gave Sydney another boost. In 1901 Britain's six colonies joined the Federal Commonwealth of Australia, which established the state of NSW with Sydney as its capital. Other key events in the 20th century include the opening of the Harbor Bridge in 1932 and the Opera House in 1973, an influx of immigrants at the end of World War II, and the construction of Darling Harbor in celebration of the city's bicentennial in 1988.

Toward the end of the century large-scale urban regeneration projects were completed in preparation for the 2000 Olympic Games, an event that allowed Sydney to take center stage and enter the new millennium with a bang.

ABOVE: *Set in the Domain parkland, the pyramid glasshouse in the Sydney Royal Botanic Gardens houses a collection of tropical plants.*
LEFT: *Sydney Opera House and Sydney Harbor Bridge.*

Sydney's Playgrounds

The real Sydney experience inevitably involves a visit to one of the beaches that lie tucked within the city boundaries. Australians worship the beach with the "Sunday arvo" excursions a national institution. At the height of summer upward of 50,000 sun worshippers and surfers have been known to visit the world-famous Bondi Beach. There is more to this Sydney institution than just sand and surf; Sydney is home to one of Australia's largest aboriginal populations and the history of the country's indigenous people is etched forever in the name Bondi, an aboriginal word that translates as "the sound of waves breaking on a beach."

Manly is another seaside playground, located on Sydney's north shore, an area that local residents have dubbed "God's Own Country." The suburb's main attraction is its white sand Pacific beach flanked by towering Norfolk pines, where surfers, swimmers, and a mass of sidewalk cafés all form part of the exciting mix. When they are not at the beach, Sydneysiders intent on having a good time head to Darling Harbor. In the shadow of the city's skyscrapers, this vast purpose-built leisure oasis boasts street entertainment, Chinese gardens, a casino, an IMAX cinema, museums, an aquarium, and a monorail that whisks visitors between the various attractions. Meanwhile those seeking a more cerebral experience can take in a world-class performance at the Opera House or head to one of Sydney's numerous galleries and museums.

ABOVE: *Tourists climbing Sydney Harbor Bridge. Opened in 1932, it is the world's largest steel arch bridge, fondly known as the "Coathanger."*

RIGHT AND OPPOSITE: *New Year fireworks display at Sydney Harbor.*

ABOVE: *Manly Beach and Manly Wharf, Stanley.*
LEFT: *Surfing on Bondi Beach.*
RIGHT: *The wrought-iron balcony of a house in Paddington, the most familiar of Sydney's inner suburbs.*

LACHLAN MACQUARIE

Born on the Scottish island of Ulva, Lachlan Macquarie (1761–1824) joined the army in 1776. His military career took him to America, India, and Egypt, as well as New South Wales (NSW), where he was governor from 1810–21. During his 11-year term Macquarie dedicated himself to developing Sydney's infrastructure, commissioning new roads, buildings, and towns. He was also responsible for the introduction of coins in 1813 and established a bank in 1817. More controversially Macquarie championed the rights of ex-convicts (emancipists), arguing that the rehabilitated deserved the same rights as free settlers. To illustrate this he appointed the architect Francis Greenway (1777–1837)— himself a former convict—to help transform Sydney, and made two former prisoners magistrates. Outraged members of the developing society petitioned Britain to intervene, and in 1819 a British judge named John Thomas Bigge (1780–1843) opened a formal inquiry into Macquarie's administration. Bigge's conclusions were damning and criticized Macquarie for squandering money on public construction projects. Ill health and the inquiry's negative judgements finally saw Macquarie resign in 1821. Almost 200 years later he is fondly remembered as the man whose 265 public works laid the foundations of the modern-day Sydney, both in terms of its physical appearance and its broad-minded outlook.

Population: 6,850,000

The world's largest collection of Chinese artifacts: 700,000 objects

Taipei 101, the world's tallest building: 1,671ft (509m)

The MRT (Mass Rapid Transit) transports 1 million people per day

A REPOSITORY OF CHINESE CULTURE

Taipei's National Palace Museum has the single largest and most valuable collection of Chinese art to be found anywhere in the world. Originally established in Beijing in 1925 to house the accumulated art treasures of the Forbidden City, the huge collection was moved across China to escape the Japanese in World War II. During the final years of the Chinese Civil War the collection was moved to Taiwan by order of Chiang Kai-shek (1887–1975). Though strongly opposed by the communist government in Beijing, there seems no doubt that the removal to Taiwan saved this priceless collection from damage and destruction during the Cultural Revolution (1966–76).

ABOVE: *Exterior of the National Palace Museum.*

Taipei

Taipei is a city framed by rivers and mountains with easy access to the sea. The main downtown area is to the west, on and by the banks of the Tanshui River. Here are the main commercial streets centered on Chunghsiao Road, the largest hotels, and the Presidential Building. The Chiang Kai-shek Memorial Hall shares Chuncheng Chinientang Park with the National Concert Hall and the National Theater. Southwest is the imposing Lungshan Temple and the "Snake Alley" night market. To the north beyond the Keelung River stands Chunglie Tzu or Martyr's Shrine, as well as the National Palace Museum. In the east of the city Kuofo Chinienkuan or the Sun Yat-sen Memorial commemorates the founding father of modern China.

A Center of Finance, Industry, and Education

Taipei City is a special municipality administered directly by the central government. It is not part of, but is surrounded entirely by, Taipei County. Major industries include electrical and electronic equipment, textiles, metals, shipbuilding, and motorcycle manufacture. Taipei is an important financial center exemplified by the huge Taipei 101 Building, the tallest in the world. City communications are excellent. The MRT (Mass Rapid Transit) uses both a light rail system and a conventional metro. Unlike most railways in Taiwan which follow the Japanese practice and have trains running on the left, the Taipei public transport system runs its trains on the right. Taipei Main Station is the largest in Taiwan and also functions as the center for the MRT. Chiang Kai-shek International Airport at nearby Taoyuan serves Taipei for international flights, while Sungshan in the heart of the city handles domestic flights. An extensive city bus system runs to those areas not covered by the MRT. A popular form of transportation in Taipei is the ubiquitous motor scooter; these are not subject to conventional traffic laws, and generally thread between cars and occasionally through oncoming traffic.

Taipei has 15 universities including the Taiwan National University, the Taipei Medical University, and the Taipei National University of Arts, as well as nine colleges including the National Taipei Teachers College. Taipei has a higher proportion of

LEFT: *The Grand Hotel.*
BELOW: *View of Taipei 101. The 101st floor can be reached in 39 seconds in the fast elevators.*

mainlanders than average in Taiwan. This and the fact that the city is highly dependent on commerce and finance, which would be disrupted in case of conflict with the Chinese People's Republic, means that the city is more favorable to reunification with the mainland than other areas of Taiwan.

BELOW: *Taipei Chiang Kai-shek Memorial Hall.*

THE STORY OF...

Both the capital of the Republic of China (ROC) and the largest city on the island of Taiwan, Taipei is also a very new city. Located in the middle of the fertile Taipei Basin, it was home to an indigenous population of Ketagalan tribes until the 18th century. Han Chinese from the neighboring mainland began to settle there from around 1710. In the 19th century the area prospered through the tea trade and in 1875 a new town, Chengnei, was founded between Bangka and Dadaocheng. The resulting city was named Taipei.

In 1895 Taipei became the political center of the Japanese colonial authorities, which called the city Taihoku. Much of its architecture, including the Presidential Building, dates from the period of Japanese rule (1895–1945). In 1949 the Chinese communists forced the Kuomintang government of Chiang Kai-shek to flee Mainland China for Taiwan. They established Taipei as the "provisional" capital of the ROC. The city expanded greatly as a result, absorbing smaller townships into one large urban conurbation.

BELOW: *Illuminated fairground wheel in Taipei.*

1790
A farmer from China's Fujian Province founds a small settlement at Takala (now central Taipei)

1875
Chinese Emperor Guangxu establishes Taipei as the capital of Taiwan province

1920
Japanese overlords formally recognize Taipei as a city

1949
Generalissimo Chiang Kai-shek flees mainland China and makes Taipei the capital of Nationalist China

1996
The first section of Taipei's much-needed Mass Rapid Transit system opens

Tokyo

Population: 8,300,000 within city boundaries; 12,000,000 in Greater Tokyo

The reigning Emperor of Japan lives in the Imperial Palace in the heart of Tokyo (said to be the world's most expensive real estate)

Tsujiki, Tokyo's wholesale seafood market, is the biggest fish market in the world

30,000,000 people (one-quarter of the Japanese population) live within 30 miles (50km) of the Imperial Palace

TOKYO NATIONAL MUSEUM

Tokyo National Museum's sculpture, paintings, lacquerware, ceramics, armor, and archaeological and Buddhist artifacts make it the most complete collection of its kind. The Japanese archaeology gallery houses fourth- to sixth-century AD terracotta figures, produced to be placed in the burial mounds of powerful leaders to protect and nurture them in the after-life. Rare Buddhist artifacts and works of art from the Horyuji Temple in Nara, said to be the birthplace of Japanese Buddhism, are housed in the Horyuji Homotsu-kan gallery, while the Toyo-kan Gallery of Oriental Antiques specializes in archaeological, historical, and cultural objects from China, India, and Southeast Asia.

ABOVE: *Detail of an early figurine in the Tokyo National Museum.*

Tokyo is Japan's political, economic, and cultural capital and the country's largest city. Three rivers—the Arakawa, Edogawa, and Sumidogawa—flow into Tokyo Bay, hence the city's original name, Edo, meaning estuary. Tokyo is divided into 23 wards (*ku*) and many smaller administrative divisions. The Kanto region, which includes Tokyo and the linking port cities of Kawasaki and Yokohama, is the most highly industrialized area in Japan. Unlike Nara and Kyoto, Tokyo is not a place of obvious historical sights and traditional charms; few old buildings survived the bombing during World War II. However, the city is a powerhouse of creative energy, global influence, and wealth.

A City of Traditions

Tokyo is a captivating mix of old and new traditions and Tokyoites have embraced the most modern technology and ideas while maintaining traditional social values and etiquette. Tokyo is perhaps unique in being a modern, densely populated, Westernized, 24-hour city that yet remains relatively free of crime, litter, and drugs. Public services are efficient and the service industry is arguably the best in the world. For Tokyoites, eating out is an integral part of everyday life and many people eat more often in restaurants than they do at home. As a result, the city has an enormous variety of eating establishments, with something to suit every taste and pocket.

RIGHT: *The entrance to the main hall of Asakusa Kannon Temple.*

LEFT: *The five-storey Asakusa Pagoda.*
BOTTOM LEFT: *Procession during Tokyo's White Heron Festival.*

Tokyo Center

The area of the city of most concentrated interest is the one bounded by the JR Yamanote loop line. In the center is the monumental 19th-century Imperial Palace, the seat of the Emperor since the Meiji Restoration of 1868. To the southwest of the palace is the Akasaka district, an area of government buildings which includes the Diet (Parliament), expensive hotels, and luxurious restaurants. Further east is the Ginza, Tokyo's world-famous shopping and entertainment district, while to the south of Akasaka is Roppongi, the city's most cosmopolitan and popular nightlife area with art cinemas and experimental theater. On the eastern edge of the area bounded by the Yamanote line is Harajuku—the site of the historically important and beautiful Meiji Shrine. Meanwhile, the Aoyama district is home to the stores of Tokyo's fashion design superstars, such as Issey Miyake (b. 1938) and Yohji Yamamoto (b. 1943).

THE STORY OF...

Tokyo, formerly Edo, was for 265 years the seat of power of the Tokugawa Shogunate, the effective rulers of Japan. In 1808 the Shogunate was toppled and during the Meiji Restoration was replaced by Emperor Meiji (1852–1912) who moved the capital from Kyoto to Tokyo. The Emperor reversed Tokugawa's policy of national isolation and led Japan from being an isolated, agricultural-based feudal society to a powerful modern nation. In 1941 the Japanese joined forces with Hitler's Germany and soon after bombed Pearl Harbor, so entering World War II. In March 1945 Tokyo was subject to three days of sustained bombing and much of the city was destroyed.

Tokyo's revival after the war was spectacular, and the mid-1980s saw a massive boom in the Japanese economy. Land development in Tokyo became frenzied and at one point land prices became the most expensive in the world. The bubble burst in the mid-1990s, bringing bankruptcies and the previously unknown spectre of unemployment for city workers. However, the new millennium has brought the first signs of real sustained economic growth.

LEFT: *Tokyo traffic at the crossroads of the Ginza district.*

key dates

1180
First reference to Edo (Tokyo), a fishing village on the western shores of Tokyo Bay

1603
Start of the reign of the Tokugawa family which ruled and dominated Japanese life until 1867

1868
Edo is renamed Tokyo. Imperiarule is re-established over the ruling Shogunate and Emperor Meiji moves his residence from Kyoto to Tokyo

1941
Emperor Hirohito declares war on the US, the UK, and The Netherlands. Much of Tokyo subsequently destroyed by American fire bombing

1964
18th Olympic Games are held in Tokyo

Yangon

The city of Yangon is located on the west bank of the Yangon River just north of its exit to the Gulf of Martaban. There are numerous Buddhist temples in Yangon, but the greatest by far is the Shwedagon Pagoda. The great golden dome towers 321ft (98m) above the city. According to legend the pagoda contains eight strands of the hair of the Buddha Gautama enshrined together with the relics of earlier Buddhas. Rudyard Kipling (1865–1936) saw the Shwedagon in 1889 and memorably called it "a beautiful, winking wonder that blazed in the sun", a description that still holds true today. Other temples of particular note include the Sule Pagoda, located right in the center of Yangon. It is said to be over 2,000 years old and enshrines another hair of the Buddha. Its golden dome stands 151ft (46m) high and is surrounded by small stores and the booths of astrologers, palmists, and fortune-tellers.

Buddhist architecture aside, Yangon is also remarkable for its fine collection of surviving colonial buildings, many clustered in the vicinity of the Strand Hotel near the banks of the Yangon River. Other places of interest include the National Museum, the Zoological Gardens, and the Peoples' Park on Pyay Road. Hlawga Wildlife Park is about 45 minutes drive from the city center and is home to over 70 kinds of herbivorous animals and 90 species of birds. It is a popular place for local picnickers and bird-watchers. The University of Yangon was founded in 1920 and reorganized in 1964, when it became the Arts and Science University.

AUNG SAN SUU KYI

Also known by her supporters as "The Lady", Suu Kyi (b. 1945) has come to be seen as a symbol of implacable but peaceful resistance to military oppression. She was awarded the Nobel Peace Prize in 1991. Suu Kyi is the daughter of the late Burmese nationalist leader, General Aung San who was assassinated in 1947. She became the leader of a growing pro-democracy movement in the aftermath of the brutal repression of a pro-democratic uprising in 1988. Inspired by the non-violent campaigns of the American civil rights leader Martin Luther King (1929–68), and India's Mahatma Gandhi (1869–1948), Suu Kyi remains under house arrest in Yangon. She has been offered freedom if she leaves Burma, but she refuses.

ABOVE: *Suu Kyi addressing supporters at her Yangon compound.*
BACKGROUND: *Sule Pagoda, City Hall and Traders Hotel.*

Trade and Transport

Major exports from Yangon include rice, teak, petroleum, cotton, and metal ores. There are rice mills, sawmills, and oil refineries as well as iron, steel, and copper mills in the industrial suburbs to the north and east of the city center. Links with the rest of the country are antiquated and inadequate, reflecting long years of military misrule. A rickety train service connects the capital with Mandalay—the country's second city—and with Myitkyina, the capital of Kachin State in the far north. All Myanmar's roads are in poor shape, and riverine traffic remains the norm, with the Twante Canal, dug in the 19th century under British rule, connecting the capital with the Ayeyarwady Delta—the country's rice bowl—and the great Ayeyarwady River, the traditional "Road to Mandalay." Yangon is linked by air to China, and South and Southeast Asia by Mingaladon International Airport, but there are no regular flights to Europe or North America.

THE STORY OF...

Legend has it that it was the Mons who laid the foundation stone of the Shwedagon Pagoda, in the heart of Yangon, 2,500 years ago. The settlement of Dagon was probably founded in the sixth century, but it remained a small fishing village until King Alaungpaya (1714–60) made it his capital and renamed it Yangon or "end of strife" in 1755. In 1851, after the Second Anglo–Burmese War, the British annexed the city and changed its name to Rangoon. A new city was designed by Lieutenant Fraser, a British Officer, laid out on a chessboard pattern with wide roads running north to south and east to west. Rangoon was badly damaged by an earthquake in 1930, and again after Japanese forces captured the city in World War II.

In 1948 Rangoon became the capital of independent Burma. The Burmese military seized power in 1962, and in 1989 the military State Law and Order Council (SLORC) changed the nation's name to Myanmar and Rangoon's name back to Yangon.

BELOW: *Embroidered hats for sale at Bogyoke Aung San Market.*

1755
King Alaungpaya builds a new city around the town of Dagon naming it Yangon

1885
The British establish Yangon as their capital, renaming it Rangoon

1942
Japanese forces capture Rangoon, leaving the city three years later

1988
Massive pro-democracy demonstrations in the capital end in bloodshed

2002
Ne Win, former dictator, dies in Yangon. His 26 years in power sees Myanmar almost bankrupted and no nearer being a free and democratic state

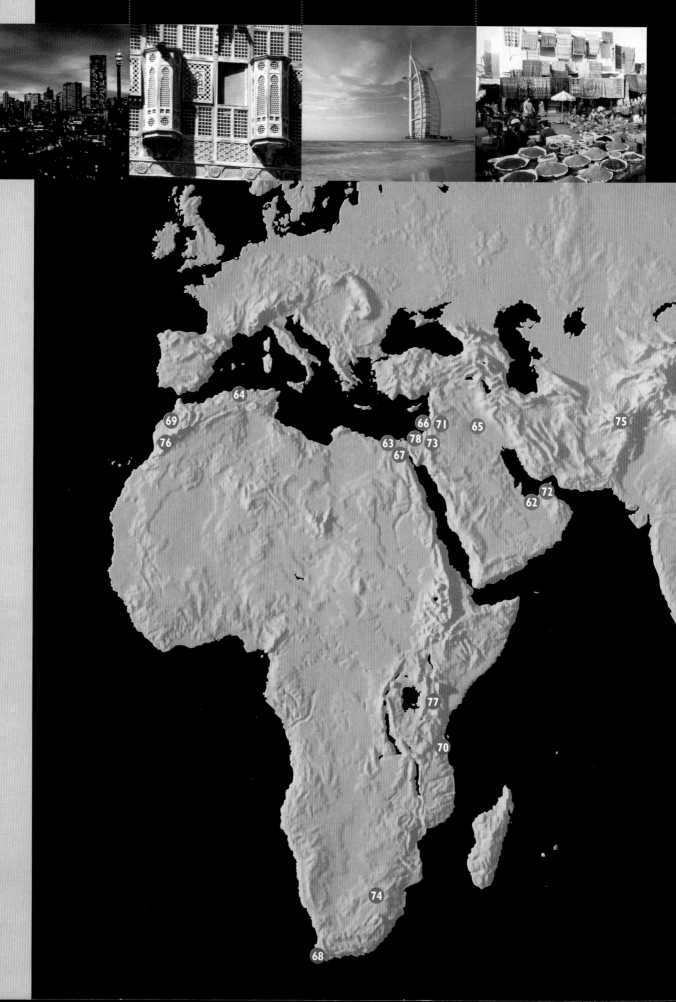

Africa and the Mid-East

The great cities of this broad swathe of territory include some of the most ancient and some of the most heavily populated areas in the world, with a little of everything else scattered in between. Wealth from that most vital of consumer products, oil, has made modern boom towns of cities like Dubai and Abu Dhabi, where innovation in architecture is a very public way to celebrate new-found wealth. The contrast with the ancient religious capital of Jerusalem, or the historic port of Casablanca, could hardly be more extreme. Clashes of religion and culture continue into the 21st century, and while war-torn Baghdad is still seeking a balance, Beirut is an example of a city which has survived a major conflict and revived.

statistics

- Population: 600,000
- 120 million recently planted, irrigated trees
- The world's highest per capita water usage
- Water table has dropped 100ft (30m) in 30 years

Abu Dhabi

To see its gleaming high-rise buildings towering over graceful mosques, lavish irrigated parklands, and countless fountains, it is hard to believe that Abu Dhabi is all so new. Its first school and hospital were built in 1967 on a small desert island: now the city center has changed out of all recognition and two causeways link swelling mainland suburbs.

Airport Road runs into the heart of the city and ends at the Corniche, a 4.5-mile (7km) seafront dotted with parks and fountains, and overlooking mangrove swamps and sandy beaches. This is where the leading hotels and restaurants are found, with the Marine Sports Club at one end and a dhow harbor at the other, backing onto a wealthy downtown area of palaces, embassies, and *souks* (markets). The island's past is acknowledged in two Heritage Villages, offering idealized recreations of Bedouin life, and the White Fort, dating back to 1793 but seriously restored since, has been preserved. Meanwhile, on one of the world's harshest coastlines is a hyper-modern, liveable city. The towering architecture of major corporations is firmly grounded amongst broad, tree-lined boulevards and shady parks, with elegant domes and minarets doing much to give the city a human scale.

A Mix of Cultures

The region's tribal tradition continues, with native families proudly retaining their family links and dynastic wealth. Swirling around the city in white robes and red headscarves, these are the city's aristocrats but they are very much in the minority. A substantial and settled middle class is made up of technicians and managers, usually from Europe or America, who often relocate complete with families. The working class, who you see driving taxis, serving at supermarkets and hotels, or fitting out the latest skyscraper, are seasonal workers from India. This gives the city a uniquely cosmopolitan air, with business and social life slipping easily between Arabic, English, Urdu, and Farsi. With most of the population imported to work and encouraged by seemingly limitless funds, Abu Dhabi has a dynamic, go-getting atmosphere where things get done—and quickly.

BELOW: *The Corniche, Abu Dhabi.*

A TALE OF OIL

Abu Dhabi is a city that is built on oil. By far the biggest oil producer in the United Arab Emirates (UAE), it controls more than 85 percent of its oil output capacity, 90 percent of its crude reserves, and 92 percent of its gas. In global terms Abu Dhabi has 9.1 percent of the world's proven oil reserves and 5 percent of its natural gas. Exports began in 1962, and its daily production is now worth $100 million each and every day.

ABOVE: *Detail of oil tank.*

Spurred by a lively competition with its neighboring Emirate, glitzy Dubai, Abu Dhabi seethes with irrigated lawns, countless construction sites, and ambitious development plans. The latest project is to enlarge the city. Each day trucks filled with sand and rock from the desert interior arrive at the Corniche to tip their loads into the Persian Gulf. The waterfront is moving. Some of the city's smartest hotels will lose their sea views, the Corniche will become an inner-city park, and a new generation of buildings will rise up over the coral-filled waters.

THE STORY OF...

Harsh and inhospitable, the desert regions of the area supported only the very hardiest tribal nomads. They traveled endlessly through the sands in search of grazing, returning each year to spend a couple of months at one of a few, scattered oases. Abu Dhabi was one of the few permanent settlements, as an important strategic trading port on a lawless shoreline known as "The Pirate Coast".

In the late 18th century the British, determined to defend their sea routes to India, imposed their rule. Control was from the sea, with a gunboat being brought in to fire on forts or encampments only when domestic feuds got badly out of hand, and the region's economy depended on slavery—an illegal trade driven inland into the desert—and fishing for pearls. In 1962, the year that oil exports began, Abu Dhabi had a population of 15,000, living in tents or mud-brick dwellings clustered around a single acacia tree. Barely a generation later, it has become one of the world's top cities.

ABOVE: *Skyscrapers in the city.*

RIGHT: *City skyline.*

key dates

AD600
Islam sweeps through the region

1819
British Royal Navy destroys 900 pirate ships and assumes distant control of intertribal disputes: the region becomes known as "The Trucial States"

1958
Anglo–French consortium discover huge reserves of oil in Abu Dhabi

1971
Britain withdraws from the region: six of the seven Trucial States merge to form the United Arab Emirates, with Abu Dhabi as capital

2004
Ruler since independence, Sheikh Zayed bin Sultan al-Nahayan dies, and is succeeded by his eldest son, Sheikh Khalifa bin Zayed

Alexandria

Population: 4,586,000, with Greek and Italian immigrants making up 4 percent of the population

Alexandria has 1,819 mosques, 36 churches, and 1 synagogue

Half a million scrolls held in Alexandria's ancient library contained the sum of human knowledge. They were destroyed by fire

Florence Nightingale trained at the Institute Saint Vincent de Paul in the city in 1850

ALEXANDER THE GREAT (356–322BC)

It is perhaps surprising that Alexandria is the only city to immortalize the name of its founder, Alexander the Great, who briefly united most of the (then) known world. From the age of 13 he studied under Aristotle (384–322BC), and by 20 had been crowned King of Macedonia. After consolidating his rule over Greece he went on to conquer the Persian Empire. With this came Egypt, where Alexander was welcomed as a liberator. He engaged an architect to draw up a city plan for a new city on the Mediterranean's Nile Delta in 331BC, before going on to invade northern India, establishing a new empire uniting East and West with its capital in Babylon. When he died at the age of 33, his body was returned to be entombed in Alexandria.

Alexandria's site was originally chosen to link the civilization of classical Greece with the ancient world of the Pharaohs, and in many ways it still fulfils Alexander the Great's original dream. Even today it has a breezy, cosmopolitan atmosphere, as much a part of Mediterranean Europe as Islamic Egypt. Its setting, with the sea on one side and a lake on the other, is a far cry from Egypt's desert heartlands.

Egypt's Second City

In biblical days Alexandria was perhaps the world's most important city, with its lighthouse, built of white limestone under the Ptolemies, considered to be one of the Seven Wonders of the Ancient World. Few of its ancient monuments survived its centuries of decline and the city is predominately new. The hub of city life is at Tahrir Square, where the Law Courts, St. Marks Church, and the old Exchange are found. From here a narrow tongue of land, originally constructed as a causeway to Pharos Island but since silted into a significantly useful piece of real estate, juts out to sea. On one side is the Western Harbor, known in antiquity as "the harbor of safe return" and on the other is the principle harbor of the ancient city, ringed by a beautiful Corniche. This is where the oldest part of the city remains, with picturesque Arab and Turkish quarters leading the way to Fort Quaitby, which guards the city's twin harbors. Meanwhile, the modern city stretches inland, squeezed by the sea and the calm expanse of Lake Mareotis in an orderly grid of boulevards and avenues greened by parks and palms.

BELOW: *The latticed oriel windows of Abu el-Abbas Mosque.*

LEFT: *A jewel-encrusted brooch in the Royal Jewelry Museum.*

A Buried Past

Alexandria's ancient past is only now coming to light, with the excavation of a Roman amphitheater and baths in the city center, and the discovery of Cleopatra's Palace beneath the waters of the Mediterranean. Much is still not known. The tomb of Alexander the Great has never been found, and nor has the ancient library. For most Alexandrians, however, the past is truly another country. For those in search of ancient history, Egypt has stacks of it, beautifully preserved, inland. There's no need to dig around looking for the old library when the city has a new one, a landmark architectural masterpiece that opened in 2001. Egypt's second city has a lively café culture and beaches warmed by an endless desert sun and a buoyant economy. Sophisticated and successful, Alexandrians prefer to look to the future.

LEFT: *The esplanade, lined with palms and fishing boats.*
BELOW: *Alexandria Library.*

THE STORY OF...

Founded by Alexander the Great to link the civilizations of Greece with those of the Pharaohs, Alexandria was strategically placed between the Mediterranean Sea and the Nile. Under the Ptolemies, Alexandria became perhaps the largest city in the world and an intellectual magnet. Its library was filled with half a million scrolls that distilled all that was known or thought in countless languages. This intellectual wealth was destroyed under Roman, and later Christian, regimes.

When Islam swept across the region in AD642, Alexandria fell to the Arab armies. Although they found a city of "4000 palaces, 4000 baths, and 400 theaters", the new rulers preferred to site Egypt's capital at Cairo, in the desert.

As trade routes opened up the southern oceans, Alexandria declined and over a thousand years later Napoleon Bonaparte discovered the city as little more than a fishing village. Under Egypt's Albanian dictator Mohammed Ali (1769–1849), the harbor was rebuilt and, later, the Suez Canal constructed. Once more Alexandria controlled 94 percent of Egypt's international trade, and the city prospered, for 70 years under British rule and then as part of an independent Egyptian state.

key dates

331BC
The city of Alexandria is founded on the site of a fishing village called Rhakotis

AD642
Alexandria is peacefully won by the Arabs in a settlement negotiated by Arab general Amr Ibn-el-'Aas

1798
Napoleon invades to find a ruined and depopulated city

1867
The Suez Canal is inaugurated, allowing Alexandria to control 94 percent of Egypt's exports

1944
Delegates from seven independent states sign the Alexandria Protocol here, founding the Arab League

Algiers

The city of Algiers is made up of a string of communities overlooking the clear waters of the Baie d'Alger. The oldest part of the city is the Casbah, set on a hill overlooking the port. This labyrinthine warren of Ottoman palaces and ancient dwellings is an atmospheric region where the ancient past seems to live on, an impression strengthened by the fact that even today only donkeys can navigate the steep narrow lanes. In 1992 it was recognized as a World Heritage Site by UNESCO. Inland from the Casbah is the city's teeming heartland of Bab el-Oued, a densely inhabited area where countless families share run-down apartments packed around streets with broken paving. The colonial city stretches south of the Casbah along the port, with its grand colonial buildings looking out to sea—its arches and stately windows putting a brave face on France's favorite colony. This leads down to an elegant colonial city center. French-inspired mansions are laid out on spacious boulevards, with only the veiled women to remind one that this is very much a Muslim country. Two major landmarks make navigation easy. The hill rising steeply behind Bab el-Oued is topped by the vast church of Notre Dame d'Afrique, while the city center is surveyed by a huge independence monument, visible from everywhere but especially, in case of future invaders, from the sea.

The Colonial Legacy

When almost a million colonists fled Algiers in 1962, they left a major city on Africa's northern coast but made no attempt to leave the infrastructure or civil institutions to maintain it. Despite being the capital city of Africa's second largest country and enriched by considerable oil underneath its huge southern desert, Algiers remains a small city at heart, with many families relying on remittances from relatives overseas.

Like all of the country, Algiers has seen its share of the political violence that has followed independence, and the city remains beset by problems, including floods in 2001 and an earthquake in 2003. Such problems, however, are smoothed by the city's residents themselves, who are outstandingly kind and hospitable. Signs of hope are beginning to emerge. The construction of an underground railway, stalled by security fears and a lack of foreign investment, is once more underway; a tramway has transformed the urban transit system; and a huge new container port is under development.

THE WAR FOR INDEPENDENCE

Algeria's war for independence was fiercely resisted by the French colonists, and Algiers was at the heart of the violence. Many Algerians would have been content with a greater assimilation with France, but this was rejected. World War II saw the occupation intensify, as Algiers became the Allied headquarters in Africa and the seat of the French government in exile. Resistance escalated, but by the 1960s there were more than a million Algerians of European extraction in control of most of the prime farmland, and they saw assimilation with France as their only hope. France was far less keen. President Charles de Gaulle (1890–1970) took on the colonists and the Algerian Army itself, with the Secret Army Organization (OAS) orchestrating many attacks on Muslims. On independence, a million colonists fled the country.

ABOVE: *Anti-French anti-independence supporters in the early 1960s.*

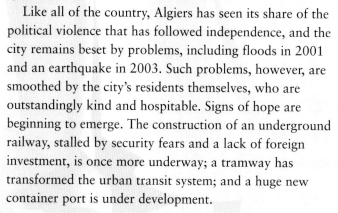

ABOVE: *Monument to the Martyrs.*
RIGHT: *Notre-Dame d'Afrique Cathedral on a hilltop.*

RIGHT: *The Casbah, the old quarter of Algiers.*

THE STORY OF...

Hunter-gatherers and fishermen were resident in Algiers as early as 8000BC, but it was not until 200BC that power was consolidated in the Kingdom of Numidia, first as an ally of Rome, then as a Roman colony. After conversion to Islam, the region became part of the Almoravid Empire that took over the Iberian Peninsula, but the situation was reversed in the 16th century, when Spain captured Algiers.

Soon after, the city became part of the Ottoman Empire, which allowed it more independence. Piracy was the major industry, supplemented by the slave trade, but this caused resentment: it was bombarded by the British, and then invaded by the French. European immigration followed, and the Muslim majority were disenfranchised. Pressure for independence intensified after both World Wars but was steadily resisted, being granted only in 1962.

Algeria's recent history has been somewhat troubled. An election in 1992 was won by an Islamicist party, which openly intended to establish a religious state and dismantle democracy. The result was annulled. Years of violence followed, with up to 150,000 deaths, mainly civilians. A 1999 amnesty seemed to cool the situation, allowing the citizens of Algiers to look nervously toward the future, though sporadic bombings still occasionally rock the city.

AD670
Arab conquest. Kahina, a formidable woman, leads the Berber resistance

1060
The Almoravids take power, extending Moorish power across Spain

1830
French forces occupy Algiers but take 50 years to subdue the rest of the country

1962
Independence. Ahmed Ben Bella forms the first government of a free Algeria

2003
On 21 May an earthquake to the east of the city kills more than 2,000 people and causes widespread destruction

Baghdad

HARUN AL-RASHID (AD763–809)

Harun al-Rashid was the fifth caliph of the Abbasid Dynasty (AD750–1258). The greatest ruler of the longest-lived caliphate, Harun and his fabulous court have been immortalized in the classic work *One Thousand and One Nights*. The son of Caliph al-Mahdi and a former slave-girl, Khayzuran, Harun ruled an empire that stretched from Persia to Morocco from his capital in Baghdad. His reign is generally considered to have been a golden era of Arab power and prosperity. Harun was a great patron of the arts and of scientific learning; during his reign, Baghdad was the ealthiest and most sophisticated city in the world.

Strategically located on the River Tigris, Baghdad is Iraq's largest city and the social and cultural heart of the country. It is a transportation hub, served by major highways west to Jordan and Syria, and east to Iran. There is an important rail link to Turkey, and both the Tigris and the nearby Euphrates are busy waterways, linking Baghdad to Iraq's second city, Basra, and the Persian Gulf. Baghdad has for centuries been the richest and most economically important city of Iraq, a position reinforced by the discovery of oil, as almost all of the country's trade is administered through the capital. Baghdad has a wide variety of products, including leather goods, furniture, wood products, chemicals, electrical equipment, textiles, clothing, bricks, cement, tobacco, processed food, and beverages. Among the main industries are oil, food-processing, tanneries, and textile mills. Baghdad's workshops have an extensive production of handicrafts, including cloth, household utensils, jewelry, leather, felt, and rugs.

The city is also a center of financial operations and the headquarters of the Central Bank of Iraq. Most of the national bureaucracy is located here, as are the leading institutions of learning, including three universities. The population of Baghdad is ethnically diverse, reflecting that of Iraq as a whole. The majority are Arabs, mainly Muslim, but with a substantial Christian minority. There is a tiny Jewish community, most Jews having migrated to Israel or North America in the 1950s. Other ethnic groups present include Kurds, Armenians, Turkomen, Indians, Afghans, and Turks.

BELOW: *Baghdad traffic.*

A Riverine City

The River Tigris snakes through the heart of Baghdad. The main downtown area, which is centered on Saadoun and al-Jamoun Streets on the east bank of the Tigris, is predominantly modern, having been built in the 1970s. There are fine examples of traditional architecture in the older suburbs. Some of the best old houses are found along Rashid Street, though many of these are now in poor condition. First-floor wooden bays with latticed windows and open inner courtyards distinguish many such houses. Government buildings, major hotels, and banks lie mainly on the west bank of the Tigris, while to the east impoverished Sadr City is home to almost 2 million Shia Muslims. Baghdad has many parks, of which Zawra Park is the largest. A few monuments of old Baghdad survive, the oldest of which is the 12th-century Abbasid Palace. The Mustansiriyah School and Sahrawardi Mosque both date from the 13th century. Baghdad's most important religious monument is the 16th-century Kadhimayn Mosque, containing the shrine of the seventh imam of Shia Islam.

THE STORY OF...

In AD762, the Abbasid ruler al-Mansur chose the small village of Baghdad, or "God's Gift" in Persian, to be the capital and administrative center of his Caliphate. Over the next 500 years Baghdad grew to be one of the world's greatest cities and a major international center of learning during a period widely considered to be the classical "Golden Age" of the Arab World. In 1258, however, the city was conquered and razed by the Mongol ruler Hulagu Khan. Hundreds of thousands were killed, including the last Abbasid caliph, al-Mustasim.

Baghdad regained much of its importance in 1534, when it was incorporated into the Ottoman Empire. In 1870 the old city walls were torn down and a process of modernization began, leaving few old buildings intact.

In 1917 the British occupied the city and in 1920 it became the capital of the new state of Iraq. Baghdad gained considerable wealth from oil in the 1970s, but was damaged in the Gulf War of 1991 and once again in the US-led invasion of 2003.

BELOW: *A man disembarks after crossing the River Tigris, a way of avoiding the often congested roads.*
RIGHT: *Kadhimain Shrine.*
FAR RIGHT: *Brass souvenirs on a Baghdad market stall.*

AD762
The Abbasid Caliphate founds the city of Baghdad, which soon becomes the focal point of the Islamic world

1055
The Seljuqs, originally Turkic nomads from Central Asia, establish themselves as the rulers of Baghdad

1258
The Mongols, led by Hulagu Khan, sack the city, a serious setback for Islamic civilization; 800,000 inhabitants massacred

1534
The Ottoman Turks incorporate Baghdad into their empire; a time of great creativity in the arts

2003
The United States and its allies enter Baghdad and unseat Iraqi dictator, Saddam Hussein

Beirut

statistics

Population: 2,0250,000

The cost of rebuilding and developing Beirut International Airport: $450 million

Beirut ranks number one in the Arab world for aesthetic plastic surgery operations

Beirut produces 70 percent of the publications in the Arab world

KAHLIL GIBRAN (1883–1931)

The poet, philosopher, and artist Kahlil Gibran was born in Beirut. Millions of Arabic-speaking people familiar with his writings in that language consider him to be the genius of his age, but he was a man whose fame and influence spread far beyond the Arab World. His poetry has been translated into more than 20 languages, while his drawings and paintings have been exhibited in many of the great capitals of the world; these were compared by Auguste Rodin (1840–1917) to the works of William Blake (1757–1827). His masterpiece *The Prophet* and his other books of poetry, which are illustrated with his mystical drawings, have made him Lebanon's best-loved writer.

Built by a fine natural harbor, Beirut is Lebanon's largest city and the social and intellectual heart of the country. Traditionally a meeting place between the Middle Eastern and Mediterranean worlds, the city was once known as the Paris of the Middle East, though it suffered badly during the Lebanese Civil War (1975–1990). Beirut has undergone a major transformation in the years following the cessation of hostilities, particularly in the downtown area. It is a city of contrasts: beautiful architecture exists alongside concrete monstrosities; traditional houses set in jasmine-scented gardens are dwarfed by modern high-rise buildings; winding old alleys lead off from wide boulevards; and expensive new cars vie for right of way with donkey carts.

ABOVE: *View of the Beirut Marina.*
OPPOSITE: *The interior of the Al-Omari Mosque, the oldest mosque in Beirut.*

A City of Vibrancy and Charm

The Hamra area, in the northwest of the city, is home to many of the city's banks, hotels, restaurants, cafés, and the main post office. Beirut Central District, also known as Solidère, has undergone major reconstruction and is once again the vibrant heart of the city. North of Hamra, the prestigious American University of Beirut has a small museum of archaeology, although it is not as extensive as Beirut's National Museum which re-opened, post-reconstruction, in 1999. The museum's collection of Phoenician figurines is particularly interesting. The Sursock Museum in east Beirut is housed in a splendid 19th-century villa; exhibits include Turkish silverware, icons, contemporary Lebanese art, and a library. In Beirut Central District the Al-Omari Mosque, also known as the Grand Mosque, is one of the few historic buildings still standing. Originally built in the 12th century as the Church of St. John the Baptist of the Knights Hospitallers, it was converted to a mosque in 1291. The Corniche, Beirut's coastal road, offers fine views of Pigeon Rocks. These offshore rock arches are a beautiful complement to Beirut's dramatic sea cliffs, and locals congregate here every evening to watch the sunset over the Mediterranean Sea.

ABOVE: *Façade of the National Museum, considered to be one of the most significant Near Eastern museums.*

Since the civil war, Beirut has been struggling to regain its position as a center of commerce and banking in the Middle East. Silk and cotton fabrics, as well as gold and silver articles, are the chief manufactures. Major exports are silk, cotton textiles, fruits, hides, livestock, and wool. Imports include building materials, clothing, and foods. In addition to air connections through Beirut International Airport, Beirut is linked by rail and road to Damascus in Syria and other cities in the Middle East.

THE STORY OF...

Originally named Beroth or "city of wells" by the Phoenicians, Beirut has long been a major trading center. For much of the Middle Ages it was overshadowed by Acre as a port, but in the 18th century Beirut supplanted Acre as the main port of the Levant.

Beirut became a cosmopolitan city and developed links with Europe and the United States. It also became the center of Arab intellectual activity in the 19th century. After the collapse of the Ottoman Empire, following World War I, Lebanon was placed under French administration.

It was given its independence after World War II and became the capital city. Beirut remained the intellectual capital of the Arab world and a commercial and tourist center until 1975, when civil war broke out. During the war, the city was divided between the largely Muslim west and the Christian east. Since the end of the war in 1990, Beirut has regained its status as a tourist and cultural hub, as well as a center for commerce and media.

BELOW: *Shoppers wandering through downtown Beirut.*

1400BC
First historical mention of Beirut found on engraved stone tablets in Egypt

140BC
Diodotus Tryphon destroys Beirut, but the city is soon rebuilt on a Hellenistic plan

AD635
The city passes into the hands of the Arabs

1918
Following World War I and the collapse of the Ottoman Empire, Beirut becomes capital of French protectorate

2009
The city will host the Winter Asian Games

key dates

statistics

Population: 15,100,000

The Great Pyramid at Giza contains 2.3 million stone blocks, each weighing on average 2.5 tonnes

Largest indoor film and television shooting facility in the world: 12,950 sq ft (5,000 sq m)

The Egyptian Museum holds the largest collection of Egyptian antiquities in the world: 120,000 objects

Cairo

Cairo is located on the banks of the River Nile in northern Egypt, immediately south of the point where the river leaves its desert-bound valley and divides into the three branches of the fertile Nile Delta. The oldest part of the city lies to the east of the river in the neighborhood of old Fustat. This older, eastern section of the city has grown haphazardly over the centuries and is filled with small lanes and crowded tenements.

Western Cairo, by contrast, was built by Isma'il Pasha (1830–1895) in the mid-19th century. It is much more modern than eastern Cairo, having been designed loosely along the lines of Paris, with wide boulevards, public parks, and open squares. While western Cairo is dominated by government buildings and modern architecture, the eastern half is filled with hundreds of ancient mosques that act as landmarks. Extensive water systems have permitted the city to expand east into the desert. Bridges link the Nile islands of Gezira and Roda, where more government buildings are located and civil servants live. Bridges also cross the Nile linking the city center to the extensive western suburbs of Giza and Imbabah.

Historic City

Cairo's main square and focal point, Midan Tahrir, is packed with people and traffic. The Egyptian Museum and a number of Cairo's most upmarket hotels are clustered nearby. Just to the northeast, centered on Midan Talaat Harb, lies the noisy, bustling commercial area known as Wust al-Balad, the busy heart of downtown Cairo. The streets are packed with stores and thousands of small businesses. Further out, the Manial Palace Museum, built in the early 20th century for an uncle of King Farouk, is set in magnificent grounds; with a diverse variety of trees and plants, it is the largest private garden in Cairo. The most important historic mosques are centered on the Al Gamaliya, Bab al-Khalq, and Al-Darb al-Ahmar quarters, all to the east of the city.

ABOVE: *Crowds of tourists outside the Pyramids of Giza.*

THE STORY OF...

There has long been a settlement in the region occupied by modern Cairo, though the city's location has naturally moved to follow the shifting course of the Nile.

About 3100BC the Pharaoh Menes established the city of Memphis just south of modern Cairo, after unifying the Kingdoms of Upper and Lower Egypt.

The first settlement to have been built on the site of modern Cairo was a fort called Babylon, established in about AD150 and settled mainly by Coptic Christians.

In AD642 the fort was captured by the great Arab conqueror of North Africa, Amr Ibn al-As. Amr's forces set up a tented encampment next to the fort, which was given the name Al-Fustat or "the tent". In time this became the first Arab city in Egypt, as well as the site of the first mosque in Africa.

In AD969 the Egyptian Fatimid established a new dynasty, seizing Al-Fustat and changing the area's name to Al-Qahirah, "the conqueror", subsequently shortened to Cairo in European usage. The Al-Azhar mosque was founded one year later and this, together with the accompanying university, soon made Cairo an important center of Islamic learning and philosophy.

The sack of Baghdad in 1258 increased the importance of Cairo and it became the leading intellectual and artistic center of the Arab World. In 1517 Cairo passed to the Ottoman Empire, though for most of the Ottoman period it was indirectly administered through the Turks' nominal vassals, the Mameluks. Modernization took off in 1851, with the completion of a railway between Alexandria and Cairo.

The construction of the Suez Canal between 1863 and 1869 continued this process. Cairo passed under British rule in 1882 and remained the capital of modern Egypt through independence in 1946 and to the present day. Today it is the largest city in Africa, and the cultural and political heart of the Arab World.

LEFT: *Tut'ankhamun's death mask in the Egyptian Museum of Antiquities.*

Further south along the Nile is Masr al-Qadima, or Old Cairo, with its historic Coptic Churches. West of Giza, on the edge of the Sahara Desert, lies the ancient necropolis of Memphis, centered on three huge pyramids. The most celebrated of these is the Great Pyramid of Giza, the last surviving of the Seven Ancient Wonders of the World.

Economy and Communications

As Egypt's capital and largest city, Cairo is the heart of the country's economy. The public sector, including government and social services and the military, make up the city's largest industry. Cairo is the center of Egypt's growing trade, finance, and insurance sectors, while tourism and servicing the Suez Canal are the major elements in the service industry. Tourism is Egypt's largest source of foreign currency and has shown remarkable growth. Most visitors come from Europe, especially Germany, Italy, and the UK, and from the wider Arab World. Other key industries, including metals (aluminium, iron, and steel), petrochemicals, cement, automobiles, textiles, consumer electronics, and pharmaceuticals, are rapidly expanding under private sector management. The

LEFT: *The delicate upper section of a late Mameluke-style minaret.*
BELOW: *The shining domes of the Citadel and the slim minarets of Muhammad Ali's mosque.*

BELOW: *Detail of handprints impressed in blood on one of the tombs in the City of the Dead.*

key dates

2560BC
Construction of the Great Pyramid of Khufu (Cheops) begins at Giza

AD969
The Fatimids seize Egypt and found Al-Qahirah, modern-day Cairo

AD970
Mosque of Al-Azhar founded, regarded as the oldest university in the world

1811
Muhammad Ali Pasha begins a massive modernization campaign in Cairo

1869
At the inauguration of the Suez Canal plans are unveiled for a new-look city along the lines of modern Paris

1987
The Cairo Metro opens; the first and still the only underground system on the African continent

government has promised to make the development of high-technology a priority, and to attract export-oriented manufacturing firms to establish bases in Cairo. The city stands at the hub of Egypt's 3,125-mile (5,000km) railway network. Ramses Station in central Cairo links the southbound line from the Nile valley and Upper Egypt (including Assiut, Luxor, and Aswan) with lines that spread out across Lower Egypt to serve Alexandria and the main cities of the Delta, as well as Ismailia and Port Said on the Suez Canal.

Cairo's roads are notorious for being congested and dangerous. The underground train system, by contrast, is modern and efficient, currently being Africa's only fully-fledged metro system.

BELOW RIGHT: *Mosaic decoration on the front of Ramses Station.*
BELOW: *Men enjoying refreshments outside the gates of Bab el-Futuh (Gates of Conquest).*

EGYPT'S MOST FAMOUS WRITER

Naguib Mahfouz (b. 1911), the best-known living Egyptian (and probably Arab) novelist, was born in the Hamaliya Quarter of Cairo. A long-time civil servant, Mahfouz served in the Ministry of Endowments, then in the Bureau of Art, as Director of the Foundation for the Support of the Cinema, and finally, as a consultant to the Ministry of Culture. He was awarded the Nobel Prize in Literature in 1988.

As both a modernist and a moderate Muslim, Mahfouz's works have often been banned in more conservative Middle Eastern countries for alleged blasphemy. Although both famous and generally popular in Egypt and beyond, Mahfouz was attacked by two extremists outside his Cairo home, at the age of 83. He now lives under constant bodyguard protection. The author of more than 30 books between 1938 (*Whisper of Madness*) and the present,

Mahfouz's most famous work is probably *Midaq Alley* (1947). Many of the writer's works have been written in serialized form, and most are set in and around his native Cairo. The American composer Dave Douglas entitled a song on his album *Witness* (2001) "Mahfouz". The 25-minute track features singer Tom Waits (b. 1949) reading an excerpt from Mahfouz's work.

BELOW: *Naguib Mahfouz is one of the foremost writers of modern Arabic literature.*

Cape Town

ocated at the southern tip of Africa, with the hulk of Table Mountain looming in the background, Cape Town enjoys one of the most dramatic locations in the world, with rugged cliffs and sun-kissed Atlantic beaches adding to its appeal. Away from its high-rise Central Business District (CBD) and the tourist hub of the Victoria and Albert Waterfront, Cape Town is actually a collection of distinctive suburbs. Close to the CBD is the colorful and traditionally Cape Malay (a name given to Cape Town's non-white and non-black Muslim population) dwelling of Bo-Kaap and the vibrant De Waterkant, while around the bay there are glamorous Atlantic beachfront suburbs such as Camps Bay. In stark contrast to these wealthy suburbs, you will also find the Cape Flats townships, where most Capetonians live—many in makeshift tin-shack

BELOW LEFT (TOP): *A township on the marshy, sandy Cape Flats.*
BELOW LEFT (BOTTOM): *Cableway at Table Mountain.*
BELOW AND OPPOSITE: *The view from Signal Hill.*

NELSON MANDELA (B.1918)

Nelson Mandela is renowned for his stance against South Africa's Apartheid regime and his role in reconciling the country after becoming the country's first democratically elected president in 1994. The Nobel Peace Prize winner joined the African National Congress Youth League in 1944 and supported strikes, civil disobedience, and mass defiance against the white regime in search of equal rights for all. In 1963, Mandela was imprisoned for leaving South Africa without permission and for inciting a strike. While behind bars, he was found guilty of sabotage and his sentence increased to life. Mandela spent the next 27 years in prison, serving the first 21 years on Robben Island.

ABOVE: *The Nelson Mandela statue, overlooking Nelson Mandela Square in Johannesburg.*

houses that line the side of the main N2 highway as it runs from the airport to the city. Each of Cape Town's unique suburbs has a vitality that is missing from many of South Africa's cities, with beach volleyball, gleaming skyscrapers, and bustling craft markets all being part of the mix.

The driving force behind Cape Town's economy is tourism. The end of Apartheid and the rise of the "Rainbow Nation" under the leadership of Nelson Mandela brought curious visitors to the city. Then, as South Africa's currency weakened, Cape Town became a cheap sunshine destination. Despite a stronger Rand and inflated prices in peak season, the city remains an affordable destination for many.

Reconciliation

Cape Town holds a special place in the hearts of many South Africans, simultaneously symbolizing the best that life has to offer, yet also remaining a poignant symbol of the country's recent troubled past. As part of what Nelson Mandela so aptly described as the "Reconciliation" of the South African people, his former prison, Robben Island, has re-opened as a museum. Former political prisoners act as guides, demonstrating to the world how even the worst hardships can be overcome. In a similar vein, the city's prized District Six Museum is an eternal reminder of the forcible relocation of some 60,000 people from their homes (which were later flattened by bulldozers), to the Cape Flats, as the district was declared a white-only area in 1966. The townships have also opened up to visitors in recent years, with an increasing number of guided tours providing a safe way to explore these poor neighborhoods.

RIGHT: *Local man wearing a colorful costume in Greenmarket Square.*
BELOW RIGHT: *Brightly colored house exteriors in Bo-Kaap, a lively suburb in the Islamic quarter of Cape Town.*

THE STORY OF...

Evidence of human habitation near Cape Town dates back 100,000 years, with the Kohikoi and San tribes settling on the Cape around 30,000 years ago.

Portuguese exploration of the Cape in the late 15th century opened up trade routes with Europe and India, and in 1652 the Dutch East India Company (VOC) established a settlement in Cape Town. By the 18th century, Cape Town was home to a culturally and ethnically diverse population – from European VOC employees, to Asian sailors, and slaves.

British occupation in 1795 (the Cape joined the British Empire in 1814) saw the abolition of slavery and liberal reforms. By the late 19th century, prejudice reared its head and the population became increasingly segregated according to race. The unification of South Africa in 1910 intensified racial discrimination and in 1948 Apartheid was formally introduced; a policy that affected most aspects of life.

Apartheid has gone but crime, unemployment, and poverty, combined with poor education, mean that significant economic and residential segregation remain.

BELOW: *Flowers growing on top of Table Mountain.*

1486
Portuguese explorer Bartholomew Diaz discovers the Cape Peninsula

1652
The Dutch East India Company establishes a trading base on the Cape

1840
Cape Town officially becomes a municipality

1948
The National Party establishes a formal system of Apartheid (racial segregation)

1994
Nelson Mandela becomes president of post-Apartheid South Africa

key dates

Casablanca

statistics

Population: 3,900,000

Casablanca has 60 percent of Morocco's total population and its citizens pay more than 50 percent of the nation's taxes

Casablanca has 1,400 miles (2,240km) of road lighting

The city uses 30 percent of Morocco's electricity and phone lines

THE SECOND LARGEST MOSQUE IN THE WORLD

Casablanca is home to the Mosque of Hassan II, completed in 1993. The second largest mosque in the world, this structure was built around superlatives. Designed by a French architect, Michel Pinseau, the mosque is designed to look as though it floats on water. Its 688ft (210m) minaret is the tallest in the world. Up to 25,000 worshippers can pray inside, while a further 80,000 can be accommodated in the courtyard. More than 2,500 of Morocco's finest master craftsmen were engaged in the mosque's construction, and the overall cost has been estimated at $1,000 million, all of which was raised by private donations.

RIGHT: *Fruit and vegetable stall in the souk in the Medina.*
FAR RIGHT: *The waterfront.*

nlike most Moroccan cities, Casablanca is a relatively modern city. Named by the Portuguese in the early 16th century and largely built by the French as a major port, its name in Arabic is Dar al-Beida, or "white abode", hence Casablanca, or "white house", often shortened to Casa even by Moroccans. Casablanca is the largest port in the Maghrib, or north-west Africa, and it boasts the Hassan II Mosque—but this apart it has little in the way of historical antiquities to distinguish it. Casablanca is in fact the least "Moroccan" of cities, with a distinctly European feel to it. Many people, perhaps most outside Morocco, will associate Casablanca with the classic film of the same name. Made in 1942 by the director Michael Curtiz and starring Humphrey Bogart (1899–1957) and Ingrid Bergman (1915–82), the movie was in fact shot entirely in Hollywood—and for a very good reason, as the city of Casablanca, like all Morocco, was controlled by pro-Nazi Vichy forces at the time.

Casablanca has good highways and rail links connecting it with Rabat, Fez, and Tangier to the north and with Marrakesh to the south. The port, which is one of the largest artificial harbors in the world, handles most

of Morocco's trade, including phosphate exports. Casablanca's industries include fishing, fish-canning, saw-milling, furniture, construction materials, glass, textiles, electronic goods, leather, processed food, beer, spirits, soft drinks, and cigarettes. The city is also home to more than half the bank transactions in Morocco. Casablanca has focused on developing a substantial tourist industry, though terrorist attacks in 2003 have hampered efforts to promote tourism.

Casablanca Today

Casablanca is Morocco's largest metropolis, distinguished both by its cosmopolitan atmosphere and Franco-Moorish civic buildings. The city, centered on Place Mohammed V and Boulevard Mohammed V, manages to be both Moroccan and European. The Old Medina contrasts with the French-built New Medina or Quartier Habous, while the huge Marché Central, which is also French-built, is the largest fresh fruit and vegetable market in the country. Casablanca's seafront is distinguished by the palm-lined Boulevard Houphouet, while the city's Aéroport Mohammed V—Morocco's largest airport—is located in the Anfa District. The city has various modern sports facilities, including a Formula One circuit at Ain Diab and a world-class golf course to the north of the city. Locals and visitors alike favor Ain Diab Beach for swimming and other water sports.

THE STORY OF...

The history of Casablanca dates back more than a thousand years to the Arab invasions in the 7th century AD, when it was a small Berber principality called Anfa.

The indigenous Berbers embraced Islam, but they also retained their own language and cultural traditions. Anfa become a haven for pirates, and attracted the wrath of the Portuguese in 1468, when Lisbon sent a fleet to raze the city. The Portuguese returned in 1515, this time establishing a new port under Portuguese control called Casa Branca.

The port remained a backwater until the mid-19th century, when regular maritime services were established between Marseilles and Morocco, and the city prospered. In 1907, when nine French citizens were massacred at the dockside, France took over the city by force.

In 1912, General Lyautey was appointed Resident-General. He completed the construction of the harbor, establishing Casablanca as a major port and industrial center.

LEFT: *The sea defence wall of the Mosque of Hassan II.*

key dates

1468
The ancient town of Anfa—on the site of present-day Casablanca—is destroyed by the Portuguese after becoming a pirate haven

1515
The Portuguese rebuild Anfa and rename it Casa Branca

1755
Town destroyed by an earthquake, rebuilding begins in 1757 under the direction of Sultan Sidi Mohamed Ben Abdallah

1943
The Casablanca Conference. Roosevelt, Churchill, and de Gaulle meet to discuss the direction of World War II

2003
Suicide bombers attack Spanish, Jewish and Belgian sites in the city, killing 39 people

Casablanca

155

Dar es Salaam

statistics

Population: 2,850,000

The majority of Dar es Salaam's population live in low-cost rented accommodation; mean household size is 3.8

Dar es Salaam is the largest port in East Africa, handling more than 9 million tonnes a year

The University of Dar es Salaam enrols around 5,000 students a year; 85 percent of which are male

ar es Salaam is Tanzania's most important city and the largest port on the coast of eastern Africa between Suez and Cape Town. Developed in the mid-19th century as a deep-water harbor and trading center, first by the Omani sultans of Zanzibar and then by the Germans, it expanded into a major port and trading center operating under British rule in the 1940s and 1950s. Today it is a busy metropolis with almost 3 million inhabitants, principally of African (Bantu) origin, but with people of Indian, Arab, and European descent comprising an economically significant 1–2 percent.

Dar es Salaam was established as a port and still looks to the sea. In its busy harbor Arab and Swahili dhows mingle with huge ocean-going container ships and tankers. Like many African cities, there are major contrasts between various parts of the city. Commerce is centered on a grid of streets in and around busy Kariakoo Market and the central clock tower. To the north are the cooler, shaded boulevards of the government administration and bureaucracy, an area also home to many embassies. There are poorer districts to the south and west of the city center, but Dar es Salaam is fortunate in not having endless slums and shanty dwellings.

SULTAN BARGHASH OF ZANZIBAR AND THE SLAVE TRADE

Sayyid Barghash ibn Said (r. 1870–88), succeeded to the throne of Zanzibar on the death of his brother, Majid. Having spent some years in exile in Bombay, Barghash understood more of European power and was more disposed to the British than his deceased brother Majid. In 1872, Zanzibar was devastated by a fierce hurricane, obliging Barghash to concentrate on the regeneration and development of Dar es Salaam. One year later, under firm British pressure, Barghash closed the Zanzibari slave market and prohibited the slave trade in East African coastal waters. Barghash died in 1888, three years before Dar es Salaam became the capital of German East Africa.

ABOVE RIGHT: *Oyster Bay.*
FAR RIGHT: *The port of Dar es Salaam.*

Exports and Education

As well as being a major seaport, Dar es Salaam is Tanzania's principal commercial, manufacturing, and educational center. Products include processed food, textiles, clothing, footwear, refined petroleum, and metal goods. Railways extend inland to Arusha in the north, to Lake Tanganyika and Lake Victoria, and to Zambia. Exports from Dar es Salaam include coffee, sisal, cotton, and copper—the latter from landlocked Zambia. Among the educational institutions in the city are the University of Dar es Salaam (1961), Kivukoni College (1961), and the College of Business Education (1965). Also here are the National Archives, the National Central Library, and the National Museum of Tanzania, located next to the Botanical Gardens in the city center. The latter features various important collections of archaeology and East African history, including the fossil discoveries of Zinjanthropus ("Nutcracker Man"), and the sad history of the Zanzibar slave trade. About 6 miles (10km) from the city center, the Village Museum is also notable, featuring a "living village" of authentic dwellings from various parts of Tanzania. Traditional dances are performed here on the weekend. Oyster Bay, a beautiful stretch of tropical coastline, is the city's nearest beach.

LEFT: *Bargaining for the daily catch at the fish market.*
BELOW RIGHT: *Container ship in the port of Dar es Salaam.*

THE STORY OF...

Until the middle of the 19th century, the coastal trade of Tanzania was dominated by the small port of Bagamoyo, at the time a slave and ivory trading post controlled by the Omani Sultanate of Zanzibar.

Some 44 miles (70km) to the south, the tiny fishing village of Mzizima or "healthy town" was all but ignored by the outside world until 1866, when Sultan Majid of Zanzibar (r.1856–70) decided to build a new, deep water port on the East African coast. The site chosen was Mzizima, and Majid gave it the auspicious Arabic name Dar es Salaam or "Abode of Peace".

In 1887 the German East Africa Company established a station here, and in 1891 it became the capital of German East Africa.

The city passed under British control in 1916 and became the capital of newly independent Tanganyika in 1961. Three years later, when Tanganyika merged with Zanzibar, it became the capital of Tanzania. Today it remains the country's major port and city, although the National Assembly moved inland to Dodoma in 1996.

1862
The Sultan of Zanzibar founds the city as a summer residence

1891
Becomes capital of German East Africa

1916
The British occupy the city, but German forces resist until 1918

1961
The British grant Tanganyika independence, Dar es Salaam becomes the new capital

1998
The al Qaeda terrorist network bombs the US Embassy; 10 people killed, mostly Africans

157

Damascus

- Population: 2,750,000
- The prayer hall in the Umayyad Mosque is one of the largest in the Islamic world: 447ft (136m) wide by 450ft (137m) long
- Damascus's National Archaeological Museum covers more than 11,000 years of history
- The city hosts a critically acclaimed international film festival every two years

A MODEL OF CHIVALRY

Salah al-Din Yusuf Ibn Ayyub (1137–93), better known in the West as Saladin, was born to a Kurdish family at Tikrit on the River Tigris in Iraq. He studied in Damascus before becoming Sultan of Egypt in 1171, making Damascus his capital in 1174. Saladin recaptured Jerusalem in 1187, after 88 years of Crusader rule. He became renowned in both the Christian and Muslim worlds for his chivalry and military prowess, especially in his relationship with Richard I ("The Lionheart", 1157–99) of England. A man remarkable for his even-handedness and lack of bigotry, Saladin died in 1193 and was buried with great honour in Damascus.

ABOVE: *Statue of Salah al-Din Yusuf Ibn Ayyub.*

Damascus is situated on a plateau 2,263ft (690m) above sea level, bordered by the Anti-Lebanon Mountains to the west, and the Syrian Desert to the east. The city lies in Ghutah Oasis, and is supplied with water by the Barada River. Although geographically close to the Mediterranean Sea, the intervening mountain ranges isolate Damascus from the coast and have made it an eastward-looking city, as befits one of the great termini of the historic Silk Road. Ancient Damascus is centered on an extensive Old City, divided into the huge *suq* or market area, a large Muslim quarter, a smaller Christian quarter, and a tiny Jewish area. All three groups are still represented in Damascus, even though the Jewish community now stands at only a few hundred. The modern city is located to the west of the Old City and dominated by the huge Presidential Palace and surrounding brown cliffs. Damascus University, numerous museums, and the diplomatic area are all located here.

Damascus's significance as a trading hub has been reduced over the centuries, while its importance as an administrative center remains. Beirut used once to be the main port for Damascus, but in the years since Lebanon's independence and civil war, has been replaced by Latakia further to the north. Damascus is well connected to the rest of the country with modern highways, as well as with Lebanon, Iraq, Jordan, and Turkey. Damascus International Airport lies 12.5 miles (20km) east of the city center, providing links with Europe and the rest of the Arab World. The economy of Damascus is chiefly based upon government administration, processed food, clothing, and printed material. The city has a handicraft tradition of considerable importance, producing high quality textiles, silk cloth, leather goods, filigreed gold, silver objects, inlaid wooden, copper, and brass articles. Ghutah, the oasis surrounding the city, produces fruit, especially olives and grapes, as well as cereals and vegetables. Among the livestock are cows, goats, and sheep.

ABOVE (TOP): *The Temple of Jupiter.*
ABOVE (MIDDLE): *Al Takieh al Suleimaniyeh mosque with its elegant minarets, built in 1554.*
ABOVE (BOTTOM): *Damascus street scene.*

THE STORY OF...

Damascus, settled about 2500BC, is thought to be the oldest continuously inhabited city in the world. It was the capital of a powerful Aramaic state in the 9th century BC, before being captured in turn by Assyrians, Persians, Seleucids, and Romans.

In AD636 the city fell to the Caliph Umar and in AD661 it became the capital of the Umayyad Caliphate (AD661–750).

In 1174 it became the capital of Salah al-Din. In 1260 the Mongols captured Damascus, and the city was subsequently sacked by the conqueror Timur in 1400.

The city passed to the Ottoman Empire in 1516 and remained under Turkish rule for the next four centuries. In 1918, the Arabs and their British allies entered Damascus at the end of the First World War.

An attempt to create an Arab kingdom under Amir Faisal was pre-empted by the French in 1920, who made Damascus the capital of a mandated Syria under the League of Nations. When Syria became independent in 1946, Damascus remained the capital. The Arabic name for the city is al-Shams, or "The Sun".

ABOVE: *Umayyad Mosque, the oldest existing monumental architecture in the Islamic world.*
ABOVE RIGHT: *Arabesque detail.*

A Center of Culture through the Ages

From AD661 to AD750, Damascus was both the capital of the Umayyad Caliphate and the center of the Arab World. This eminent history is apparent from the city's many fine buildings, especially the Umayyad Mosque, Islam's fourth holiest shrine (after the great mosques of Mecca, Medina, and Jerusalem). The Old City is bisected by the biblical "Street Called Straight" (Bab al-Sharqi), probably the oldest surviving street in the world. Other buildings of major importance include the Tomb of Salah al-Din, the House of Ananias (now a church), and the elaborately ornate Hijaz Railway Station.

key dates

2500BC
The name Dimashqa (Damascus) first appears in written records

732BC
Assyrians conquer Damascus

AD661
The Umayyad Empire, which extends from Central Asia to Spain, makes Damascus its capital

1400
Mongol leader Timur (Tamerlane) pillages and burns the city, relocating most of its craftsmen to Samarkand

1946
With Syrian independence from France, Damascus remains the capital

statistics

Population: 1,040,000

60 percent of the population is made up of immigrant workers from India, Pakistan, and the Philippines

Dubai International Airport is one of the fastest growing airports in the world

Annual rainfall: 11.75 inches (300mm)

Dubai

ubai has emerged in recent years as a playground for the rich and famous, with numerous international celebrities buying property in the city. Just like the tourists, who flock to the emirate in ever-increasing numbers, celebrities are attracted to Dubai by the sandy eastern shores of the emirate with their warm seas and year-round sunny skies. Inland the deserts await, with the adventures of camel trekking and four-wheel driving across the dunes. Then there are the atmospheric old *souqs* (markets), where the aroma of spices fills the narrow lanes and mountains of gold are on sale at knockdown prices. In addition, traditional dhow boats ply Dubai Creek. Dubai also offers first-class golf courses, and some of the world's best duty-free shopping in gleaming new air-conditioned malls that are mini-cities in themselves.

Grand Designs

Dubai does not do things by half measures and, as the emirate's aspirations grow, top designers are being brought in to supervise ever more elaborate projects. The Burj al Arab hotel, or Arab Tower, which rises like something out of a James Bond movie from its own man-made island in the Arabian Gulf, is one of the most instantly recognizable symbols of the new Dubai. This multi-storey monster is an oasis of true luxury that is symbolic of the emirate itself.

Ambitious construction projects in the emirate include "The Palm", which, when completed in 2007, will bring 75 miles (120km) of new beachfront through the creation of two enormous man-made and palm-shaped islands. The developers claim that it will even be visible from space. Plans are also afoot for the creation of the world's tallest tower, a giant underwater hotel, and the first desert ski center featuring real snow. The latter is part of the multi-million dollar Dubailand theme park (due for completion in October 2006), which will also have an artificial rainforest, the largest zoo in the Middle East, and the region's biggest and most spectacular water park.

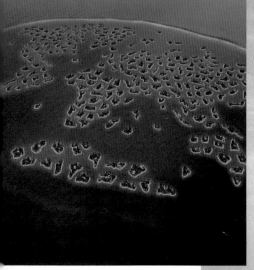

THE WORLD

Investment in real estate in Dubai has ballooned in recent years, with building projects occurring on a grand scale. "The World" is currently the most elaborate development in progress and, when it is completed at the end of 2005, it will be a collection of up to 300 islands made from land reclaimed from the Arabian Gulf. What is as impressive as the engineering feat required to reclaim the land, which will fit into a rectangular area measuring 5.5 miles (9km) by 3.75 miles (6km), is the fact that The World will, from the air, resemble a map of the world.

RIGHT: *Jeep safari in Dubai.*
CENTER RIGHT: *The Dubai World Trade Center.*

BELOW: *The luxury 28-storey Burj al Arab hotel.*
BELOW RIGHT: *Satellite view of The Palm hotel development.*

The discovery of oil in 1966 changed the face of Dubai forever. However, petroleum products now account for just 10 percent of Dubai's economy, with trade, service industries, finance, light industry, real estate, and tourism all becoming increasingly important. With the multi-starred luxury hotels of Jumeirah Beach, the high-tech skyline of the business district, and inventive new projects all integral to Dubai's image, it is hard to imagine that only a century ago it was a desert of shifting sands and nomadic Bedouin tribesmen. As the outlandish development of the emirate continues apace, who knows what the next century will hold for Dubai.

THE STORY OF...

It is tempting to think of Dubai as a thoroughly modern city, but the emirate's history dates back to the third century BC, when nomadic tribes eked out a living in the arid deserts. Dubai gradually emerged as an trading hub on the route between Mesopotamia and the Indus Valley, and by the 19th century a fishing village had taken root at the mouth of Dubai Creek. The village was inhabited by the Bani Yas tribe, led by the Maktoum family who still preside over Dubai today.

As Europe embarked on the mass destruction of World War I, Dubai still had no running water, no real roads, and the main mode of transport was the camel. Dubai's remarkable success began in 1966 when oil was struck, setting the scene for the emirate's rapid generation of incredible wealth. As Dubai earnt billions of dollars from oil, it invested in the country's infrastructure and conjured up a city to match its newfound riches.

BELOW: *The Dubai World Cup is the world's richest horse-racing event.*
BELOW LEFT: *The Jumeirah Mosque.*

Dubai

1833
Members of the Bani Yas tribe settle near Dubai Creek

1966
Oil is discovered

1969
Dubai exports oil for the first time

1971
Dubai becomes part of the newly formed United Arab Emirates (UAE)

2001
Construction work begins on The Palm development

key dates

statistics

- Population: 692,000

- Area: 48.75 sq miles (126.4 sq km), the largest city in Israel by area

- The Al-Aqsa Mosque is the oldest extant mosque in the world, built in AD715

- The Church of the Holy Sepulchre is shared by six Christian denominations. To prevent any arguments, the keys have been entrusted to a Muslim family since 1187

Jerusalem

Jerusalem lies about 34.5 miles (55km) to the east of the Mediterranean Sea, and 15.5 miles (25km) from the Dead Sea. About 2,750ft (850m) above sea level in the Judea-Samaria Mountains, the city enjoys subtropical climate, with warm and dry summers and rainy winters. In some years there is even a substantial snowfall. Jerusalem is divided into an Old City, a New City, and various satellite towns which are scattered around it on all sides. On the eastern side, the towns have been built on land taken from Palestinian owners, and populated with Jewish settlers with the aim of making a return of East Jerusalem to Palestinian control as difficult as possible. Jerusalem's main sources of income are state institutions and government activities, building services, and tourism. The latter has declined since 2000, due in large part to the Palestinian *intifada*, or uprising, in protest against continuing Israeli occupation. Other service sectors include banking, finance, and insurance. Important light industries in the city are diamond cutting and polishing, as well as printing and publishing. Jerusalem is linked to Tel Aviv on the coast by highways and railways. Jerusalem International Airport lies in occupied Palestinian territory to the north.

A Mix of Religions and Cultures

The historic Old City is divided into Armenian, Christian, Jewish, and Muslim quarters. The most holy Jewish and Muslim sites are located at Temple Mount, while the Church of the Holy Sepulchre in the Christian quarter is said to be built over the site where Jesus was crucified, buried, and resurrected. Most visitors arrive here after walking down the Via Dolorosa (The Way of Suffering), the route Jesus followed as he carried the cross on his way to Calvary. Beyond the Old City lies bustling, traffic-filled Arab East Jerusalem, or the modern streets and shopping centers of Jewish West Jerusalem. Also to the west of the city is Yad Vashem, a moving memorial to the Jewish dead of the Nazi Holocaust. Fine views across the city may be had from the Mount of Olives, where Jesus is believed to have ascended to heaven. Jerusalem is administered as a cultural heritage site. New building work in the city is strictly controlled. Even if the construction style is modern, only a limited range of stone types and colors are allowed, and the height of buildings is strictly controlled. Culture in Jerusalem is predominantly oriented toward religion. Virtually all major sights and important buildings are of a religious character. One rare exception is the Knesset parliament building, an example of modern architecture from the early days of the modern state of Israel.

THE HOLIEST PLACE

Temple Mount, or Har Habayit in Hebrew, is the site of the last Jewish Temple, though only the Western Wall survives. It is also the site of the Dome of the Rock and Al-Aqsa Mosque, and is known in Arabic as al-Haram as-Sharif, or the "Noble Sanctuary". The political status of Temple Mount remains bitterly contested, but all sides agree on its sacred nature. Some Jews wish to relocate the Dome to Mecca and replace it with a Third Temple, but since the Dome is built around the Rock where Islam teaches the Prophet Muhammad rose to heaven, such an act would be nothing short of sacrilege to Muslims.

ABOVE: *The minaret and domes of the Al-Aqsa Mosque.*

ABOVE LEFT: *The Muslim Dome of the Rock, on Temple Mount.*
FAR LEFT: *The ruins of the Hurva Synagogue in the Jewish Quarter.*
LEFT: *The Shrine of the Book.*
RIGHT: *Faience tiles on the front of the Dome of the Rock.*

THE STORY OF...

The city, called Yerushaláyim in Hebrew and Al Quds in Arabic, has a long history. Biblical records state that King David captured Jerusalem from the Jebusites 3,000 years ago.

King Solomon built the first Jewish Temple in the 10th century. In 598BC Jerusalem was captured by the Babylonians and the Temple destroyed. The Temple was rebuilt by King Herod about 515BC and then destroyed by the Romans around AD70.

The city passed to the Christian Byzantines around AD326, and nine years later the Church of the Holy Sepulchre was built. Jerusalem fell to the Arabs in AD638, and 60 years later the Dome of the Rock was built.

Between 1099 and 1187 it was the capital of the Crusader Kingdom of Jerusalem. In 1517 Jerusalem passed to the Ottoman Turks and in 1918 became the capital of British-mandated Palestine. In 1948 West Jerusalem became the capital of Israel, and in 1967 Israel seized and unilaterally annexed Arab East Jerusalem, a move not recognized in international law.

BELOW: *The Children's Memorial for young Holocaust victims.*

1005BC
The United Kingdom of Israel, under King David, establishes Jerusalem as its capital

AD70
The Romans destroy the city of Jerusalem, leaving little standing

AD638
Arabs led by Caliph Umar ibn al-Khattab capture Jerusalem

1099
Crusaders briefly establish the Kingdom of Jerusalem

1967
Israeli forces occupy Arab East Jerusalem

statistics

- Population: 3,200,000
- Elevation: 6,000ft (1,753m) above sea level
- 40 percent of the world's gold has been mined in the Johannesburg area
- Johannesburg has more than 10 million trees

Johannesburg

Located in the northeastern part of South Africa on a high plateau, Johannesburg is one of Africa's most important economic hubs. The city that flourished after the discovery of gold just over a century ago is still dominated by money, with the rich barricading themselves behind high-rise walls and gates topped with barbed wire, and protected by burglar alarms and armed response units. Meanwhile, African immigrants who come to eGoli (the City of Gold) in search of wealth are often disappointed, with many finding themselves unemployed and often living in crime-ridden and deprived areas, such as Hillbrow. Despite South Africa's economic problems—around 40 percent of the population is unemployed—development in Johannesburg has continued apace, with the hurriedly built shantytown of 1886 now replaced with a sprawling metropolis that spans some 635 sq miles (1,645 sq km), comparable in scale to Los Angeles. Despite its social and economic problems, Johannesburg remains an energetic and cosmopolitan city, with all 11 of the country's official languages spoken by its inhabitants, as well as the Portuguese and French tongues of residents from across Africa. The city also has a significant Asian population, particularly from India and China.

BELOW LEFT: *The Metro Mall, the largest market in Johannesburg.* BELOW CENTER: *Musician at the African Craft Market in the Rosebank Shopping Mall.* BELOW RIGHT AND OPPOSITE (INSET): *The Johannesburg skyline by day and by night.* OPPOSITE (FULL PAGE): *Figures at the African Craft Market in the Rosebank Shopping Mall.*

HECTOR PIETERSON MUSEUM

Commemorating the tragic events of 16 June 1976, the Hector Pieterson Museum is Soweto's most poignant sight. Opened in 2002, it is dedicated to the memory of 12-year-old Pieterson, who was gunned down during a student protest against the forced use of the Afrikaans language in education. Photographs, eyewitness accounts, and video footage replay the events that led to the death of over 500 black civilians at the hands of the security forces. The iconic photograph—a powerful reminder of the madness of Apartheid that cast a shadow over South Africa throughout the 20th century—shows a fellow student running through the streets carrying the dead boy as Pieterson's sister runs alongside screaming.

Reconciliation and Regeneration

Often perceived as an endless, and still growing, sprawl, Gauteng's (a Sesotho word which means "place of gold") largest city also boasts tranquil parks and world-class museums. The Apartheid Museum evokes the struggles of those living in Johannesburg's townships in the 1970s and 1980s. Constructed on an impressive scale, the museum has 2,317 sq miles (6,000 sq m) of floor space and bombards the senses with harrowing photographs and multimedia displays; it also seeks to expose the futility of Apartheid policies and demonstrates how the city and the South African nation have survived them.

Another museum showing that Johannesburg is working hard to overcome the problems of the past is Constitution Hill. Opened in March 2004, just after the country's Human Rights holiday, the complex combines a working Constitutional Court with an educational insight into life for the former inmates at the notorious Fort Prison Complex. Guided tours and interactive displays in the former prison cells bring to life the hardships suffered by prisoners during the jail's 80-year history. The exhibits, dedicated to the newfound and protected freedoms afforded to all South Africans, emphasize the belief that Johannesburg can, and will, go from strength to strength.

THE STORY OF...

Prior to the discovery of gold in 1866, Johannesburg was little more than open grassland. Three years later, as prospectors from North America and Europe flocked to the region, Johannesburg became the biggest town in South Africa.

By 1875 the population had swelled to 100,000, around 75 percent of whom worked in the mines. As the gold mines increased the city's fortunes, tensions between the ruling Afrikaners and the British grew, finally culminating in the Boer Wars. At the end of the wars in 1902, Britain had won the Transvaal and declared the union of South Africa in 1910. After this time mining became more organized.

Instead of creating wealth for all, the gold mines actually increased the subjugation of black workers, who were barred from skilled jobs and therefore forced down the mines, charged heavy taxes, and paid poorly. Racial segregation and Apartheid policies dominate the city's more recent history.

When Apartheid ended in 1991, non-whites finally received political freedom, but further work is needed to ease the poverty of the masses.

BELOW: *Cakes and pastries in Fourno's Bakery.*

1866
Johannesburg is founded with the discovery of gold

1922
A white miners strike (the Rand Revolt) leads to a bloody three-month conflict

1940
Many blacks start to be forcibly relocated to the South-Western townships (Soweto)

1948
The National Party establishes a formal system of Apartheid (racial segregation)

1976
Police gun down student protestors in Soweto as unrest against Apartheid grows

key dates

Kabul

- Population: 3,150,000
- More than 24 percent of all imports to Kabul are from Pakistan
- The Kabul Central Bank managed to save 20,000 pieces of gold jewelry from the fundamentalist Taliban government
- The Afghan Mine Detection Center in Kabul employs 244 mine sniffing dogs

AFGHANISTAN'S FOUNDING FATHER

Ahmad Shah (1724–73), the founder of Afghanistan's Durrani Dynasty, was the son of a chief of the Abdali tribe. While a boy, he fell into the hands of the rival Gilzai tribe. In 1738, Ahmad was rescued by Nadir Shah and given command of a body of cavalry. On the assassination of Nadir in 1747, Ahmad persuaded the Afghan tribes to assert their independence and was elected King (Shah) by an assembly of Pashtun chiefs. His rule was marked by repeated invasions of the Punjab and Kashmir. At the height of his power, in 1756, his forces sacked Delhi. He is considered the founder of modern Afghanistan.

Kabul is Afghanistan's capital and its largest city. An important economic and cultural center, it is strategically situated in a narrow valley by the Kabul River, in high mountains west of the Khyber Pass. Highways link Kabul with Pakistan (via Jalalabad and Quetta), as well as with Iran (via Kandahar and Herat). Another highway leads north, through the Salang Tunnel—the highest road tunnel in the world—beneath the Hindu Kush Mountains to Mazar-i-Sharif and Uzbekistan. Kabul's main products include armaments, textiles, furniture, and sugar beet, though continual warfare between 1979 and 1981 has limited the economic productivity of the city.

Old Kabul is a city of crowded bazaars and narrow, winding streets. Kabul has a university, established in 1931, and a number of colleges. Major cultural sites include the Tombs of Babur and Timur Shah, the Mausoleum of Nadir Shah, and various important mosques. Outside the city proper stand a citadel and the royal palace, both badly damaged by years of warfare. Kabul Museum, which used to have one of the finest

BELOW LEFT: *Children in the streets of Kabul.* BELOW RIGHT: *The Kabul Museum, which houses the most comprehensive record of Central Asian history.* BOTTOM: *A busy market scene.*

collections of antiquities in Asia, has had nearly three-quarters of its collections looted or destroyed. It is still possible to see the remaining artifacts, but museum hours are erratic. It was once possible to walk the five-hour length of the crumbling mud walls of the ancient citadel, Bala Hissar, but these are now off limits and considered dangerous due to unexploded bombs and landmines. The pleasant Gardens of Babur are a cool retreat near the city walls, and one of the most peaceful and beautiful spots in the city.

Reconstructing the City

Public transportation in the city is currently overcrowded, with fewer than 200 public buses for a population of between 2 and 4 million. A US$23 million project to restore and expand the public electric bus system is currently re-establishing some 30 miles (50km) of track and 50 vehicles. The goal is to have buses running along one line by mid-2005. Expertise and training are coming from the Czech Republic; in addition, India, Iran, and Japan have agreed to provide more regular buses for the city. Three banks currently operate in Kabul: the Standard Chartered Bank, Punjab National Bank, and the Habib Bank of Pakistan. The Kabul Hotel stands in the center of town and has been restored at a cost of US$25 million, while the prestigious Intercontinental Hotel is currently undergoing major reconstruction.

BELOW: *View from Nadir Shah's mausoleum toward the Queen's mausoleum.*

THE STORY OF...

Arab Muslim forces captured Kabul in AD664. Over the next six centuries, Samanid, Ghaznavid, and Ghorid Dynasties controlled the city in turn.

In the 13th century the Mongols passed through, causing great destruction. In the 14th century, Kabul rose again as a trading center under Timur. The city was captured in 1504 and made into a capital by the Mughal Emperor Babur. Nadir Shah of Persia captured it in 1738; during the mid-18th century Ahmad Shah Durrani reasserted Afghan rule.

The British captured Kabul in 1839, but were driven out in 1841. A year later they returned, sacking Bala Hissar fort before retreating to India. In the early 20th century, King Amanullah (1892–1960) introduced electricity, and schooling for girls.

The Soviet Union occupied the city in 1979, starting a 10-year civil war. Kabul fell to mujahideen forces in 1992, but tens of thousands of civilians were killed in factional fighting. Taliban fundamentalists captured the city in 1996, but were driven out by United States forces and the Northern Alliance in 2001.

BELOW: *Souvenirs for sale in a market in Kabul.*

300BC
Records of the Persian Achaemenids refer to a settlement known as Kabura

1504
Zahiruddin Muhammad Babur, the first Mughal emperor, captures Kabul and makes it his capital

1738
Nadir Shah of Persia, founder of the Afsharid dynasty, captures Kabul

1939
The USSR invades Afghanistan and occupies Kabul on 23 December

2004
Hamid Karzai presides over the first democratically elected Afghan legislature

Marrakesh

Population: 848,000

Highest mosque: Koutoubia Mosque, at 230ft (70m)

Largest conference center in Morocco: le Palais des Congrès, taking 5,500 people

Number of gates: 8 (Bab Agnaou, Bab el Khémis, Bab Aghmat, Bab Er Rob, Bab Aylen, Bab ed Dbbagh, Bab Ahmar, Bab Doukkala)

Situated in southwestern Morocco in North Africa, at the foot of the Haut Atlas (High Atlas) mountains that reach to over 13,000ft (4000m), Marrakesh has always been a place of strategic importance. At one time, the city was the rendezvous for trade caravans traveling through the Sahara Desert with salt, gold, sugar, and slaves, and it is still used as a meeting point and trading post for Berbers and tribesmen from the south. The largest population of Marrakesh are actually Berbers, followed by Arabs, then migrants, nomads and former slaves from the desert and beyond in Africa, and finally Europeans. In recent years, more Europeans have bought property, captured by the stylish architecture and artisan lifestyle. Behind the thriving bustle of Marrakesh is high unemployment, although tourism plays a major part in the economy. The tourist trade has been significantly boosted by

ABOVE (TOP): *The Djemma El Fna (the main town square) at night.* ABOVE (BELOW): *View over the Djemma El Fna from the Café de France.* RIGHT: *Berber carpets and spices in the Criée Berbère market.*

ANCIENT SOUQS

Set out in a labyrinth of narrow streets within the old city, Médina, are the ancient souqs (markets) of Marrakesh. Lit by shafts of light through thatched roofs, the stalls and stores hum with workers who are busy at the important local industries of leatherwork, woodturning, metalwork, and the tanning of animal skins. Just about everything is sold here, from tortoises, lizards, and chameleons, to olives, spices, and silver from the Sahara. Hedgehogs are sold as a delicacy and the famed Moroccan carpets woven by the Berber tribes are bought by many foreigners, who are expected to follow the custom and haggle over the price.

Morocco's modern King, who plans new museums, attractions, and living quarters to take the city into the 21st century.

In the past Marrakesh attracted artists, including the former British Prime Minister Sir Winston Churchill (1874–1965), who went there to paint. The white of the winter snow on the mountains is one of four colors which make up the city, the others are the blue of the sky, the ocher color of the city walls, and the green of the palms and mandarin trees. The city is split into two. The Médina is the old city, which has the palaces and the souqs, while outside is the Guéliz, the modern city built by the French. Africa meets Europe with camels and cars in the traffic, and dusty streets mixed with wide boulevards. Piercing the skyline is the 12th-century Koutoubia Mosque, described as the most perfect Islamic monument in North Africa, which sets the scene for some of the finest architecture of the Arab world. Legend has it that when it was built it bled its spirit into the city, giving the buildings their rose red hue. The Palais de la Bahia (Palace of the Brilliant) is a lavish royal palace, with a harem for the Grand Vizier's wives and concubines. Tombeaux Saadiens (Saadian Tombs) is a preserved mausoleum built by Sultan Ahmed el Mansour.

The Greatest Circus on Earth

The most famous attraction is Djemma El Fna, a huge square nicknamed the greatest circus on earth. Marrakesh has yet to build dedicated theaters or dance institutions and so the city's best performers put on shows here. The square buzzes with storytellers, acrobats, jugglers, water sellers, magicians, and musicians, performing amidst the aroma from bubbling cauldrons of lamb stew.

BACKGROUND: *Ramparts with the Haut Atlas Mountains behind.*

BELOW: *Musicians in the Djemma El Fna in Marrakesh.*

THE STORY OF...

For 1,000 years the area was ruled by Phoenicians, Romans, Byzantines and Greeks, although the high mountains remained in the hold of the first Berber tribes (from the Greek "barbarian")—a tribe of warriors who took root in the Atlas Mountains and from there defended their bastion.

In 1062, Marrakesh was founded by the Almoravid Berbers of the Western Sahara. Kingdoms, dynasties, wars and feuds followed until the Treaty of Féz (1912) made Morocco a protectorate of France.

In 1956, Morocco became independent from France and Sultan Mohammed became King Mohammed V. During the 1960s Marrakesh became very popular with Westerners and a playground for rock musicians, photographers and artisans.

Under King Hassan II much of the economy was nationalized and poor decisions led to poverty, resulting in mass migration in the 1980s. Hours after his death in 1999, Hassan's son, King Mohammed VI, promised to tackle the country's poverty, corruption and human rights record.

BELOW: *Men in traditional dress on the Djemma El Fna.*

1062
City is founded

1912
Morocco becomes a protectorate of France

1956
Morocco gains independence

1961
Hassan II becomes King

1999
Mohammed VI becomes King

statistics

- Population: 2,850,000

- 40 percent of Nairobi's population are Kikuyu, Kenya's largest ethnic group

- The Bomas (homesteads) of Kenya, just south of Nairobi, houses the largest theater in Africa, accommodating up to 3,500 people

- A resident of Kibera, Nairobi's largest slum, pays five times as much as the average North American for a liter of water

Nairobi

Nairobi lies about 275 miles (440km) north-west of Mombasa, on the edge of the East African Highlands, at an altitude of 5,590ft (1,700m). Once a leisurely colonial town, the Kenyan capital is now a crowded metropolis. Nairobi continued to grow at a prodigious rate throughout the 20th and into the 21st centuries and is now the largest city between Cairo and Johannesburg. Almost all of the colonial-era buildings were replaced by modern office buildings during the burst of new construction that followed Uhuru (independence) in 1963, and the skyline of downtown Nairobi is marked by high-rise apartments and offices. Most of the adult population are migrants, chiefly country people seeking work in light industries and commerce in the industrialized south of the city. Many such people are transient, maintaining close ties with their rural homes and often eventually returning to them.

Today, Nairobi is a bustling city in the grip of a seemingly endless crime wave. Heavy-handed policing and political disputes often result in violent demonstrations, particularly when the government embarks on one of its slum-clearing operations.

BELOW LEFT: *The Peace Monument at Uhuru Park in Nairobi.* BELOW CENTER: *The Langata Giraffe Center.*

KENYA'S "GUIDING LIGHT"

Jomo Kenyatta (1889–1978) was born near Nairobi. He received his primary education at the Scottish Mission Center, and in the 1930s studied in the UK and the Soviet Union. Kenyatta spent the war years in England and participated in the 5th Pan African Congress at Manchester, in the UK, in 1945. In 1946 he returned to Kenya, and was arrested in 1952 and imprisoned for insurgency. He was released in 1961 and became President of the Kenya African National Union. On 1 June 1963, he became the first Prime Minister of independent Kenya, becoming known as "Father of the Nation". He died on 22 August 1978, aged 89.

ABOVE: *The statue of Jomo Kenyatta on his Nairobi mausoleum.*

Services remain strained by the rapidly growing population and there are substantial slums on the outskirts of town, especially to the south and east. Religious violence is on the increase, and in 1998 militants linked to al Qaeda blew up the US Embassy on Moi Avenue, killing more than 200 Kenyans. More positively, the city is both culturally vibrant and economically productive. Presidential elections in 2002 were widely expected to spark a Nairobi tinderbox, yet after losing the poll, Daniel Arap Moi (b. 1924), contrary to all expectations, relinquished power to Mwai Kibaki (b. 1931) without a struggle.

An International City

The population of Nairobi is overwhelmingly African, though there are economically significant South Asian and European communities. The city is home to Nairobi and Kenyatta Universities, the prestigious Nairobi Museum, and the Kenyatta Conference Center. It is also the headquarters of two UN agencies, concerned with the environment and with human settlement. Road and rail links with Kenya's main port, Mombasa, as with Kisumu on Lake Victoria and the Ugandan capital, Kampala, are excellent. Jomo Kenyatta International Airport is one of the busiest in Africa, with continent-wide links, as well as flights to Europe, Asia, and North America. Nairobi is also unique in Africa in having a protected game reserve, Nairobi National Park, within its boundaries.

Nairobi

THE STORY OF...

Nairobi is a young city, founded in 1899 by Sir George Whitehead during the construction of the Kenya–Uganda Railway. The first camp was established by a swamp on the edge of the Rift Valley in flatlands known to the indigenous Masai people as *enhare nairobi* or "cool waters", a name later shortened to Nairobi.

It was rebuilt at the beginning of the 20th century, after an outbreak of plague and the burning of the town. The settlement grew rapidly, and in 1905 the seat of government moved from Mombasa to Nairobi.

In 1907, the city became the capital of the British East African Protectorate. As the capital, the future of the city was assured and wealth began to flow into the city.

Nairobi's Eastleigh Airport became an important landing strip in the pre-jet airline era, being used as a halfway stop on the 1930s and 1940s British passenger and mail route to Cape Town.

Nairobi became the capital of independent Kenya in 1963. Going from strength to strength, the city continues to expand.

BELOW: *Flowers on display at the market in Nairobi.*

key dates

1899
Founded originally as a railroad camp for the Uganda Railway

1907
Becomes capital of the British East Africa Protectorate, replacing Mombasa

1963
On 12 December, the flag of newly independent Kenya is raised in Nairobi

1998
The al Qaeda terrorist network bombs the US Embassy; 213 are people killed, and more than 5,000 injured

2004
Nairobi hosts first UN Security Council meeting ever to be held in Africa

171

Tel Aviv-Yafo

statistics

- Population: 365,000 (1.1 million in greater Gush Dan area)
- Religious affiliation: 80 percent Jewish, 18 percent Muslim, 1.7 percent Christian, and 1.3 percent Druze
- Tel Aviv's Central Bus Station is said to be the largest in the world, covering 0.09 sq miles (0.23 sq km)
- The Tel Aviv suburb of Ramat Gan is home to the world's largest diamond exchange, with 1,000 offices and 2,500 members

Tel Aviv lies at the center of a major urban conglomeration on the eastern shore of the Mediterranean Sea. This urban sprawl, which is known in Hebrew as Gush Dan, includes Bat Yam, Holon, Ramat Gan, Givatayim, Bnei-Nrak, Petah-Tikvah, Rishon LeZion, Ramat Ha-'Sharon, and Herzliya. The city of Tel Aviv-Yafo is Israel's commercial, financial, communications, and cultural center. Right by the sea, it is also an important tourist resort. Despite Yafo's long Arab past, today virtually the entire population is Jewish. Construction is the main industry; textiles, clothing, and processed food are the chief manufactures, and pharmaceuticals, electrical appliances, printed materials, and chemicals are also produced. The city is a major diamond-processing center.

The main access route for Tel Aviv is the Ayalon Highway, which runs north-south through the city providing excellent road links to Haifa in the north and Jerusalem to the southeast. Tel Aviv has four railway stations along the Ayalon Highway, and it is estimated that about 1 million people use the train from Rishon LeZion and Petah-Tikva to central Tel Aviv each month. The city's huge Central Bus Station is located in the southern part of town. Tel Aviv's airport is Dov Hoz, located at the north of the city, and this serves as a major airport for domestic flights. Ben Gurion International Airport, which is Israel's main international hub and also serves Tel Aviv, is located 9 miles (15km) to the southeast, near the city of Lod.

BELOW: *Stopping for a conversation in the street.*
RIGHT: *View over the city.*
OPPOSITE: *The Corniche.*
OPPOSITE BELOW: *Crowded Jaffa Market.*

YITZHAK RABIN (1922–95)

Born in Jerusalem, Yitzhak Rabin began his political life as a soldier, joining the Jewish Palmach guerrillas in 1940. Between 1948 and 1968 he fought in all Israel's wars, commanding the Israeli Defence Forces during the 1967 Six-Day War. Later, as a politician, he twice served as Israeli Prime Minister (1974–77 and 1992–95). In 1992, he played a leading role in the Oslo Peace Accords, and in 1994—along with Shimon Peres (b. 1923) and Yasser Arafat (1929–2004)—he was awarded the Nobel Peace Prize. In 1995, he was assassinated by a Jewish extremist in Tel Aviv's Kings of Israel Square, since renamed Yitzhak Rabin Square in his honour.

A Center of Culture

Tel Aviv University has a reputation for academic excellence, particularly in science and computer technology. Cultural centers include the Opera House and the Tel Aviv Culture Hall. The Eretz Israel Museum is famous for its archaeological and historical exhibits, and the Tel Aviv Arts Museum for its fine-art exhibitions. The Israeli Defence Forces Museum documents the history of Israel's struggle to survive, while the Palmach Museum offers an experience of Israel's military struggles against the British and the Palestinian Arabs. In Yafo there is a small museum dedicated to the forces who conquered Jaffa in the Arab–Israeli War of 1948. On the campus of Tel Aviv University, the Diaspora Museum is dedicated to Jewish history and culture worldwide.

THE STORY OF...

The twin cities of Tel Aviv-Yafo have very different histories. Yafo—Yafa in Arabic—dates back at least as far as the 16th century BC. According to legend, its name derives from Japheth, a son of Noah who settled here. It is also believed that Jonah sailed from Yafo before being swallowed by the whale.

It has long been an important port, controlled at different times by Phoenicians, Greeks, Arabs, Turks, and Crusaders. It was captured by the Arabs in AD637, and briefly occupied by Napoleon Bonaparte (1769–1821) in 1799.

Yafo remained an almost exclusively Arab city until the foundation of Israel. Yafo's larger twin, Tel Aviv, was established in 1906 as Ahuzat Bayit ("Housing Estate") by the Convention of the Jews of Yafo, a group of around 60 families. Later the name was changed to Tel Aviv, or "Hill of Spring". The new city, contiguous with Yafo, grew rapidly and soon became a major Jewish center.

In 1948, Tel Aviv became the first capital of modern Israel and then, in 1950, Tel Aviv and Yafo were united to become Tel Aviv-Yafo.

1906
City of Tel Aviv is founded (as Ahuzat Bayit) by Jewish settlers, near the ancient Palestinian port of Yafa (Jaffa)

1948
Jewish forces seize Yafo and proclaim Tel Aviv the first capital of independent Israel

1950
Tel Aviv and Yafo unite in a single municipality, Tel Aviv-Yafo

1970
Israel unilaterally transfers its capital to Jerusalem, but the move is not recognized in international law and most embassies remain in Tel Aviv

2004
Tel Aviv's White City is declared a World Heritage Site by UNESCO

The Americas

The great cities of the so-called New World are new enough to reveal their colonial origins, whether in the Spanish culture of Havana, the French traditions of Québec, the Portuguese in Rio, or the British in Boston (but glittering Las Vegas, in its present form, is surely all-American). The regular block grids of New York and Washington DC show a degree of planning that has been long lost in older, apparently more organic cities, while shanty fringes of hubs such as Mexico City and Caracas, created as poverty drives people from the land and into town, show the uneven spread of wealth in emerging cities. Yet there is a vibrancy about these places that is the envy of the rest of the world, whether it's seen in the spirit and energy of the south, or the confident new sky-towers of the north.

Boston

- Population: 589,141
- The Big Dig is a 14-year tunnel project, designed to ease congestion and reshape the city
- The Big Dig is creating 300 acres (121 ha) of landscaped parkland
- Boston has 34 institutes of higher education

I n Boston, centuries of history stand side-by-side with brick townhouses, church spires, gleaming skyscrapers, and expansive highways. Each district has a story to tell, from the Italian enclave of North End, with its excellent restaurants and former home of Paul Revere (1734–1818)—a key player in the American Revolution—to Beacon Hill, with its white upper-class houses and the seat of the Massachusetts state government. Downtown, mirrored office blocks and busy malls dominate, as much of the original infrastructure was wiped out by fire in 1872, while the leafy Cambridge suburb is monopolized by Harvard University. Like many cities throughout the world, the communities living in Boston's suburbs are polarized, with Malcolm X being one of the former residents of the largely African American area of Roxbury, and a sizeable Chinatown springing up in the early 20th century. These ethnic ghettos underline Boston's complex history, with immigrants from all over the world flocking to the city in the late 19th century. Despite its racial diversity and history as the place where slavery was abolished, racial harmony in the 20th century was largely absent from the city. The disharmony from the race riots that arose in the 1970s, as a result of the authorities' attempts to better integrate white and black children in schools, still hangs over Boston.

Twenty-first century Boston is doing well for itself, with the city's colleges turning out highly educated and well paid graduates, many of whom go on to work in the city's other key fields—health care, financial services, insurance, and federal or state government.

BENJAMIN FRANKLIN (1706–90)

Benjamin Franklin was born in Boston. At the age of 12, he worked as a typesetter for his brother, before moving to Philadelphia in 1723. After a brief period in London, Franklin opened his own publishing house and bought the *Pennsylvania Gazette*. In the 1730s he opened the nation's first subscription library, in Philadelphia. In 1748 Franklin turned to science, inventing bifocals, armbands, lightning rods, and the Franklin Stove. He entered politics in the 1750s, working as a diplomat in England before returning to Philadelphia to draft the Declaration of Independence, which he signed in 1776. From 1785–87, Franklin worked in Europe negotiating treaties with France and Britain. Returning home, Franklin focused on the abolition of slavery.

ABOVE (LEFT TO RIGHT): *Acorn Street in Beacon Hill; an 18th-century statue in front of the Bunker Hill Monument;* USS Constitution; *the sign identifying the home of the Boston Red Sox; the dome of the Old State House.* OPPOSITE: *The John Hancock Tower.*

City of Firsts

Bostonians are proud of their "City of Firsts", staking claim to the oldest underground train system, the oldest university (Harvard), the oldest public park, and the oldest botanical garden in America. Perhaps this pride contributes to the residents' love of outdoor spaces, with Boston Common, Boston Garden, and the city's arboretums (The Bonsai Garden at the Harvard Arboretum is over 200 years old) being popular leisure venues. With 43 miles (69km) of coastline, a revamped waterfront, 30 offshore islands, and the city's lifeblood, Charles River, Boston is a city that is very much dominated by water, with whale watching and harbor cruises among the many activities available. Sport, culture, and nightlife—this is a city with more than 30 universities and colleges after all—are also important to the average Bostonian; Boston has its own theater district and a local passion is supporting the city's Red Sox baseball team.

THE STORY OF...

Puritan-dominated Boston was characterized by intolerance, marginalization of the native population, and the witch trials of the 1660s. Eighteenth-century slaves fared no better, with merchants exporting rum distiled using sugar yielded by unpaid labor. The year 1705 saw the first slaves arrive in the city. In the mid-18th century England increased taxes levied on the colony, sparking early calls for independence from the British Empire. The Boston Massacre and the Boston Tea Party proved a catalyst for the American Revolution, with battles taking place in Boston from 1775 to 1781.

As part of the newly independent United States of America, Boston emerged as a prosperous city, which welcomed immigrants, expanded its territory, and pioneered the abolition of slavery. The city's fortunes declined dramatically after World War II when, as it was no longer a major port, its heavy industry declined and its population fell. Replacing traditional industries with high-tech alternatives and finance, Boston rose to the fore once again in the 1980s.

BELOW: *Rubbing the left foot of John Harvard's statue in front of University Hall is thought to bring good luck.*

1630
Puritans from Britain settle at Shawmut

1770
Boston Tea Party—locals throw 342 chests of tea into the harbor in a political protest

1776
John Hancock signs the Declaration of Independence

2004
The Boston Red Sox win the World Series for the first time in 86 years

key dates

177

Buenos Aires

On the east coast of Argentina, bordered to the north by the Rio de la Plata (River Plate) and by the vast pampa grasslands to the west, Buenos Aires is the country's capital. Forty percent of the Argentine population lives in the city's sprawling suburbs. Known as *porteños*, making reference to the city's port, these people are gregarious and expressive. Roman Catholicism is the main religion, and the language is Spanish.

Designed on a Spanish colonial grid system, the city is divided into 47 *barrios* (neighborhoods). The city center is known as Capital Federal (federal district) and boasts beautiful European architecture, wide boulevards, cobbled streets, and landscaped parks. It also suffers pollution, overcrowding, and the faded elegance that comes with an historic city. Central points are the Plaza de Mayo (May Square) and its landmark building Casa Rosada (Pink House) the presidential palace beneath whose balcony mass rallies cheered former president Juan Perón (1895–1974) and his charismatic wife, Eva "Evita" Perón (1919–52). The Catedral Metropolitana holds the remains of Argentinian liberator José de San Martín (1778–1850), and the Teatro Colón is one of the world's best known opera houses. The bohemian streets of San Telmo, the birthplace of the tango, are in sharp contrast to the hectic Avenida 9 de Julio, (the world's widest street), which is usually choked with 16 lanes of traffic.

A local culinary custom is to hold an *asado* (barbecue) with a whole lamb roasted on a spit. This is followed by the ritual of making and drinking maté, an infusion made from the leaf of the Paraguayan tea plant. Fashionable *porteños* dine in the plethora of restaurants, cafés, and bars of what has become the cosmopolitan and cultural capital of South America.

TANGO

Originating in brothels in the working-class quarters of 19th-century Buenos Aires, the tango is the national dance of Argentina and practised in countless bars, theaters, clubs, and schools. From 1902, when the city's Teatro Colón launched tango balls, the dance became a craze and by the 1920s had spread to high society in Paris. In Buenos Aires today, Sundays are devoted to tango shows and the city also holds an Annual Tango Day in December.

ABOVE: *The Avenido 9 de Julio, the world's widest street.*
OPPOSITE: *La Boca is a famous walkway where artists exhibit their work.*

A Passion for Soccer

Capital Federal is the financial, industrial, and commercial center of Argentina, with one of the busiest ports in the world and industries such as oil refining, car manufacturing, and metalwork. It also processes and manufactures meat (though beef is no longer the dominant trading commodity it once was) plus wool, grain, tobacco, and animal skins for export. Arguably Argentina's best export is soccer and in Buenos Aires it is a serious passion. Many city teams are in the first division of the major league and there is high rivalry between River Plate and Boca Juniors. The most famous Argentine soccer player, Diego Maradona (b. 1960) came to prominence with Boca Juniors, before his infamous "Hand of God" goal for Argentina against England in the World Cup of 1986.

THE STORY OF...

Buenos Aires was founded twice, first by Don Pedro de Mendoza, a Spanish gold-hunter in 1536 (the settlers, however, were forced away by the indigenous people, the Querandí Indians), and then again in 1580 by the Spaniards of the nearby city of Asunción, led by Juan de Garay. In 1810 the people of Buenos Aires ousted the Spanish Viceroy and established a provincial government. Six years later, independence from Spain was granted, although not officially recognized until 1862. The railways came in the 19th century, during which time Spanish, Italian, Russian, and Polish immigrants began arriving in the city.

By the 20th century, migrants from other Latin American countries had settled and their descendants give the city its cosmopolitan feel. A huge modernization program during the 1930s brought the broad avenues that give Buenos Aires its visual character. More recently, deep recession led to economic collapse in 2001, but by 2003 a recovery was underway.

BELOW: *Captain Daniel Passarella holds the 1978 World Cup trophy.*

1536
First settlement is founded

1580
Second and final settlement is founded and becomes Buenos Aires

1862
Independence from Spain is recognized

1978
City hosts and wins World Cup

2001
Economic collapse

key dates

179

Caracas

statistics

- Population: 5,500,000
- The Museum of Contemporary Art houses the largest collection of Picasso etchings in South America
- Venezuela is the fifth-largest exporter of oil in the world and the only Western member of OPEC
- More than 60 percent of the population lives in *barrios,* or illegal settlements

Set in the shadow of Mount Avila, Caracas is a vast metropolis that follows the sprawling progress of fast-moving expressways that link 12.5 miles (20km) of suburbs and districts, each with their own character and atmosphere, along a narrow coastal valley. The city has some outstanding modern architecture, with leading works by Gio Ponti (1891–1979) and Fernand Léger (1881–1955). Its beautifully landscaped parks make it one of South America's greenest capitals, but it also has some shockingly austere concrete buildings and some of Latin America's most impoverished *barrios*. Downtown, the city stretches for 5 miles (8km), from El Silencio to Chacao. The remnants of the city's historic center are to the west—museums, theaters, and cinemas are clustered around the Parque Central and hotels, stores, and restaurants run along the bustling Sabana Grande shopping district. Further to the east, the smart suburbs of Altamira, El Rosal, and Las Mercedes offer a mixture of residential buildings, nightclubs, and restaurants.

FAR LEFT: *The National Pantheon, where Simón Bolívar is buried.*
LEFT: *The Ayacucho Colonial Theater.*
BELOW: *A sculpture by Alejandro Otero called "Abra Solar" in Plaza Venezuela.*

SIMÓN "EL LIBERTADOR" BOLÍVAR (1783–1830)

Caracas is the birthplace of Simón "El Libertador" Bolívar, hero of Latin America's independence movement and now immortalized in countless statues, street names, and folklore. Though he led the military resistance against the Spanish, his vision of a "Gran Colombia" (uniting Venezuela, Colombia, and Ecuador) did not match the regional ambitions of the newly independent states. He finally died in poverty in Colombia, and it was 12 years before his body was returned home. Now his contribution is newly recognized: Venezuela's currency is the bolívar and the country has been renamed the Bolivarian Republic of Venezuela.

ABOVE: *Simón Bolívar statue.*

Living Art

Caracas is a vital center for modern art and sculpture. It has some of the continent's most outstanding buildings, including the University—a World Heritage Site designed by Carlos Raúl Villanueva (1900–75), and some of its finest museums, especially the Museum of Contemporary Art. But it is also very much a city of the modern age, with a thriving artistic scene where civic sculptures, quietly sophisticated galleries, and public murals combine with a lively tradition of street art and graffiti. It is also intensely musical, blending the influences of Africa, the Caribbean, and Spain into a hectic mix that blares from every car and bus, and fuels a lively, energetic life.

Green City

Few residents live far from a park of some sort, with the most popular being the Parque del Este, designed by Brazilian landscape architect Robert Burle Marx (1909–94) in 1956. Every Sunday huge crowds hike or take the cable car into the brooding wilderness regions of Mount Avila in a sort of dawn *passeo*, where being seen is as important as the exercise. Set 3,000ft (900m) above sea level, Caracas has a pleasant climate of perpetual spring and the sparkling metro system, as clean now as when it opened in 1983, makes it easy to get around. Most Caraqueños believe they have the best of all possible worlds, with an open attitude that looks equally to their own vast and beautiful southern hinterland, the Caribbean Sea at their feet, and the sophistication of America's Miami beyond.

THE STORY OF...

Though the city was first founded by colonial Spain in 1560, resistance by indigenous Toromaima Indians meant it only became established seven years later. Failing to find gold or silver in Venezuela, the Spanish turned to cocoa for revenue, but this labor-intensive crop required skills the indigenous people could not, or would not, provide. Spanish immigrants flooded in alongside slaves from Africa, altering the country's racial makeup. Always at the center of the rebellion against colonial rule, Caracas was also the focus of the most determined Spanish military campaigns, but emerged in 1830 as the capital of an independent Venezuela.

Oil was discovered in 1920 and the revenue from this resulted, in the 1950s, in the city being almost completely rebuilt according to the vision of modernist architects, while further waves of immigrants from rural areas and neighboring Colombia have set up contrasting slums, teetering on sheer slopes and filling in spaces between rich suburbs. Caracas remains one of South America's most divided cities.

1560
Explorer Francisco Fajarda discovers a verdant valley farmed by local Indians and founds the city

1810
Caracas becomes the center for the first revolt against Spanish rule. Two years later it is destroyed in an earthquake, blamed by the church on its rebel sympathies

1920
Oil money brings a rush of development, gathering pace in the 1950s, when leading architects are invited in to replace most of the old city

1999
Mudslides destroy hillside slum dwellings, killing between 30,000 and 50,000 people

2002
A right-wing media campaign to destabilize the government of Hugo Chavez results in a coup. Despite American backing, it lasts only one day, but the political situation remains unstable

181

Chicago

Chicago is situated in Illinois, the heart of the American Midwest, and sits on the shores of Lake Michigan. Although it is easily the largest city in the state, it is not the capital (which is Springfield). Chicago is nicknamed the "Windy City," most likely because of the frequent winds blowing through the city streets, but also, possibly, because of the boasts by the inhabitants about their city after it was rebuilt following the Great Fire of 1871, or even as a reference to the blustering of early local politicians.

Because of its reputation at the turn of the 20th century as a place full of opportunity, Chicago attracted many black people from the Deep South, as well as Irish and Eastern European immigrants. Even today, it is said to have the largest Polish population outside Warsaw. Criminal activity increased in Chicago during the Prohibition era of the Roaring Twenties, with gangsters Al Capone (1899–1947) and George "Bugsy" Moran (1893–1957), major figures during a time when the city had a wild reputation.

Fine Buildings and Music

Regarded as the birthplace of modern American architecture, Chicago claims that the nine-storey Home Insurance Building, erected in 1885, was the world's first skyscraper. Today, Chicago's many fine structures include the Wrigley Building (home of the chewing-gum company), the Sears Tower (formerly the world's tallest), the John Hancock Center (with huge Xs on each side), the Gothic-style Tribune Tower and the Beaux-Art Chicago Cultural Center. In the lakeside Millennium Park, the curved metal forms of the Pritzker Music Pavilion were designed by Frank Gehry (b. 1929).

Chicago is steeped in music, with jazz and blues pouring out of a host of bars and clubs, the Chicago Symphony Orchestra delighting audiences, and summer festivals attracting thousands every year. Claimed to be the blues capital of the world, Chicago can trace its musical roots back to the sounds of the slaves and folk "hollers" of the 1920s. The city's "urban-style" of music developed after the Wall Street Crash of 1929, but really came to prominence in the 1940s and 1950s, with the rise of artists such as bluesman Muddy Waters (1915–83). He was an inspiration to, and influence on the Rolling Stones, who named themselves after his first single, "Rollin' Stone."

LEFT: *A street performer on the 1916 Navy Pier.*
BELOW: *Alexander Calder's "Flamingo" in Chicago's business district.*

statistics

Population: 2,896,016 (Nine-county Metropolitan area: 8,272,768)

Chicago has three of the world's tallest buildings

The third largest city in the United States, with 29 miles (47km) of lakefront parks and 15 miles (24km) of beaches

The city's O'Hare Airport is the second busiest in the world

FRANK LLOYD WRIGHT

Chicago's architecture is world-famous, as is architect Frank Lloyd Wright (1867–1959), who lived in the city suburb of Oak Park and, during his lifetime, designed more than 1,000 buildings, around 100 of which are in the Chicago area. Described as the "pioneer of the Prairie style of architecture"—horizontal designs inspired by the flat landscapes of the American Midwest—he is probably best known for the Robie House in Chicago's Hyde Park, which is considered to be one of the most important buildings in American architecture. His former home (and studio) is now a museum, restored to its 1909 appearance.

ABOVE: *A view of the spiral staircase in The Rookery.*

Chicago is the home of many international American companies, among them United Airlines, McDonald's, and Motorola. It has two world-class universities—the University of Chicago, known for its research in economy, medicine, and sciences, and Northwestern University, famous for its Kellogg Business School.

BELOW (INSET): *A turret on the Historic Water Tower, a pseudo-Gothic creation in yellow limestone, overlooked by modern skyscrapers.*
BELOW: *The high-rise skyline of Downtown Chicago contrasts with the beaches and the expanse of Lake Michigan.*

THE STORY OF...

Chicago's first settlement was built at the mouth of the Chicago River in 1779 by Jean Baptiste Point du Sable, a fur trader of French-African descent from Santo Domingo. In 1830, Chicago was connected with the Mississippi River with the opening of the 100-mile (161km) Illinois and Michigan Canal. The Great Chicago Fire, in 1871, claimed 300 lives, left 90,000 homeless, and caused $200 million worth of damage, but allowed the city to be rebuilt.

In 1893, to provide transportation for the World's Columbian Exposition—which drew nearly 26 million visitors—the Chicago Transit Authority introduced the city's first elevated train system, "the Loop", which encircles the central business district. The World's Fair in 1933 marked 100 years since Chicago was incorporated. Twenty-two years later, Richard J. Daley was elected Mayor of Chicago for the first time. He served as mayor for 21 years and was later followed, in 1989, by his son, Richard M. Daley, who was re-elected for the fourth time in 2003.

1779
A trading post is established on the north bank of the Chicago River

1833
Chicago is incorporated as a town

1871
300 Chicago residents are killed and 90,000 made homeless in The Great Fire

1974
The Sears Tower is completed, at 1,450 feet (442m) the world's tallest building (until 1996)

2004
The Millennium Park is opened to the public

key dates

Havana

- Population: 2,300,000
- Old Havana has the largest concentration of classical Hispanic architecture anywhere in the New World
- Every primary school student takes a minimum of 2 to 3 hours physical education a day
- Jardín Botánico Nacional is the largest botanical garden in Latin America

JOSÉ MARTÍ, THE FATHER OF CUBAN INDEPENDENCE

José Martí (1853–95), the poet, essayist, and journalist, was born in Havana. He joined the independence movement while still at school and, in 1869, was deported to Spain. In 1874 he graduated in law and moved to Mexico, where he continued his anti-colonial activities. In 1878, after the first Cuban War of Independence, he returned to Havana but was re-arrested and again deported to Spain. In 1895 he landed clandestinely in eastern Cuba, but was killed in the first skirmish of Cuba's Second War of Independence. Today he is regarded as the father of the nation and there is a memorial to him in every settlement across the island.

ABOVE: *Monument to José Martí.*

Strategically located astride a natural harbor, Havana is Cuba's largest city, and the social and cultural heart of the island. The city is divided into three distinct sections: historic La Habana Vieja (Old Havana), Centro or Central Havana, and the more wealthy Vedado. Further west, most embassies are located in the relatively affluent Miramar and Playa Districts. The city faces north, toward the Straits of Florida and the United States mainland, and is defined by the two huge Spanish-period castles of El Morro and La Cabaña, as well as by the renowned 5-mile (8km) long Malecón, or sea wall. La Habana Vieja is the oldest, largest and most impressive historic site in Latin America, with a magnificent cathedral dating from 1748, as well as numerous museums, memorials, art galleries, churches, and bastions. Centro is dominated by the Capitolio Nacional, unashamedly modeled on the Capitol Building in Washington, while Vedado is home to the Plaza de la Revolución, Havana University, and the monumental Necrópolis Cristóbal Colón, Cuba's most important cemetery, named after the intrepid navigator Christopher Columbus (1451–1506).

The population of Havana is predominantly of Spanish descent, though there is a considerable black presence originating from West Africa, notably the descendants of Yoruba people from present-day Nigeria. As a result of long years of intermarriage, there is a substantial *mestizo*, or mixed-race, population and racism, once prevalent under the Spanish authorities and during the first decades of independence, has greatly diminished under the government of Fidel Castro. Central Havana is an elegant but run-down metropolis, which suffered serious neglect in the decades following the Cuban Revolution of 1959. The situation has slowly improved since La Habana Vieja was declared a UNESCO World Heritage Site in 1982, but large areas to the south and east of the city remain crumbling, Soviet-style slums.

ABOVE (TOP): *Souvenir stall at El Morro.*
ABOVE (BOTTOM): *Restored building in La Habana Vieja (the old city).*

Commerce and Culture

Havana is a sophisticated city, with an international reputation as a center for the fine arts, music, and dance. Two of the most famous products of the city, indeed of the island itself, are rum and cigars. The city also serves as Cuba's center of government, medicine, education, scientific research, communications, and trade. It is home to much of the island's heavy and light industry, including power stations, chemical plants, paper mills, textile factories, and shipyards. Until 1989 the former Soviet Union was a major trade partner and source of aid. However, since the collapse of the USSR, Havana has emerged as a major tourist destination, earning millions of dollars annually for the Cuban economy.

BELOW AND OPPOSITE: *The beach at Havana's Playa del Este.*
BELOW RIGHT (INSET): *Women in traditional Cuban dress in Havana's Plaza de la Catedral.*

The exact date of the founding of La Habana (Havana) is unclear. A settlement called San Cristóbal de Habana was established by the conquistador Pánfilo de Narváez in 1514. Over the next five years it was moved three times, finally relocating to its present position in 1519. The city soon became Spain's major port for expeditions to the nearby mainland, and it grew rapidly in prosperity. In 1533 Havana became the official residence of the Spanish governor, but this did not stop English privateers from sacking the city in 1622, 1623, and 1638.

By the 18th century, Havana was the third largest city in Latin America, though still at the mercy of the English, who occupied it for six months in 1762. Havana reached the height of its wealth on the back of the sugar boom in the 19th century, becoming capital of independent Cuba in 1902. By the middle of the 20th century, Havana had acquired a reputation as a corrupt playground for North Americans, but this ended with Fidel Castro's (b. 1926) victorious revolution in 1959.

BELOW: *Shopping in Havana's Mercado Agropecuario.*

Havana

1519
Havana founded in its present position

1607
Becomes official capital of Cuba

1762
The British capture the city, but return it to Spanish rule the following year

1898
US battleship *Maine* blown up in Havana harbor; precipitates Spanish–American War

1959
A victorious Fidel Castro enters Havana

185

Las Vegas

statistics

Population: 535,000

Marriage ceremonies performed each day: 150

Number of hotel rooms: 130,000 and growing

Average spend by tourists on gambling: $480 each

WEDDINGS

Almost 40 wedding chapels exist in Las Vegas. Couples can marry in a traditional ceremony or with an Elvis Presley impersonator singing as the bride and groom walk down the aisle. Marriages are also performed in the hotels, in hot air balloons, or during a bungee jump. Around 100,000 couples are married here each year because in Las Vegas it is quick and easy. No blood tests, birth certificates, or waiting periods are required and marriage licences can be obtained for a small fee 24 hours a day. Famous people that have got married in Las Vegas include Elvis and Priscilla Presley, Frank Sinatra and Mia Farrow, and Bruce Willis and Demi Moore.

Seen from the air, day and night, as a crowd of flashing lights, the largest city in the state of Nevada in the United States sits in an arid basin surrounded by rocky mountains and desert. Former playground of the gangsters of the 1930s, the city that they say "never sleeps" is now a major tourist resort, existing to satisfy the needs of its visitors. Las Vegas was created with the fun and fortune seeker in mind, rather than as a city in which to set up home. However, this is the fastest growing metropolis in the US and its hotels and gaming casinos demand a multitude of workers. More schools are opening and Las Vegas has more churches and places of worship than any other city in any US state, at least 580. Added to this, the rise in banking, real estate, and light industries such as textiles, together with an influx of Asian businesses setting up shop, means that the city is diversifying.

Downtown is the famous "Strip", a 4.5-mile (7km) long avenue, cruised by stretch limousines and lined with ultra-extravagant hotels that are attractions in themselves. Luxor replicates the Sphinx and the pyramids of Egypt, and has a spotlight at its apex which can be seen from space. New York City replicates the New York skyline and Caesar's Palace has an enormous shopping mall, and now a replica of the Roman Coliseum. The Venetian doubles as the Guggenheim Hermitage Museum, with priceless artworks from various permanent collections. The Bellagio is fronted with dancing fountains, and The Mirage has an erupting volcano.

The Business of Tourism

Costing $2.5 billion, the Wynn Las Vegas is the most expensive hotel in the world to date, with an in-house Ferrari and Maserati dealership. Each hotel contains a casino, ringing with the sound of slot machines disgorging nickels and quarters. People are poised around tables playing blackjack, poker, or baccarat. Over recent years, Las Vegas has boosted tourism numbers by changing from "Sin City" and a source of adult entertainment, into a massive family attraction and theme park for children. Tourism brings in $32 billion a year, with an average spend by each tourist of $480 on gambling. By the end of 2004, Las Vegas was expected to host a record-breaking 37 million visitors, with an additional $6 billion being spent on new construction.

CLOCKWISE FROM TOP: *The Bellagio Hotel immortalized in the movie* Ocean's Eleven; *view down the Las Vegas Strip; the Riviera Hotel; the Vegas Vic in Fremont in the oldest part of the city.*

THE STORY OF...

Desert Indians used Las Vegas as a base and the Paiutes hunter-gatherers occupied the valley. Las Vegas, meaning the fertile valleys, was named by Spanish travelers who would stop at the springs for water on the Old Spanish Trail from Texas. In 1854, Mormon fathers settled at the oasis, although they abandoned the site a few years later. The US Army built Fort Baker and Las Vegas continued to be an important water spot on the wagon trails and the railroad.

In 1905, when 110 acres (44.5 ha) of what later became Downtown was auctioned off, Las Vegas city was officially founded. After gambling was legalized in 1931, Las Vegas grew bigger and brighter. Huge hotels, each with a gambling casino at its core, were built; many allegedly backed by money from notorious gangsters of the time. Gamblers, fortune seekers, and tourists began flocking to the city, swelling both population and profit, and turning Las Vegas into the "Entertainment Capital of the World"—a boom which shows no signs of abating.

BELOW: *Harley Davidson café.*

key dates

1854
A town is first settled by Mormon fathers

1864
US Army builds Fort Baker

1905
The City of Las Vegas is officially founded

1931
Gambling is legalized

2000
MGM Grand Inc. announces purchase of Mirage Resorts Inc., the largest corporate buyout in gaming history

Lima

THE GOLD OF PERU MUSEUM

It was gold that fired the Spanish conquistadors in their conquest of South America, and Peru was their richest source. Gold sculptures and artifacts were looted from Andean temples and graves, and almost all were immediately melted down and shipped to Europe. In the process, incalculable artistic treasures were lost. A museum was founded in 1968 to collect what remained, and the privately owned Gold of Peru Museum now has the best selection of surviving gold, silver, and gilded copper artworks. More than 5,000 necklaces, funerary masks, sceptres, ceremonial cups, tumis (sacrificial knives), nose rings, earrings, and idols reflect Peru's different pre-Columbian cultures, including Lambayeque, Chimú, Mochica, Nazca, Frias, Huari, Vicus, and Inca civilizations.

ABOVE: *The golden Tumi, symbol of Peru at the Gold of Peru Museum.*

Originally designed for tens of thousands of people to live around a neat grid of colonial streets, Lima has grown far beyond its borders. It now runs for more than 31 miles (50km) from north to south and 25 miles (40km) following the Rímac River inland from the ocean. Most of the city is low-rise, new suburbs, and shanty-towns spreading modestly over more and more of the arid coastal hinterlands. As befits a commercial lifeline, the Rímac River is not a tourist attraction: industrial development lines its banks from the coast inland as far as the Andean foothills. Lima's racial make-up reflects its colonial past: although nationally 45 percent of Peruvians are classed as pure-bred Indians, in Lima more than 90 percent of the population are *mestizos*, combining Indian and European bloodlines. Unemployment is officially low, and yet underemployment is widespread; this is a city where drivers can hardly pass through a set of traffic lights without being offered the chance to buy a new watch, packet of tissues, or a daily newspaper.

Historic Center

Until recently the colonial center of Lima was neglected, dirty, and crime-ridden. That has all changed. The main square, with the Town Hall (Cabildo), Cathedral, and Government Palace overlooked by the latticed wooden balconies of elegant Spanish colonial mansions, has been designated a UNESCO World Heritage Site and cleaned up for the 21st century. At the heart of one of South America's most fervently Christian countries, Lima is renowned for its churches and monasteries, many of which have survived earthquakes

ABOVE (TOP): *Palacio de Gobierno.*
ABOVE (BOTTOM): *The Museu e Iglesia de San Francisco, a prime example of Baroque colonial architecture.*

and invasions. At least ten major churches dating back to every age of Lima's colonial history are busy with supplicants and worshippers to the present day, still richly decorated with Inca gold and Andean silver. The Museum of the Inquisition, with its frescoed audience chamber and preserved prison cells, recreates some of the more extreme tortures designed to root out heresy.

Escape to the Suburbs

As the rural population flocks into the city, wealthy Peruvians have escaped. Miraflores and San Isidro—previously merely wealthy suburbs—have become glossy, high-rise cities in their own right, with their own international banks, skyscraping office buildings, and internal economies. Looking out over the Pacific Ocean and scarcely glancing at the low-rise sprawl on every side, these are the powerhouses of a new Lima, content to leave the historic center basking in the distant memories of its colonial glory.

THE STORY OF...

Some of the world's greatest civilizations were established on Peru's Pacific coast, but in the 16th century invading Spanish armies found the region controled by the Incas from their Andean stronghold. Francisco Pizarro first conquered the Incas, and in 1535 founded Lima. Linked to its Spanish motherland through the port of Callao, it quickly became the most important settlement in Latin America, as capital of the Viceroyalty of Peru. Until the 1713 Treaty of Utrecht opened up world trade, all the plundered gold and mined silver from the Andean nations were funneled through the city, which became the financial and social center of the New World.

However, as the Spanish Empire crumbled, so did Lima's fortunes. Much of the city was destroyed in 1746 by an earthquake, and as a royalist stronghold it was on the losing side in the battle for independence. Even today, this coastal implant of central government struggles to maintain control over separatist movements in the country's mountainous hinterlands, but it remains Peru's most important city and state capital.

TOP LEFT: *Quecgua girls in Plaza de Armas.* LEFT: *Lima Cathedral.*

key dates

1535
The city of Lima is founded by Francisco Pizarro, two years after his conquest of the Incas

1746
A major earthquake destroys most of Lima and its port of Callao is swept away by the tidal wave

1821
Lima—and Peru—is liberated by two "outsiders": the Venezuelan Simón Bolívar and the Argentinian José de San Martín

1881
Chilean forces invade the capital and occupy it for two years, looting many national treasures

1990
President Alberto Fujimori is elected, to begin a ten-year term that sees significant progress against Maoist insurgents, played out in the face of economic deterioration

Los Angeles

statistics

Population: 3,800,000

Height of the HOLLYWOOD lettering: 50ft (15m)

Largest publicly owned city park in the United States: Griffith Park 4,000 acres (1,600 ha)

Annual income generated in California motion picture industry: $31 billion

Los Angeles, or LA, is in the state of California on the west coast of the United States. Its vital trading ports face the Pacific Ocean, and it spans 81 miles (130km) of coastline. The metropolitan area is edged by the San Gabriel Mountain range and divided by the Santa Monica Mountains. Despite being rich in native plant species, areas of wilderness and pockets of wetland, LA has a reputation for being glamorous, a home to movie star legends who leave their handprints in the sidewalk of Mann's Chinese Theater, and people forever seeking eternal youth. However, the city is gradually becoming known for its fine and contemporary art, its architecture (movie palaces and modernist buildings), and the new Getty Center for arts. Away from the crowded neighborhoods are the upmarket beaches of Santa Monica and Venice Beach, where image-conscious locals go rollerblading, surfing, and weight lifting.

Central LA appears to be an urban sprawl of wide boulevards and fast freeways, with no central point or typical "town center". In fact, Los Angeles city is just one of 88 independent cities in LA County, including Beverly Hills and its multi-million dollar mansions. Because it is the largest entry point for immigrants to the United States, the population of LA is diverse, with residents from 140 countries including the largest populations of Mexicans, Armenians, Koreans, Filipinos, Salvadorans, and Guatemalans outside of their respective countries. Downtown LA is the largest government center outside Washington DC and is considered the hub of the city, where thousands work.

ABOVE: *Angels Flight Railway.*
ABOVE RIGHT: *Crowds in Venice Beach, west of Downtown LA.*
RIGHT: *The Beverly Hills Hotel, Sunset Boulevard.* OPPOSITE: *Night time in Downtown LA.*

HOLLYWOOD

The most famous sign in the world is the white lettering on Mount Lee, which spells HOLLYWOOD. First built in 1923 at a cost of $21,000 on the side of Mount Cahuenga, the original sign said "Hollywoodland" and promoted the sale of homes in the area. It is now a designated Cultural-Historical Monument. The period from the 1920s to the 1940s was the golden age of Hollywood, with the arrival of sound in motion pictures in 1927. Big producers Paramount, Fox, Warner Brothers, and Metro-Goldwyn-Mayer (MGM) made hundreds of movies a year. Walt Disney (1901–66) and brother Roy launched Disney Brothers Studio, creating short cartoons, the first full-length animated movie, *Snow White*, and the most famous cartoon character of all, Mickey Mouse.

ABOVE: *Look-a-likes posing on Hollywood Boulevard.*

Movie City

The entertainment, automotive design, and aviation industries lead the economy, and LA is home to the largest retail sales market in the United States, with the greatest concentration of retail stores per capita in the nation. Though Hollywood itself lost most of its major film companies, which are now located outside the city for tax purposes, movies are still big business, and numerous television and cable television production companies are also based in the city. On average 50 productions are filmed daily on LA's streets and the Academy Awards ("the Oscars") is the annual event when awards are given to those working in the industry. It is a massive gathering of who's who and no expense is spared.

THE STORY OF...

The Spanish arrived in 1542 to a land occupied by Native Americans, and in 1769 they put down roots. On 4 September 1781, settlers from Mexico founded the small mission town of El Pueblo de Nuestra Señora Reina de los Angeles de la Porciuncula. American pioneers were drawn to the Californian Gold Rush of 1848 and in 1850 California was admitted to the United States.

By 1876 the transcontinental railroad, the Southern Pacific, was in operation, and discovery of oil a few years later made Los Angeles a supplier of a quarter of the world's petroleum. In 1965 racial tensions, overcrowding, and unemployment were high. The arrest of a 21-year-old African American helped spark five days of intense rioting and looting in the Watts neighborhood, which left 34 people dead and was responsible for $40 million worth of property damage.

Since the motion picture industry boom in the 1920s, the town has become the undisputed movie and television entertainment capital of the world.

BELOW: *Stars and signatures on the Hollywood Walk of Fame on Hollywood Boulevard.*

1542
Spanish explorers arrive

1781
Settlers from Mexico establish a town

1911
Hollywood's first film studio opens near Sunset Boulevard

1965
Watts Riots rage for five days

1984
City hosts the Olympic Games

key dates

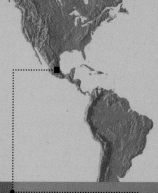

Mexico City

MARIACHI

When the Spanish conquered Mexico in 1521 they brought their instruments with them—namely guitars, violins, harps, brass horns, and woodwinds. Over time the different regions of Mexico developed their own distinctive styles of folk music, which combined these European instruments with those of Mexico. The Mariachi music that is performed across Mexico City today dates from the 19th century, with Mariachi groups typically consisting of six violinists, two trumpeters, and one guitarist, as well as musicians playing the Mexican vihuela (five-stringed guitar with a concave back and high pitch), the deep bass guitarró, and the folk harp.

ABOVE: *Statue of a Mariachi with guitar in Plaza Garibaldi.*

M exico City is known throughout the world for two things: its sprawling urban conurbation and its high altitude. The Mexican capital has one of the largest metropolitan areas in the world, yet despite its size it is also one of the most densely populated places on earth. Meanwhile its altitude is staggering, with experts estimating that there is up to 30 percent less oxygen in the air at 7,347ft (2,239m) than there is at sea level.

Mexico City is at the heart of the Mexican economy and has one of the strongest economies in Central America, built on manufacturing, construction, services, finance, and tourism. The city's success has a downside, with thousands of job seekers descending on it each week. With inadequate resources or jobs to sustain its booming population, Mexico City has become home to shanty-towns, and poverty within the city is pronounced.

Despite its problems, Mexico City has a vibrant Latin American pulse, with bustling street markets, lively bars, and a thriving cultural scene. The latter includes world-class galleries and museums, which delve deep into the history of city and country with stunning artifacts from the Aztec civilization through to collections of fine and contemporary art.

Architectural Treasure Trove

Modern life revolves, as it did during Aztec times, around the Centro Histórico (Historic Center). Here majestic Spanish architecture stands alongside the ghosts of Aztec civilization, with the Catedral Metropolitana and Templo Mayor (Great Temple)—just one of five Aztec temples in the city—located on the main Plaza de la Constitución (El Zócalo). The cathedral is a colossal house of prayer that evolved over three centuries, while Templo Mayor was the most important building in Tenochtitlan. The square, the second largest in the world after Moscow's Red Square, is also home to Mexico's government buildings, and has therefore been the site of numerous political demonstrations over the years.

While the Catedral Metropolitana and Templo Mayor have a special significance for the citizens of Mexico City, UNESCO believed that the whole of the historic center was so important that it placed it on the World Heritage List in 1987. In fact, more than 1,500 buildings have been identified as having artistic or historic significance. Alongside all this ancient history and colonial architecture, visitors also find the city's Torre Mayor on nearby Paseo de la Reforma. This towering skyscraper reminds visitors that Mexico City is a thoroughly modern and commercial city. Beyond Mexico City's historic core there is also a wealth of fine palaces, grand mansions, and monuments.

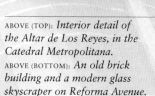

ABOVE (TOP): *Interior detail of the Altar de Los Reyes, in the Catedral Metropolitana.*
ABOVE (BOTTOM): *An old brick building and a modern glass skyscraper on Reforma Avenue.*

BELOW (INSET): *A musician in Conchero dress playing a pipe and drum .*
BELOW: *Stalls outside the Catedral Metropolitana in El Zócalo.*

THE STORY OF...

Mexico City and its environs have been inhabited for over 20,000 years, with the city rising to the fore as the power center of Aztec culture in 1325, when the Mexica tribe established Tenochtitlan on an island in the middle of Lago de Texcoco (Lake Texcoco). Less than 200 years after they first settled Tenochtitlan, the Mexica had subjugated other tribes, forcing them to pay tributes (a form of tax), and expanded their territory. They constructed an impressive city, complete with sacrificial temples, palaces, markets, homes, and even an aqueduct. The civilization came to an abrupt end in 1521, when the Spanish, under Hernando Cortés (1485–1547), laid siege to, and then took control of, the city, with much of it reduced to rubble.

The following year, Cortés became the governor of New Spain, with colonization bringing Hispanic culture, Catholicism, and European architecture to the city. Money generated by mining helped the city prosper and a raft of religious and public buildings was constructed during the 18th century. After 1821, newly independent Mexico City experienced rapid industrialization and population growth, a phenomenon which has continued into the 21st century.

BELOW: *The exterior of the Teatro de los Insurgentes.*

1629
Floodwater up to 6.5ft (2m) high devastates city

1910
The resignation of Díaz sparks the Mexican Revolution, bringing violence to the city and other parts of the country

1968
Student protests end in the massacre at Tlatelolco

1968
Mexico City plays host to the Olympic Games

1985
A powerful earthquake reduces parts of the city to rubble

193

- Population: 362,000
- Number of Art Deco buildings: around 800
- Southernmost barrier island in the United States: Key Biscayne
- First planned community in the US: Coral Gables

Miami

iami sits on the banks of the Miami River in southeast Florida in the United States of America. Its name is a Native American word for "sweet water", in reference to the Miami River, which acts as a funnel for water from the Florida Everglades National Park to the Atlantic Ocean. Miami is made up of small towns, such as Miami Beach and Key Biscayne; the latter are actually barrier islands, linked to the Miami mainland by causeways. Nicknamed the "Ameribbean", Miami is where fast food and MTV America meets subtropical Caribbean, palms, and banana trees. Many Latin-American companies base their headquarters here, as the port is close to South America. Traditionally a nightlife and beach town, Miami's eco-tourism is a big attraction. Annually, an average of 43 million out-of-state visitors holiday here, with 12.5 million

RIGHT: *The Cardozo Hotel and Cavalier Hotel in Miami Beach.*
BELOW LEFT: *The Metromover.*
BELOW RIGHT: *Lummus Park in South Beach.*

ART DECO

The Art Deco parade of buildings stretches along the ocean frontage of Miami Beach, particularly Ocean Drive. Around 800 buildings dating from the 1920s and 1930s, portray the decorative art movement of the period. Painted in shocking pink, lemon, and turquoise, the buildings are styled with geometric verticals, horizontals, portholes, neon signs, and hammered aluminium. In 1976, appalled at the derelict condition of the once elegant buildings, a group of residents formed the Miami Design Preservation League and had the entire Art Deco District placed on the National Register of Historic Places.

ABOVE: *An Art Deco detail on the side of a building in Miami Beach.*

THE STORY OF...

Native Americans, predominantly the Tequesta Indians, lived in this swampy territory for thousands of years. The Spanish arrived in 1513. In 1763 Florida was ceded by Spain to Great Britain, and land in Miami was offered up for British colonial plantations. By 1783, Miami had been returned to Spain, until the United States acquired the territory in 1821. In the late 1800s the Florida Coast Railroad was expanded southward to Miami. During the 1920s, thousands of migrants from the northern United States arrived in search of their fortune, attracted by the lax gambling rules. This was followed in the 1960s by a mass influx of Cuban refugees. In the 1980s Miami both suffered and prospered from the drugs industry, as cocaine came through its port from South America, and unleashed a violent crime wave. Miami's efforts to boost tourism and smarten the city's architecture have increased the number of tourists. In 2003 the city held the FTAA, a collaboration of 34 democratic governments in the Americas to ensure prosperity, democracy, and free markets.

ABOVE LEFT: *The Vizcaya Villa next to the waters of Biscayne Bay.*
ABOVE: *In-line skating along the paths of Lummus Park.*
LEFT: *A trompe l'oeil mural on the wall of the Fountainbleau Hotel.*

BELOW: *The Miami skyline viewed from the Rickenbacker Causeway.*

of those visiting one or more of the state's parks and nature reserves. Miami's parks show how important the mangrove and migratory bird systems are to the coastline and inland areas.

Miami Beach is the focal point of the city and incorporates famous South Beach, which in turn has Ocean Drive. Downtown Miami has skyscrapers lit with neon and the Freedom Tower, the immigration center that filtered Cuban refugees in the 1960s. Recently, Craig Robins, a real-estate developer and art collector, has transformed Miami into a city of culture, by turning 18 blocks of a neighborhood into a design district for exhibiting contemporary art, and to play host to the annual Miami Art Basel festival of contemporary international art.

Little Havana

Only a small number of Miami's residents are originally from Miami. Some Americans say that to get ahead in life, you have to move to Miami. When Fidel Castro ousted dictator General Batista of Cuba in 1959 and declared himself President, he ordered the arrest and execution of Batista supporters. Thousands of Cubans fled from Havana, Cuba's capital, first by air, then in flotillas. In the 1970s, the Mariel Boatlift was the largest flotilla to cross the 90 miles (145km) of ocean between Cuba and Miami, carrying 150,000 Cubans. Little Havana was born and today is a colorful Spanish-speaking, Cuban-American community, alive with salsa music, Cuban cooking, and the craft of cigar rolling. Maximo Gomez Park, named after the famous Cuban revolutionary Maximo Gomez (1836–1905), is a main meeting point where locals congregate to play dominoes and chess.

1513
The Spanish arrive and settle in Florida

1763
The Spanish cede Florida to Great Britain

1821
Spain cedes Florida to the US

1896
Miami is incorporated into a city

1992
Hurricane Andrew hits, causing 52 deaths and $30 billion worth of damage

2003
Miami hosts Free Trade Area of the Americas (FTAA)

key dates

statistics

- Population: 3,575,000 (Metropolitan Montréal)

- Second largest French-speaking city in the world, after Paris

- 994 miles (1,600km) from the Atlantic; the largest container port on the East Coast of North America

- Employing 9,000, its film industry is worth $1.6 billion annually

Montréal

Only 45 miles (72km) from the US border, Montréal is a city of many faces: historic Vieux-Montréal, the modern skyscrapers of Downtown, greenery of Mont Royal and the Olympic venues. Down by the Old Port is a maze of cobbled streets and old stone warehouses, many now converted into galleries, restaurants, and boutique hotels. The original settlement was at Pointe-à-Callière, now the site of an excellent history and archaeology museum. For Montréalers, however, the heart of the city and of their Roman Catholic faith is the Basilique Notre-Dame, an impressive 1829 Gothic Revival church. Like many North American cities, Downtown is laid out on a grid pattern. The main avenues include Rue Sherbrooke and Rue Sainte-Catherine, where major department stores include Ogilvy, the Eaton Center and La Baie.

La Baie is a direct descendant of the Hudson's Bay Company, the English fur trading company, formed in 1670. Underground is the *Ville Souterraine*, some 20 miles (33km) of brightly-lit walkways linking Métro stations, shopping malls, hotels, movie theaters, and museums with offices, apartment buildings, and universities. This network enables life to carry on as normal during the bitterly cold winters and hot summer days.

BELOW (INSET): *Late 19th-century townhouses in Montréal.*

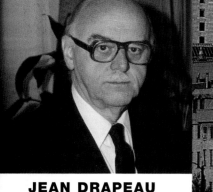

JEAN DRAPEAU (1916–99)

A lawyer turned politician, Jean Drapeau served as mayor of Montréal from 1954 to 1957 and from 1960 to 1986. By supporting two major international projects, he helped elevate the city from a provincial city to a world-renowned metropolis. Expo 67, the Montréal World's Fair, and the 1976 Olympic Games provided the catalyst for upgrading the city's infrastructure, particularly the swift, clean, and safe Métro (underground train system). Although Drapeau was criticized for lavish spending on these projects, he also encouraged a major league baseball franchise (that lasted for 36 seasons), and he hosted major museum exhibitions. Drapeau's advancement of the city was recognized in his re-election to mayor a record seven times.

CROISIERES DU PORT DE MONTREAL

M.V. MONTREAL
MONTREAL

Culture and Sport

The lively cultural scene revolves around the Place des Arts, while St. Denis, known as the Latin Quarter, buzzes with restaurants, nightlife, and students from nearby McGill University and the University of Québec at Montréal. Overlooking the city is Mont Royal, more hill than mountain at 764ft (233m) high, and known for its park and affluent homes. Signposting the Olympic Park is the world's tallest leaning tower (575ft/175m), with its panoramic views. More legacies of the Games are the 55,000-seat stadium, still used for sport and concerts, and the Biodôme. With its four different ecosystems, this high-tech indoor museum of natural sciences is an imaginative conversion of what was the cycling stadium. Festivals are a regular feature, with the Just for Laughs (comedy) and the International Jazz Festival among the biggest in the world. Ice hockey is a passion: the Montréal Canadiens Hockey Club has won the Stanley Cup 24 times up to 2004, making it one of the most successful championship sports teams in the world.

A Thriving Economy

In Canada, Montréal is second only to Toronto as an economic powerhouse. For North America, it ranks first in the aerospace industry, second only to New York for fashion and food, third in the biopharmaceutical industry, and fourth in technology. Most of Montréal's economy (about 78 percent), however, is in the service industry.

THE STORY OF...

Second only to Toronto in size, and with immigrants making up 30 percent of the population, Montréal is one of North America's most international cities. Not long after New France was ceded to Britain in 1763, loyalists fleeing the new United States, plus immigrants from Scotland and Ireland, arrived in the French-speaking community, set on the mighty St. Lawrence River. The resulting tension between the anglo and francophone communities has flared off and on for two centuries. Although the once-lucrative fur trade waned in the early 1800s, Montréal developed into one of the world's major grain ports, as well as Canada's premier commercial, manufacturing, and financial hub.

Although it lost that position to Toronto in the 20th century, the 1967 World's Fair and 1976 Olympics placed the city in the world spotlight. The French nationalist movement brought important political changes, such as making French the official language in 1977. Today, both communities enjoy the vibrant cultural life, encompassing museums, ballet, and music, as well as 40 major festivals.

FAR LEFT: *The Biosphere on Ile Sainte Hélène.*
LEFT: *Montréal Tower at Olympic Park.*

BELOW: *Fountain at Place des Arts in Downtown Montréal.*

CROISIERES DU PORT DE MONTREAL

VILLE-MARIE II

M.V.CONCORDIA
MONTREAL

1535
Traveling up the St. Lawrence River, the French explorer Jacques Cartier lands on a large island and names its mountain Mont Royal

1642
Paul de Chomedey, Sieur de Maisonneuve, founds the colony of Ville-Marie, soon to be known as Montréal

1763
After the Seven Years' War, New France becomes a British colony

1844
Montréal is named capital of the united Canada

1976
Montréal hosts the 21st Olympic Games

New Orleans

statistics

- Population: 1,106,000
- New Orleans has more than 3,000 restaurants, with spicy Cajun food the most popular on the menu
- Over 40,000 buildings are listed on the National Register of Historic Places, more than Washington DC
- The city is 8ft (2.5m) below sea level, and pumps work 24 hours a day to keep it dry

Known as "The Big Easy" or pronounced "N'Awlinz" in a lazy southern drawl, this is one of America's most charming cities, with its old town center still occupying a grid of six-by-thirteen streets laid out by the original French engineer, Adrien de Pauger. Known as the "French Quarter," this still retains the atmosphere of its French and Spanish architects, with some notable buildings including the St. Louis Cathedral, America's oldest continuously active cathedral. Today New Orleans is better known for the bars, stores, and clubs of Bourbon Street, which runs through the city's heart and is busy 24 hours a day with tourists, musicians, and hustlers. Hemmed in by a crescent curve of the Mississippi River and Lake Pontchartrain, the city center is small enough, and safe enough to explore on foot. Wealthy residents live outside the center in elegant white-painted mansions that surround the St. Charles Streetcar route, running out through the Garden District into genteel suburbs, where white picket fences and wooden façades epitomize the image of southern plantation living. The city does have an undeniable but under-reported underclass. Racial segregation continues to the present day, and the city's substantial African American population is concentrated in low-cost out-of-center housing settlements, known as "projects." These fill in the gaps between swamps and lakes, ensuring the city remains very much the island it was when first settled.

Inevitable City – Impossible Location

The strategic reasons that caused the city to be set in its swampy location mean its survival is dependent on constant engineering works. The slow-flowing Mississippi raises its level through sedimentation, while the city itself is sinking 3ft (1m) every century.

CITY OF JAZZ

In the early 20th century, New Orleans became the birthplace of jazz. Congo Square was the only place in the South that African drums were allowed to be played, and the musical form that is now known as jazz—combining elements of Ragtime, marching-band music, and Blues—grew up here and in the bars and brothels nearby. Early jazz pioneers such as Louis "Satchmo" Armstrong (1901–71), Charles "Buddy" Bolden (1877–1931), Ferdinand "Jelly Roll" Morton (1890–1941), and Joe "King" Oliver (1885–1938) got their starts in the nightclubs of Storyville, a red-light district that flourished between 1897 and 1917. Today the Neville Brothers, the Marsalis family, Harry Connick Jr., and others continue the tradition at small bars and clubs, with jazz festivals and Mardi Gras celebrations keeping the atmosphere at street level very much on the boil.

ABOVE RIGHT: *Mardi Gras Night in New Orleans.*

Levees, or earth banks, 15ft (5m) high keep the river and lake at bay, while 22 massive pumps churn out groundwater. One of the city's stranger tourist attractions is Lafeyette Cemetery, where the dead are buried in raised tombs. Buried underground, the bodies would float back to the surface overnight.

Economic Powerhouse

Once the third largest city in America, New Orleans is now not even the state capital of Louisiana—that is in the smaller and blander city of Baton Rouge, upstream. This doesn't bother New Orleans' residents. It is one of America's most popular tourist destinations, maintaining an easy-going atmosphere fueled by a mixture of music, cuisine, history, and a reputation for hedonism. Forget government, is the general attitude. "*Laissez les bons temps roulez*"—let the good times roll—is not just the city's motto: it's an article of faith.

THE STORY OF...

The Mississippi, with its tributaries, drains North America from the Rockies to the Appalachians; control of this river promised control over much of the trade from the New World. This was enough for the French to make the efforts necessary to raise a city on a disease-ridden swamp. A street-plan was laid out by a French engineer, but it was nearly 100 years before enough people arrived to populate the city. Normally, French colonies received little investment. However, New Orleans was different, thanks to a marketing scam by British financier John Law, who ramped up interest in the colony in an investment bubble that burst in 1720. After France lost the Seven Years' War (1756–63), Louisiana was ceded to Spain, but as a colonial outpost in English-speaking America it was unsustainable.

In 1803 Thomas Jefferson (1743–1826) bought the State of Louisiana, including New Orleans, in the Louisiana Purchase. Unshackled from colonial protectionism, the city grew prosperous exporting cotton and sugar and importing slaves. By 1852 it was the third largest city in America, with bars and flophouses (cheap lodging houses) attracting early tourists, and tourism continues to be an important source of revenue.

ABOVE (TOP)): *The Natchez Steamboat paddle wheeler.*
ABOVE (BOTTOM): *The French Quarter is an area which nestles on the bend of the Mississippi River.*

statistics

Population: 8,000,000

The New York Stock Exchange annual trading volume: $5.5 trillion

John F. Kennedy Airport: the USA's second busiest airport with over 31,000,000 passengers per year

Statue of Liberty: 305ft (93m) from ground to tip of torch

New York

New York is located on the East Coast of the United States of America, opened by natural and man-made waterways to the Atlantic Ocean. It is considered the birthplace of the American nation, the city that welcomed immigrants into its increasing "melting pot" with a towering statue proclaiming liberty and freedom. One of the most densely populated places in the US, New York is home to people from many cultures, and a multitude of languages are spoken. The pace is fast; New Yorkers flit beneath the soaring architectural icons that symbolize the city, and hail one of the 12,000 yellow taxicabs. They are known for a no-nonsense approach to life and for working and playing hard.

The Statue of Liberty

New York's main attraction was opened on 28 October 1886. A gift from the people of France to the United States, the statue was designed by sculptor Frederic Auguste Bartholdi (1834–1904) to commemorate the centennial of the American Declaration of Independence of 1776. In France, Bartholdi consulted with Alexandre Gustave Eiffel (1832–1923), designer of the Eiffel Tower. Eiffel was commissioned to design the Statue of Liberty's massive iron pylon and secondary skeletal framework, which allows the statue's copper skin to move independently and stand upright. The statue arrived from France in 350 individual pieces, packed in 214 crates, and took 4 months to re-assemble. Her crown has 25 windows to symbolize gems of the Earth, and 7 rays to represent the 7 seas and continents of the world. The tablet in her hand reads, in Roman numerals, 4 July 1776.

RIGHT: *Detail of the Statue of Liberty. Located on Liberty Island, it is one of the most recognizable symbols of political freedom and democracy.*

THE STORY OF...

European explorer Giovanni da Verrazano (1485–1528) visited the harbor and its Native American population in 1524, and in 1609 English explorer Henry Hudson (1565–1611) arrived. However, it was the Dutch who settled in what they named New Amsterdam, to rule their much larger colony of New Netherland in 1624. The British took New Amsterdam in 1664 and renamed it New York City. Word spread that this was the promised land, attracting many immigrants. The last British troops departed in 1783 and New York City briefly became the capital of the new nation, with President George Washington (1732–99) inaugurated in 1789. In the following years, canals and waterways were created and the city grew into a busy Atlantic Ocean seaport.

In 1792 a group of merchants began meeting under a tree in Wall Street, which eventually became the New York Stock Exchange. The 19th century saw a population explosion, boosted by further European immigration, including Irish immigrants fleeing the potato famine in 1843. New arrivals passed through the immigration station on Ellis Island beneath the torch of the Statue of Liberty. During the early 1900s, skyscrapers built here were, for a time, the tallest buildings in the world. In 1993 Republican candidate Rudolph Giuliani (b. 1944) became mayor and the city saw a reduction in crime. Times Square was a major tourist draw, art flourished, and the city became an international hub.

On 11 September 2001 (9/11) a terrorist attack on the twin towers of the World Trade Center brought New York to a standstill. Two hijacked aeroplanes, flown by terrorists linked to the al-Qaeda organization, crashed into both towers. The towers eventually imploded, and approximately 2,800 people perished. In 2003, New Yorkers began plans for a new World Trade Center.

BELOW: *A distinctive yellow cab crosses Brooklyn Bridge.*
LEFT: *Looking up at the cables of Brooklyn Bridge.*

Manhattan

Five boroughs make up New York City: Manhattan, Brooklyn, Queens (part of Long Island), the Bronx (part of the North American mainland), and Staten Island. The twin Gothic arches make the Brooklyn Bridge a recognizable attraction, while Queens has neighborhoods of South Americans, Indians, Greeks, Chinese, and Irish. The Bronx has more parkland than any of the other boroughs, and the most fun way to arrive at Staten Island's parks, beaches, and wetland preserve is by ferry. Manhattan, a long, slender island bordered by the Hudson River and East River, is the "in place" to live if you are a New Yorker, and is where everyone jostles for space. It is the city's business and entertainment area, and home to its skyscrapers.

The Chrysler Building, at 1,046ft (318m), was the tallest skyscraper in the world until the Art Deco Empire State Building, at 1,453ft (443m), transformed the skyline. These were followed in 1972 and 1973 by the twin towers of the World Trade Center, which were at that time the tallest buildings in the world. During a ceremony on July 4, 2004, the ground was broken at Ground Zero, on the construction site of the World Trade Center. Designed primarily by architect Daniel Libeskind, the new 1,776ft (540m) Freedom Tower will reflect the posture of the Statue of Liberty and will be taller than the tallest of the twin towers, at 1,368ft (417m). Scheduled for completion in 2008, the Tower will keep the footprints of the original twin towers as a memorial site to those who died there.

1609
Henry Hudson sails into New York's harbor

1664
The British capture the city

1783
Evacuation Day, when the last British troops leave

1883
Brooklyn Bridge built

1929
Stock Market Crash

2001
World Trade Center twin towers destroyed in a terrorist attack

TOP: *The World Trade Center Globe Statue Memorial in Battery Park.*
ABOVE: *Central Park*
ABOVE LEFT: *The stainless-steel spire of the Chrysler Building.*
LEFT: *The spires of St. Patrick's Cathedral seen against a glass skyscraper.*
FAR RIGHT: *Grand Central Station.*
BACKGROUND: *The Flatiron Building, the oldest remaining skyscraper in New York.*

Entertainment and Economics

Times Square is the tourist and theater hub, known for shows in the district of Broadway. Nearby is Grand Central Terminal, opened in 1913 as the world's largest train station. Lower Manhattan is the commercial heart of New York City and the financial center of worldwide finance. Here is Wall Street, the New York Stock Exchange, and the Federal Gold Bank. At the heart of Manhattan is New York's green open space and playground, Central Park, where locals escape from the city pollution and jog in its 843 acres (337 ha).

ST. PATRICK'S DAY

On 17 March 1756, New York's Irish community celebrated St. Patrick's Day for the first time. Ten years later, the first official parade by Irishmen from the military stationed in the city marched through the streets. Since then, each year on the same day, New York hosts the largest St. Patrick's Day celebration in the world. Ironically, dozens of Irish citizens travel across the Atlantic Ocean from Ireland to join in the festivities and revelry, which continues into the early hours.

Traditionally a religious holiday to honor St. Patrick, the patron saint of Ireland, these days the celebrations are more about having a good time. Known as "Green Day", 17 March in New York is a mass of people wearing green clothing and hats, and carrying green flowers to signify their ancestral home's national colors.

In typical American style, even the Empire State Building and the city fountains, beer, and bagels take on a shade of green.

A major parade of more than 150,000 people of Irish descent, including people from 30 Irish county societies and the Ancient Order of Hibernians, marches up Fifth Avenue in Manhattan, headed by a unit of soldiers from the Irish 165th Infantry.

- **Population: 672,000** (Greater Québec)

- **95 percent speak French** as their first language

- **The only fortified city in North America**

- **The annual Winter Carnival is billed as the world's biggest**

ROBERT LEPAGE (B.1957)

Playwright, actor, film maker, and director Robert Lepage is Canada's Renaissance man. He first made international headlines with the cult classic, *Trilogie des Dragons* (Dragons' Trilogy, 1986–90). In 1992, Lepage was the first North American to direct a Shakespeare play—*A Midsummer Night's Dream*—at London's Royal National Theater. Eager to embrace new technology and new theatrical techniques, he has won awards for directing a diverse range of arts and projects, from modern opera to popular music (he staged Peter Gabriel's 1993 and 2002 world tours). In 1994, Lepage founded his own multidisciplinary production company, Ex Machina. As well as directing productions in Japanese and Spanish, he has worked with Québec's acclaimed Cirque du Soleil.

BACKGROUND: *The banks of the St. Lawrence River and the Château Frontenac.*

Québec

The French phrase "*Je me souviens*" (I remember) is on every Québec car licence plate, a reminder that the region's French past lives on in the present. Ringed by massive walls, its narrow cobbled streets lined with 17th- and 18th-century houses, Québec City looks more European than any other North American city.

BELOW LEFT: *A restaurant in the Old Town, with the Château Frontenac hotel behind.*
BELOW CENTER: *Place Royal.*
BELOW RIGHT: *The red-tiled roof of the Place d'Armes restaurant.*

Just as it did in the old days, Vieux-Québec, the Old City, splits into the Haute-Ville (Upper Town, within the walls) and the Basse-Ville, the Lower Town. Running along the riverfront, this area is being revamped and revitalized, with stores, restaurants, and living spaces. The hub is the elegant Place Royale, the site of the first permanent settlement in New France. Nearby, the contemporary Musée de la Civilisation, one of Canada's finest museums, reflects both French-Canadian and First Nation (Amerindian) culture. A steep funicular connects the Lower with the Upper Town, where Samuel de Champlain (1567–1635) built his fort in 1620. The city's most famous icon is the 618-room Château Frontenac hotel, built in 1893, during the heyday of the grandiose Canadian Pacific hotels.

Cultural Heritage

Contrasting with the twisting lanes within the walls of the Upper Town is the broad Grande Allée leading to the splendid 19th-century Hôtel du Parlement, home of the provincial government. Nearby stands La Citadelle, a star-shaped fortress. Built by the British (1820–32) to a French design, it is still a working military headquarters, with a daily Changing of the Guard in summer. The neighboring parkland is the main site for the famous Carnaval de Québec, or Winter Carnival where events such as snowshoe competitions and snow sculpture take place on the Plains of Abraham, where General Wolfe's victory changed the course of history. Beyond the historic quarters, this lively city extends to modern suburbs and shopping malls. As nearly 30 percent of the population is under 25 and the Great Outdoors is on the doorstep, locals can easily go cycling, skiing, and hiking; but they also value their cultural heritage. So, morning coffee is served in traditional *bols*, small bistros serve French cuisine, clothing styles are French and French is the first language, though many words are different to those heard in France itself.

Industry

Although many English-speaking companies abandoned Québec during separatist agitation a few decades ago, the city thrives as the capital of a vast province rich with mineral mining. Manufacturing is also vital, from petroleum refining to motor vehicles. While tourism is a major industry, Québec has managed to avoid turning into a romantic, historic theme park.

RIGHT: *The star-shaped fortress, La Citadelle.*

THE STORY OF...

In French, Québec can refer to both the city and the province; to avoid confusion, the city is known as Québec City in English. The city commands the St. Lawrence River, its name deriving from the Algonquian "where the river narrows." First developed as a fur trading post, the well fortified town, high on Cap Diamant, soon attracted French administrators and religious orders. Strategically important, it was attacked both by local Iroquois and by the British, who finally captured it after the Battle of the Plains of Abraham (1759).

Thereafter, as capital of the British province, Québec City thrived as a port until Montréal's rise in the 19th century. Now Québec City takes pride in being the bastion of French culture and tradition in North America. Tourism is a major industry, but the determination to hold onto the past is balanced by the more educated younger Québécois.

BELOW: *The brass band of the Canada 22s regiment.*

1608
Samuel de Champlain builds a wooden fortress, called the *Habitation*

1759
Battle of the Plains of Abraham, General Wolfe's British troops defeat General Montcalm's French forces. New France becomes a British colony, with Québec City the capital

1985
Québec City is the first North American urban center to be recognized as a UNESCO World Heritage Site

1995
A narrow majority (50.6 percent to 49.4 percent) of Québec province residents votes against a mandate to negotiate secession from Canada

2008
Québec City celebrates its 400th birthday

Quito

- Population: 1,575,000
- Quito is the second highest capital in Latin America (after La Paz), at 9,000ft (2,850m)
- The city sits beneath the volcano, Pichincha, that erupted in 1999 having been dormant for 350 years
- Quito is the capital of Ecuador, lying just 14 miles (23km) south of the Equator that gave the country its name

ATAHUALPA (1495–1533)

Atahualpa was the Inca emperor of the north when a tiny band of 63 Spanish conquistadores invaded. When the Spanish leader Pizarro captured him, Atahualpa promised a ransom of gold and silver—enough to fill a room measuring 23ft by 6.5ft (7m by 5m) to the height of his raised arm. But months passed while the precious metals were brought from all parts of the far-flung empire and the Spanish grew nervous at the rumors of a great army on the march to rescue its emperor. In 1533 Pizarro decided to murder the emperor. Quito's Inca general razed the city and hid the vast ransom, which has never been found.

Quito lies in one of the most breathtaking positions of any capital. Surrounded by the high Andes—and sometimes smoking volcanoes—it is a thin strip of a city filling its mountain valley. The old colonial city is a UNESCO heritage site and the best preserved historic city in South America. It is a maze of narrow streets lined with exquisite monasteries, churches (decorated with copious amounts of gold leaf), and grand houses (all fine examples of colonial architecture), a wide range of museums and art galleries, and elegant plazas with open-air cafés. At the center of the city is the Plaza de San Francisco, also called the Tianguez (market-place) where in pre-Hispanic times maize, salt and firewood were bartered, and where the magnificent church and convent of San Francisco now stand.

About half of Ecuador's population is *mestizo* (descendants of Indians and Spaniards) and around a quarter belong to one of 14 different indigenous tribes, each with its own jealously guarded traditions. In Quito, the Andean peoples are much in evidence. Religious processions, complete with singing, dancing, bands, and statues of the Madonna frequently wend their way through the streets, the participants tossing rose petals en route (roses are one of Ecuador's main exports). There are excellent restaurants and stores selling beautiful indigenous crafts, including rugs, weavings, pottery and, most notably, the silver jewelry for which the country is famous.

The Center of the World

Quito is a city right at the middle of the world and just 14 miles (23km) north of the city center, the line of the Equator (latitude 0°-0'-0") is marked by the Ciudad Mitad del Mundo (the City at the Center of the World). There is a park, stores, restaurants, and a museum devoted to the history of the various ethnic groups. Even though Quito lies on the Equator, its climate is spring-like, rather than unbearably hot, because of its great altitude.

After a disastrous economic performance during the 1990s, Ecuador defaulted on all its debts in 1999 and the government abandoned the national currency, the sucre, adopting the US dollar instead. Now Quito is becoming a much more cosmopolitan city, the new city funded by oil-based industries (oil was discovered here in the 1960s), with tourism a rapidly growing, but still relatively new industry.

BELOW: *The Plaza Grande, the main square in Quito.*
LEFT: *The cloister of the San Francisco Church.*

BELOW: *The yellow line that divides the two hemispheres and the Center of the World Monument.*
LEFT: *Local women buying wool in Latacunga.*

THE STORY OF...

The fertile valley in the high Andes that was to become Quito was first settled in the first millennium, gradually becoming a major trading center. It became part of the Inca empire for only 80 years, when it was established as the northern capital. It was invaded by the Spanish conquistador Pizarro but the Incas razed it to the ground rather than let it fall into Spanish hands. The colonial city of San Francisco de Quito was founded on the ruins and over the next 300 years flowered into one of the most beautiful cities of Spanish America.

The city was created by the Quito School of Art, a combination of Baroque Spanish and Moorish influences, with indigenous Quiteños' creativity. After a series of failed attempts, Ecuador gained its independence from Spain in 1830 and Quito became the capital. Repeated coups and presidential assassinations followed during decades of social unrest. Nevertheless, Ecuador's great mineral and agricultural wealth ensured that its capital grew and in the 20th century an entirely new city grew up beside the old one.

BELOW: *Traditional city band in front of Quito Cathedral.*

1428
The Incas invade Ecuador

1523
Atahualpa becomes ruler of the northern Inca Empire, with Quito his capital

1562
Work begins on Quito Cathedral, (now the oldest still standing in South America)

1830
Ecuador gains independence from Spain and Quito becomes the capital

2000
A military coup lasting just three hours turns President Jamil Mahuad out of Quito and into exile

key dates

207

Rio de Janeiro

- Population: 11,950,000
- Rio has 37 white sand beaches, stretching for 56 miles (90km)
- More than 60,000 people participate in Rio's Carnaval
- The city is the center of Brazil's soccer mania and the national team is the only one ever to have won the World Cup five times

Rio de Janeiro, or Rio, is not a peaceful city. Life is lived out of doors and at full volume by the Cariocas, as Rio's inhabitants are called—and most often on the beach. By day, the beaches are used for sports—soccer, volleyball, gymnastics, surfing, windsurfing, and traditional Brazilian games such as *peteca* and *futevolei*. The beaches are just as alive at night. They are lined with bars and restaurants where diners stay late into the night, eating, talking, and partying. Dinner usually starts late here—9pm or 10pm—after a drink in a bar. Cariocas also use the beaches during the evenings for a whole range of events. Sporting competitions take place, often in specially constructed courts and stadiums, built on the sand. There are free musical concerts and extravaganzas. And, best of all—and only beaten by Carnaval into second place on the Rio events calendar—the spectacular New Year celebrations come to life on the shore.

Cariocas are a mixture of indigenous Indian, African, and Portuguese and, while the population is officially Catholic, many other religious influences come into play, such as at Reveillon, or New Year. Hundreds of *Filhas-de-Santo*, the priestesses of Brazil's African religions, burn candles on the sands and launch tiny boats filled with flowers and gifts into the sea. These are offerings for Iemanjá, the Queen of the Sea and, if the boat is taken out to sea on the tide, the wish it carries will be granted.

BELOW (TOP): *Christ the Redeemer on the Corcovado Mountain.*
BELOW (BOTTOM): *Maracanã Soccer Stadium.*

CARNAVAL

Carnaval is Rio's most famous event, a moveable feast tied to the Christian calendar, and a traditional celebration of plenty before the rigors of Lent. In Rio it always starts on a Friday and ends on Ash Wednesday, and the whole city is filled with parades, balls, singing, dancing, and music. The biggest parade takes place on the Sunday and Monday nights in a fiercely competitive event. Rio's top samba schools are judged by a government-appointed jury and each must present a display with a central theme. This may be an historical event or Brazilian Indian legend, which is taken up in the samba song, the costumes, and the huge floats that follow the dancers down the main streets.

A Spectacular Beauty

Rio's waterfront is world famous: the lush, dramatic tropical coastline of formidable natural beauty; the long, white beaches lined with skyscrapers; the bell-shaped lump of granite that forms Sugar Loaf Mountain; and, towering above it all, the outstretched arms of Christ the Redeemer standing on top of Corcovado mountain. It is the most popular tourist destination in Brazil, as well as being a major center for the country's shipping, banking, and publishing industries. It is not, however, the capital, which is Brasilia.

As in many Latin American countries, there is a wide gulf between rich and poor. State schools are notoriously sub-standard and parents who can afford it send their children to private schools. The shanty-towns, the *favelas* are full to overflowing and stretch up the surrounding hills above the coast, and there is a soaring crime rate. However, the rich and poor all meet in Rio's ultimate melting pot—the beach.

RIGHT: *Botafogo Inlet and Sugar Loaf Mountain.*
BELOW: *The view from Sugar Loaf Mountain.*

Rio de Janeiro

THE STORY OF...

When the Portuguese arrived in 1502, the coastline around the huge bay was inhabited by Indian tribes, the ancestors of many of today's Cariocas. The French soon followed the Portuguese and a series of battles culminated in 1567, when the Portuguese drove out their rivals and built the first fortified city in the bay, calling it São Sebastião do Rio de Janeiro. It soon became a trading center for sugar cane, slaves and, after its discovery in the 1690s, gold. In 1807, Napoleon Bonaparte (1769–1821) invaded Lisbon and the crown prince, Dom João VI, escaped with his entire court to Rio and began a period of building and modernization. He declared Rio the capital of the United Kingdom of Portugal and returned reluctantly to Lisbon only in 1820, leaving his son Pedro behind as prince regent.

In 1822, Pedro led a bloodless coup to gain Brazil's independence. His son, Pedro II, succeeded to the throne in 1840, aged 14, and ruled for 49 years, introducing political and economic reform and abolishing slavery. Brazil abolished the monarchy and became a republic in 1889. The 20th century saw huge development in Rio and a population explosion.

BELOW: *Colorful performers at the annual Carnaval.*

key dates

1502
Portuguese explorer Gaspar de Lemos is the first European to arrive in Rio

1570
The Portuguese begin importing slaves from Africa

1807
The Portuguese prince regent sets up his court in exile in Rio

1822
Brazil gains independence from Portugal

1960
Brazil moves its capital from Rio to Brasilia

San Francisco

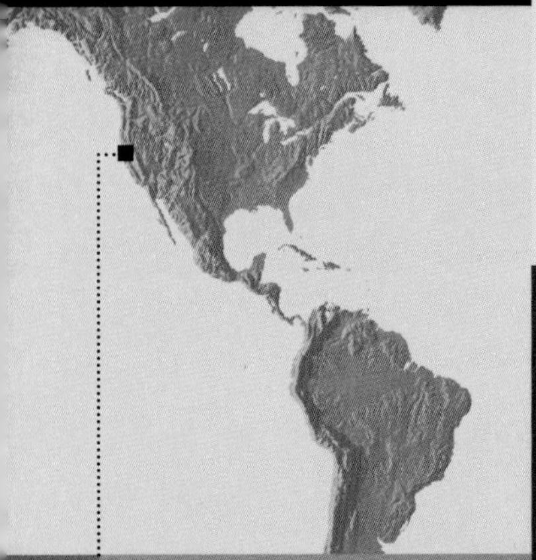

statistics

Population: 792,700

Annual average number of vehicles crossing the Golden Gate Bridge: 41 million

Number of fog signals in San Francisco Bay: 32

Number of high-rise buildings 75ft (23m) tall and above: 501

CHINATOWN

Chinatown, with around 9,000 residents of Asian descent, is the most eclectic neighborhood, with roasted chickens hanging in stores, bags of fortune cookies, and fish landed daily by fishing boats owned by Koreans and Vietnamese. Situated at the foot of Nob Hill, the district covers at least 24 blocks and is the second largest Chinatown outside Asia, second only to New York. As Chinese immigrants settled, products from the East flooded in and a market of stores and stalls grew up, as did a distinct neighborhood. Chinatown Gate, a huge archway painted with a dragon, is the entrance to the sights, smells and tastes beyond.

ABOVE: *A gift store in Chinatown.*

FAR RIGHT: *San Francisco's Bay Bridge.*
ABOVE: *A cable car.*
RIGHT: *Traffic on steep Powell Street.*

Surrounded on three sides by the Pacific Ocean, with San Francisco Bay to the northeast, the city sits on the tip of the San Francisco Peninsula. The city is built on 43 hills, the highest natural point being Mount Davidson at 938ft (286m), competing with the tallest skyscraper, the Transameric Pyramid at 853ft (260m). Nine bridges cross into the city, and the Golden Gate Bridge, often shrouded in San Francisco's frequent fog, is the most famous. In 1916 James Wilkins, newspaper editor of the *San Francisco Call Bulletin*, revived an earlier idea of building a bridge across the Golden Gate Strait. A national enquiry began, though most engineers said a bridge could not be built as it would be too expensive. Joseph Baermann Strauss, bridge designer, disagreed. On 28 May 1937, the bridge opened to traffic. Its span measured 1.75 miles (2.7km) including approach roads. The initial building cost was $35 million. The Bay itself accommodates 14 islands, including the island of the former state penitentiary, Alcatraz.

Downtown centers on Union Square bustling with locals working in the nearby financial district. Tourism is a major part of the economy, followed by retail—in 2006 the largest Bloomingdales store outside New York is due to open. Fisherman's Wharf, known for steaming bowls of clam chowder, and North Beach are popular haunts, as is a population of California sea lions that has made its home on wooden jetties at Pier 39. The mammals were rescued shortly after the 1989 earthquake and due to a plentiful herring supply and a protected environment, rest here each winter before migrating south. Also well known are the wide boulevards and beautiful Victorian houses in wealthy areas such as Nob Hill. A familiar sight climbing the steep city streets at a speed of 9mph (14.5kph) are the cable cars, which make up the only moving National Historic Landmark in the US.

Hippie Culture

San Francisco's reputation is built on its people and a liberal culture inspired by the Beats, a group of middle-class youths from the Haight-Ashbury district. Their free-thinking attitudes spawned the hippie revolution in the 1960s and a worldwide following practising peace, free love, and drugs, which was at its height in 1967 in "The Summer of Love." Today, San Francisco's multi-ethnicity enhances this bohemian backdrop, as well as the tag of gay capital of America. Whites make up the main population group, followed by Asians, Hispanics, African Americans, American Indians and Alaska Natives, Native Hawaiians, and Pacific Islanders.

RIGHT: *A row of Victorian houses known as the "painted ladies."*
FAR RIGHT: *Visitors to Boudin's, the makers of San Francisco sour dough.*

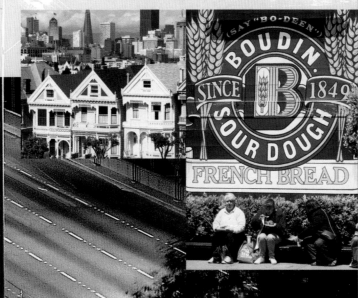

THE STORY OF...

The Miwok Indians first inhabited the coastal area around what is now San Francisco Bay. Early Spanish and Portuguese exploration began in 1542, and Sir Francis Drake (c.1540–96) came close to discovering the bay in 1579. In 1776 the Presidio of San Francisco and La Misión de San Francisco de Asis (Mission Dolores) was founded by the Franciscans, the oldest building intact in the city and one of the oldest Mission Churches in California. By the early 1800s American trappers and pioneers began arriving. The city became a prosperous transit point, experiencing a population explosion as a result of the Gold Rush in 1848 and Chinese immigration.

In the 20th century, a massive earthquake destroyed much of the town in 1906. In 1989 another serious earthquake served as a wake-up call to take seriously the seismic threat in the Bay region. The city became the center of the dot com boom which peaked in 2001, with computer giants Apple and Yahoo locating in "Silicon Valley" to the south of the city.

BELOW: *Cars negotiating the hairpin bends in Lombard Street.*

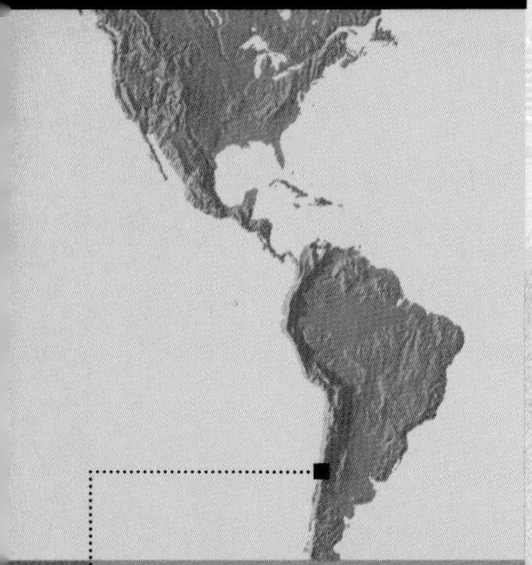

Santiago

ew cities can rival Santiago's spectacular setting, in a broad and fertile alluvial valley, framed by the snow-capped peaks of the Andes to the east and the low rolling coastal mountain range to the west. Santiago residents could, if they wished, ski in the mountains in the morning and spend the afternoon sunbathing on the fashionable beaches of Santiago's Pacific resorts of Viña del Mar and Valparaiso,

statistics

- Population: 6,000,000

- Height above sea level: 1,700ft (520m)

- Ethnic mix: White and *mestizo* (mixed parentage) 95 percent, Amerindian 3 percent, other 2 percent

- Economic growth: 15 years of growth averaging 6 percent makes Chile the envy of Latin America

PALACIO DE LA MONEDA

Built in 1805 as one of colonial Spain's final projects, the Palacio de la Moneda was the seat of government and the focus of General Augusto Pinochet's (b. 1915) 1973 coup. The sight of air-force planes bombing the stately pillared residence provided one of the iconic images of the 20th century. Shortly afterward, this was where the elected president, Salvador Allende (1908–73), met his mysterious death, though it has never been established whether this was murder or suicide. Once more the seat of government, even today the Moneda Palace's elegant frontage is dotted with patched bullet holes dating from Allende's last stand.

ABOVE LEFT: *The Palacio de la Moneda.*
ABOVE CENTER: *Iglesia de la Merced.*
ABOVE RIGHT: *Sculpture in Plaza de Armas.*

a mere 62 miles (100km) away. The city center itself is compact, with the downtown area laid out between the Avenida O'Higgins and the River Mapoche, and bounded by the landscaped hill of the Cerro Santa Lucia, where the original Spanish settlers were besieged. This is where you'll find the Plaza de Armas, as drawn out by Valvidia and still surrounded by the grandest of the city's surviving colonial buildings, including the cathedral and the wedding-cake architecture of the Central Post Office, with the Moneda Palace and the Museum of Pre-Colombian Art nearby. Historic buildings are in the minority, however, in this dynamic city, where striking modern buildings liberally reflect its prosperity. Cross the river and the smart Bellavista and Providencia suburbs offer quieter attractions away from the worst of the traffic, overlooked by the looming Cerro San Cristobal, a pine-forested outcrop of the Andes that juts into the city center. Topped by a white statue of the Virgin Mary, this peak is latticed by hiking trails but a cable car provides easier access to the summit.

An Emerging Culture

The arts are only recently recovering from years of totalitarian repression. Artists litter the Plaza de Armas in the hope of catching hold of a visiting dollar, but galleries are starting to open and the city museums have good collections of—mainly Western—art. Santiago's literary heritage, on the other hand, rivals any country in the New World. Gabriela Mistral (1889–1957) was the first Latin American to win the Nobel Prize for Literature, closely followed by Pablo Neruda (1904–73), the poet whose Bellavista home is still open to visitors. Chile's best-known contemporary writer is Isabel Allende (b. 1942), niece of the former president, but for political reasons only her books are

set in Chile: she herself was forced to flee to the United States after Salvador's death. Despite being part of South America, Santiago remains strongly attached to its European roots. The years of conflict with the indigenous Indians all but exterminated the native cultures, and the values of the Old World were reinforced by waves of immigration that continued well into the 20th century. Isolated by the Andes and the vast Pacific Ocean, and further sanctioned through years of military rule, Santiago is only now emerging to take its full place on the world stage.

LEFT: *The Cathedral Tower.*
BELOW: *View of Santiago from the Cerro San Cristobal.*

THE STORY OF...

The indigenous Indians were not remotely pleased when Spaniard Pedro de Valdivia trekked across the Andes with a small band of soldiers and founded Santiago in the fertile Mapoche valley. They razed the Spanish settlement and for two years besieged the settlers on a hill, which is now a popular city-center park called Cerro Santa Lucia. Reinforcements arrived, however, and despite 200 years of resistance the Indians, decimated by Western diseases, were forced to give way to this new society.

Set in a temperate climate and fertile land, the city grew wealthy through agriculture, with a workforce not of slaves but of voluntary immigrants from Spain. After independence in 1818, Santiago continued to grow, with mining becoming an increasingly important source of income. In the War of the Pacific (1879–83) Chile was able to defeat its old rulers, Peru, and its neighbors, Bolivia, gaining control of the copper-rich Atacama Desert and leaving Bolivia landlocked, and prospered through a long period of relative stability and democracy. The 20th century saw fluctuations between military rule and militant socialism, both fueled by substantial revenues from copper exports, but Santiago has now matured into a clean and well-planned city.

1494
All land west of Brazil is granted to Spain under a treaty with Portugal

1541
Pedro de Valdivia treks across the Andes and founds the Spanish town of Santiago

1818
Eight years of conflict with Spain ends with Chile's second declaration of independence. Bernado O'Higgins becomes the first president

1973
Socialist President Salvador Allende is overthrown by General Augusto Pinochet in a military coup

1990
Democracy is restored following free elections

Seattle

ABOVE: *The fountain outside the Seattle Center.*
BELOW (TOP): *Hammering Man at the entrance to the Seattle Art Museum.*
BELOW (BOTTOM): *The Seattle Center Monorail.*

statistics

- Population: 672,600
- Seattle has 14 museums, 28 historical sites, 25 public libraries, and 27 performing arts centers
- Tourism is Washington State's fourth largest industry and Downtown Seattle has more than 4,400 hotel rooms
- Seattle has more than 6,100 acres (2,469 ha) of city parks

WILLIAM (BILL) GATES (B. 1955)

A native of Seattle, William (Bill) Gates is the chairman and chief software architect of the Microsoft Corporation, the worldwide leader in computer software. He attended Lakeside School, where he began programming computers at 13, and later Harvard University. In 1975, he founded Microsoft with his childhood friend, Paul Allen. Under Gates' leadership, Microsoft has improved software technology, and made it easier and more enjoyable for people to use computers. Today, Microsoft employs more than 55,000 people in 85 countries and regions and it has its HQ in Redwood, on the outskirts of Seattle.

Seattle is situated in Washington, the most north-westernly state in America. Although it is the largest city in the state, it is not the capital, which is Olympia, 60 miles (96.5km) to the south. Seattle, which sits between the Puget Sound and Lake Washington and overlooks Elliott Bay, is nicknamed The Emerald City—because of its parks, greenery, and glimpses of sparkling water. Close to the snowy peaks of Mount Rainier, it frequently tops lists of the most desirable place to live. As a result, many Californians have moved there. Seattle has a reputation as a rainy city, but its annual rainfall of around 36in (91cm) is less than New York City's 47in (120cm).

When a fire in 1889 destroyed most of the city, engineers raised streets several feet above the high tide level to prevent flooding. As a result, one of Seattle's most popular tourist attractions in the city is the Underground Tour, which looks at the passages that were once the main roadways and first-floor storefronts of the old town.

Art Galleries and Coffee Houses

The city's Pioneer Square is said to be the home of the original Skid Row, or Skid Road, a term used to describe the sliding of logs down Yesler Way to a steam-powered mill on the waterfront. As the area degenerated to become a bad part of town, "skid road" became "skid row." In the 1960s, Pioneer Square was saved from demolition by protestors and now it is home to many of the city's art galleries, restaurants, and inns. Pike Place Market is the oldest continually operating farmers market in the US, having been open since 1907. It too was saved by locals when, in 1971, they objected to a decision to clear the site. In the same year, Starbucks opened its first coffee house in the market. Now the company, which has its headquarters in Seattle, has more than 8,300 coffee houses worldwide.

The Space Needle tower, 605ft (184.4m) tall, was built for the 1962 World's Fair. It can withstand wind speeds of up to 105mph (169kph) and is part of the Seattle Center, a 74-acre (30 ha) complex that is home to the Seattle Opera and the Pacific Norwest Ballet.

Boeing, Microsoft, and Amazon.com, which also has its headquarters in Seattle, have helped bring a prosperity to the city, seen in the restoration of its old center, a booming arts scene, and thriving film and music industry. Fans of legendary musician and singer Jimi Hendrix (1942–70) make their way to the city as the singer was born here.

THE STORY OF...

On 13 November 1851, pioneers from Illinois landed on Alki Point (now west Seattle) to establish a community, which they named "New York Alki" ("Alki" being an Indian word meaning "by and by"). Changing it to "Seattle"—after the local Indian chief, Sealth—the pioneers moved to Elliott Bay. During the next 50 years, the town on Puget Sound grew to become a major shipping port. By the end of the century, benefiting from the Klondike gold rush, Seattle had become the main commercial, shipping, and marketing center of the Pacific Northwest.

During World War II the city was a major naval base, and local airplane company Boeing manufactured heavy bombers for the US Army Air Force. By the 1960s, Boeing had grown to become the world's leading producer of commercial jet aircraft. Since 1962, and the Seattle World's Fair, tourism has been a major source of income, while computer software manufacturers, bio-medical industries, and aerospace have taken over from forestry, fishing, and agriculture to dominate the local economy.

ABOVE LEFT: *The sign that adorns Pier 55 along the Seattle waterfront.*
ABOVE: *Seattle's Pike Place Market, world famous for its fresh seafood.*
BELOW: *The city's most famous landmark, the Space Needle.*

- Population: 5,100,000
- Though not the capital (Ottawa), Toronto is Canada's biggest city, covering 3,861 sq miles (10,000 sq km)
- The CN Tower is the world's largest free-standing structure, at 1,814ft (553m)
- Toronto has over 120 ice rinks, for skating and ice hockey

Toronto

Toronto has become a bustling contemporary city, after many years when it was regarded as dull and provincial. Since the 1960s there has been massive regeneration and economic growth, making it Canada's foremost city. At the forefront of this change is the city's waterfront area, once a dispiriting industrial site and now a thriving commercial and residential area with excellent museums and entertainment as well as the ferry port for Toronto's islands, which are rural car-free retreats.

Toronto's Downtown area houses the banking district, the main shopping area, including the huge Eaton Center shopping mall, numerous art galleries, and the CN Tower. Uptown has even more museums, from the Royal Ontario Museum to smaller, quirkier specialist collections such as the Bata Shoe Museum and Casa Loma.

Toronto is much more than just its center. One of the features that make it such a vibrant and cosmopolitan city is its many district neighborhoods, all of which have their own distinctive appeal. These range from a sizeable Chinatown to Little India, Little Italy, and Little Portugal. There are some districts, such as Kensington Market, that are defined by their diverse stores and stalls in a multicultural neighborhood comprising Portuguese, West Indian, and Jewish cultures. The Beaches has 1.75 miles (3km) of boardwalk and lots of sand, while the oddly named Cabbagetown is full of pretty Victorian houses.

THE CN TOWER

The CN (Canadian National) Tower has become the symbol of Toronto. Though originally planned simply as a broadcasting transmission antenna, it rapidly turned into the city's star tourist attraction, with over 2 million visitors a year. The lofty slender spire has exterior glass lifts that rise at ear-popping speed to 1,135ft (346m) and the look-out galleries. Here, there is a reinforced glass floor where you can stand and look down to the ground below—though many people find it simply too scary to step on.

RIGHT: *The domed roof of the Skydome stadium viewed from the CN Tower.*

A Thriving Cultural Center

Although Toronto is Canada's foremost commercial and banking center, it also has a long history as a cultural center. Many of Canada's most prominent writers have been based here, from Margaret Attwood (b. 1939) to Robertson Davies (1913–95) to Michael Ondaatje (b. 1943), and have used the city as the backdrop to their novels. Toronto has a thriving theater scene, the third largest in the English-speaking world after London and New York, as well as out-of-town summer theater festivals in Stratford and Niagara-on-the lake. The Toronto International Film Festival is the largest in North America and the city has a billion-dollar film-making industry of its own.

Ice hockey is Canada's most popular sport and ice rinks abound in Toronto. The main team, the Toronto Maple Leafs, has the state-of-the-art Air Canada Center as its headquarters, also home to the Toronto Rangers basketball squad. Toronto's other sporting icon is the SkyDome, next to the CN Tower, where the Toronto Blue Jays play baseball and the Toronto Argonauts play Canadian Football.

)PPOSITE (INSET ABOVE): *A sign advertising the Hockey Hall of Fame.*
)PPOSITE (INSET BELOW): *Exterior of Casa Loma.*
ABOVE (TOP): *View along Bloor Street.*
ABOVE (BELOW): *A street in Chinatown.*
RIGHT: *View toward a shopping complex, Yonge Street.*

THE STORY OF...

Toronto means "place of meetings" in the language of the Huron tribe, the original inhabitants of the area. Europeans did not arrive until the 16th century when French and British fur traders began to explore with considerable rivalry, befriending opposing local tribes and arming them with muskets. In a war between the French and British that lasted from 1756 to 1763, the British were eventually the victors and their numbers grew after the American Revolution (1775–83) when thousands of loyalist Americans migrated to Canada to be under British rule.

The British divided the country into Lower Canada (Québec) and Upper Canada (Ontario) and the first capital for the latter was Niagara-on-the-Lake close to the US border. In 1793 the capital moved to the Lake Ontario shore, briefly named York before it became Toronto. The city experienced a trade and industry boom in the 19th century but had a reputation for provincialism until the 1960s brought an economic renaissance turning it into Canada's largest city and most important commercial center.

BELOW: *Detail of an Inuit mask in the Bay of Spirits Gallery.*

key dates

1720
The French establish the first settlement, a fur trading post

1791
The British Parliament passes the Canada Act establishing Toronto as capital of Upper Canada

1812
The Americans attempt to oust the British from Canada but are swiftly ejected by loyalists

1867
Upper Canada becomes Ontario with Toronto as capital

2000
"Moose in the City" exhibition generates $400 million and its website receives 4 million hits

Vancouver

Vancouver is in the province of British Columbia on the west coast of Canada, in North America. It is a sparkling city, due to the reflection of mini skyscrapers and stylish condominiums bouncing back from the channels, bays, inlets, and the mighty Fraser River. The city is also cradled by the Coast Range mountains and the Pacific Ocean, with the Strait of Georgia separating the mainland from Vancouver Island.

Home to a variety of ethnic backgrounds and neighborhoods—Indians, Japanese, and Greeks—Vancouver has a huge Chinese population, one which expanded following the handover of Hong Kong to China in 1997. Third only to Chinatowns in New York and San Francisco, Vancouver's version has the Dr Sun Yet-Sen classical Chinese garden, the first to be built outside China.

Since the late 1990s residential activity has overtaken the city, particularly in vibrant Downtown, the central peninsula that juts into the harbor and includes the Central Business District, the stock exchange, and Concord Pacific Place, North America's single largest urban waterfront development. People are moving from the suburbs to be here, close to the stores and buzz of main thoroughfare Robson Street, to wake up with the views, not having to commute and still be within reach of the mountains for weekend skiing. Notable buildings include the Vancouver Art Gallery, built in 1911 and converted in the 1970s, still with many of its original neo-classical features and works by celebrated Canadian painter Emily Carr (1871–1945). To the east of Gastown is a designated historic district, with brick streets and restored Victorian buildings. On Vancouver Island, reached by boat or seaplane, is Victoria, British Columbia's capital since 1868 and quintessentially English, with double-decker buses and a stone-built Parliament Building. Stanley Park is the city's lungs. Stretching as a dense, semi-wild forest of cedar trees and Douglas firs, the park is the largest urban park in North America. It is surrounded by ocean on three sides and is where the locals come for fresh air and to walk the old aboriginal trails.

FIRST NATIONS ART

In the late 1960s, elders of the First Nations people began to preserve and revive their history and culture, in particular their arts, which date back thousands of years. Artistic expressions were linked to the struggle for democracy and equal rights, as well as trying to improve life for their communities. Vancouver grew to become the center of First Nation and Inuit art, and its native artists are among the most recognized and appreciated of all Canadian Artists, the finest examples being on show in the Museum of Anthropology, at the University of British Columbia.

ABOVE: *Detail of Brockton Point totem pole in Stanley Park.*

The Business of Film

As Canada's largest port and gateway to the Far East, foreign export tops the economy, followed by tourism, with visitors flocking to the ocean beaches in summer and the Whistler mountain ski resort in winter. Vancouver has gained the nickname "Hollywood of the North," as American television and movie companies film against its backdrop to take advantage of the favorable exchange rate. British Columbia's film industry is now worth $1 billion a year.

FAR LEFT: *The Geodesic Dome housing Vancouver's Science World, built for Canada's Expo '86.* LEFT: *View through an archway to a Chinese-style pagoda in the Dr Sun Yet-Sen Garden in Chinatown.* RIGHT: *The marina off Vancouver's Granville Island.*

THE STORY OF...

Vancouver sprang up at the mouth of the Fraser River as a settlement of mainly Musqueam and Squamish indigenous people. From the 16th century European explorers came, with the first recorded landing on Vancouver Island by British explorer Sir James Cook (1728–79), followed by more Britons and Spanish in search of gold. In 1792, naval Captain George Vancouver (1757–98) arrived and claimed the land for Britain, and in 1849 Vancouver Island was officially designated a crown colony. News of gold on the banks of the Fraser River brought activity to the area and encouraged a bigger port to be built on the mainland, now Vancouver city.

In 1870 the colonial government of British Columbia moved to the area known as Gastown and seven years later welcomed the Canadian Pacific Railway from Montréal, linking the west to the east. Progress was interrupted with the devastating Great Fire of 1886, however Vancouver rebuilt swiftly. From the 1950s, high-rise condominium towers began appearing in Downtown, followed by a second real estate boom in the 1990s which is continuing to the present.

BELOW: *The white "sails" of the Trade and Convention Center.*

key dates

1792
Captain George Vancouver declares the area for Britain

1886
The Great Fire destroys the city

1969
The environment organization Greenpeace is founded

1986
Centenary commemorated with the World Exposition

2010
Vancouver is due to host the Winter Olympics

Washington DC

Population: 563,384

Largest employer: Federal Government

Licensed lawyers: 78,000

Cherry trees: 3,700

GEORGE WASHINGTON (1732–99)

The son of wealthy Virginia land-owners, young George Washington was trained to survey America's frontier for expansion, but gained military fame during the French and Indian War. In 1775, he was named Commander in Chief of the Continental Army and skillfully led an unskilled force of 14,000 in America's Revolutionary War, a grueling conflict that was to last six years. The British army surrendered at Yorktown in 1781, after which General Washington looked forward to retiring to his estate at Mt. Vernon. Instead, he was elected unanimously as the first president of the United States in 1789, serving two terms and establishing the fundamental tenets of American democratic government.

Americans regard Washington, DC as their country's most elegant city—the only American city that was planned with such aesthetic and order before its actual construction. Wedged between Virginia and Maryland, the diamond-shaped District of Columbia is divided into four directional quadrants (NW, NE, SW, SE), with a grid of numbered streets running north and south, and lettered streets running east and west. Diagonal avenues named after individual states cut wide thoroughfares through the city, intersecting at prominent traffic circles and offering beautiful views of the capital's most prominent neo-classical buildings. From the front of the president's pillared home—the White House—one catches a clear view down Pennsylvania Avenue, leading to the grand dome of the Capitol.

The renowned Smithsonian museums line both sides of the National Mall, featuring a grassy green park that extends from the steps of the Capitol to the glistening white obelisk of the Washington monument—the city's tallest structure at 555ft (169.3m). Unlike most American cities, Washington, DC preserves its memorial skyline by limiting building height to 12 storeys. By night, the sky is marked with the silhouetted monuments to Thomas Jefferson (1743–1826) and Abraham Lincoln (1809–65), and by day the temple-like memorials are mirrored in the reflecting pool and the Tidal Basin of the Potomac River.

Political Diversity

Washington, DC rises and falls with the tides of American government: the city keeps an accelerated pace whenever Congress is in session, and election time adds fanfare to the daily buzz of running the United States. Those who do not work for the Federal Government often work with the government in some capacity. Lobbyists form the second tier of Washington's workforce, along with World Bank employees and diplomats. More than 20 million visitors come to the US capital every year—tourists enjoy the sites and the springtime cherry blossoms for which Washington is famous, while others come to make their politics known in protests and parade demonstrations. The capital's African-American heritage represents a vibrant core of the city—over 60 percent of the city is black and Washington's Howard University is the country's oldest African American college. Other prominent ethnic communities are originally from Ethiopia, Central America, and Southeast Asia. Such a diverse population—along with the hundreds of Victorian-style embassies that grace the historic neighborhoods of Georgetown and Dupont Circle—make Washington one of America's most cosmopolitan cities.

ABOVE (TOP): *The White House, at 1600 Pennsylvania Avenue.*
ABOVE (BOTTOM): *Rotunda interior of the US Capitol Building.*

THE STORY OF...

By 1789, the brand new United States of America had already adopted a constitution but still lacked a national capital. Northern ports such as New York and Philadelphia lobbied to be the seat of government, but the southern states sought a location closer to home. A compromise was struck in 1790, allowing President George Washington to designate the site of a "Federal City" on the banks of the Potomac River. French-born artist Pierre L'Enfant (1754–1825) designed the new city of Washington with wide boulevards, Baroque vistas, and alabaster government buildings.

Washington's population doubled during the Civil War, as the government grew and thousands of runaway slaves arrived from the South. Washington was known to be an unkempt and disorderly town before Congress started governing the district in 1874. In 1901, Senator James McMillan (1838–1902) set about restoring the Mall with monuments and scenic parks. Washington's size and importance increased with the Great Depression and World War II, and today the city counts itself among the world's great global capitals.

LEFT: *The Jefferson Monument.*

key dates

1790
The United States Congress passes the Residence Act, authorizing President George Washington to choose a site for a Federal City

1814
The British attack Washington, burning the White House and Capitol, leaving Congress to meet in the Post Office

1912
The city of Tokyo sends a gift of blossoming cherry trees to beautify the American capital

1963
Marting Luther King, Jr, delivers his "I have a dream" speech from the Lincoln Memorial, to a crowd of 250,000

1990
Mayor Sharon Pratt Dixon Kelly is elected as the first black woman to head a major US city

Index

Acknowledgements

Abbreviations for terms appearing below: (t) top; (b) bottom; (c) center; (l) left; (r) right.

The Automobile Assocation wishes to thank the following picture libraries, companies and tourist boards for their assistance with the preparation of this book.

Alamy 17b (Tibor Bognar), 70cl (Robert Harding Picture Library Ltd), 72/3 (FAN & MROSS Travelstock), 72cl (Grant Farquhar), 72c (rochaphoto), 73tr (FAN & MROSS Travelstock), 73bc (Rolf Richardson), 83cr (lookGaleria), 103cb (Mark Lewis), 103b (Kalpana Kartik), 110/1 (Coral Planet), 110t (Robert Harding Picture Library Ltd), 110b (Robert Harding Picture Library Ltd), 116/7 (Iain Masterton), 117cr (Nic Cleeve Photography), 122/3 (Panorama Stock Photos Co Ltd), 130/1 (G P Bowater), 132/3 (Frantisek Staud), 138t (Mediacolor's), 138cl (Greenshoots Communications), 139cl (Peter Adams Photography), 139c (Peter Adams Photography), 139cr (Mediacolor's), 139tr (Greenshoots Communications), 140/1 (Petr Svarc), 140t (Petr Svarc), 141c (Eye Ubiquitous), 144t (Bill Lyons), 145cr (Bill Lyons), 146b (Paul Doyle), 154bc (Robert Harding Picture Library Ltd), 154/5b (Imagestate), 164cl (Julius Lando), 166/7 (Nicholas Pitt), 178t (Bill Bachmann), 178/9c (Bill Bachmann), 179cr (Popperfoto), 206b/g (Beren Patterson), 206bc (Mireille Vautier), 207 (Harryhaussen), 207tl (Beren Patterson), 212cl (Jamie Marshall), 212c (Gary Cook); **Corbis UK** 196cl (Bettmann); **CPA** 92cl, 104/5, 104t, 104cl, 104c, 105c, 105b, 105cr, 105tr, 110cl, 114/5c, 114cl, 114/5c, 120/1, 120cl, 121tr, 121cl, 121cr, 121bl, 135cl, 135tr, 135cr, 146cl, 156cl, 158/9, 158t, 158cl, 158ct, 158cr, 158b, 159tr, 159cr, 166t, 166c, 167cr, 172/3 (Madison Images), 172t (Madison Images), 172cl, 172c (Madison Images), 173b (Madison Images); **Dubai Tourist Board** 160t, 160br, 161cr, 161br; **Mary Evans Picture Library** 129cr; www.fotoseeker.com 162br; **Fundación Miguel Mujica Gallo, Museo's 'Oro del Peru', 'Armas del Mundo', Lima-Peru** 188cl; **Getty Images** 10cl (Hulton Archive), 11tl, 14cl, 46/7 (Photographer's Choice), 56cl (Hulton Archive), 86cl (Hulton Archive), 90cl (Hulton Archive), 95c (Taxi), 102cl (Time Life Pictures), 134cl (AFP), 142cl (Hulton Archive), 144cl (Hulton Archive), 145b (AFP), 145c (Lonely Planet), 145tr (AFP), 146t (AFP), 146b/g (AFP), 147 (AFP), 147tr (AFP), 151cr (Time Life Pictures), 180ccr, 181tr, 206cl (Hulton Archive), 214cl; **Domingo Giribaldi/Promperu** 188ctr, 188cbr, 189tr; **Hill & Knowlton** 160cl, 161c; **Hong Kong Tourism Board** 88tcl, 100/1t, 100/1b, 100/1 b/g, 100b, 101cl; **Japan National Tourist Office** 116r, 116br, 117tl, 117tr; **Jumeirah International** 136tcr, 160/1, 161tr, 224tcr; **La Citadelle of Québec** 205c; **Las Vegas Convention & Visitors Authority** 4vii, 186/7c, 186/7b, 187tc, 187tr; **Ljubljana Tourism** 46t, 46cl, 46c, 46cr, 46bc, 47bc, 47cr, 47tr; **Leonard Magomba** 156t, 157tr, 157cl, 157cr; **Robin McKelvie** 26cl, 34cl, 41c, 160bc; **Munich Tourist Office** 56/7; www.neworleansonline.com 198t; **Pictures Colour Library** 32/3, 32t, 32cl, 33tr, 33cl, 33cr, 41tr, 64cl, 76c, 77, 86/7, 102bl, 114cr, 115cr, 123cr, 130cl, 130br, 133, 134/5, 134t, 138/9, 174tcr, 188t, 188/9b/g, 189l, 189cl, 198/9, 198cl, 198c, 199ct, 199cb, 199tr, 213cl; **Rex Features Ltd** 16l, 142t, 142b, 143, 143tc, 144/5, 166cr, 166b, 167tr, 203cr, 204cl; **Rio Convention & Visitors Bureau** 208t, 208ccl, 208bc, 209c, 209tr, 209cr; www.salzburg.information 68t, 68bl, 69tr, 69cr, 69bc, 84cl; **Seattle's Convention & Visitors Bureau** 5tc, 214c (Tim Thompson), 214bc (Tim Thompson), 215tc, 215tr; **Jonathan Smith** 34/5, 34t, 34bl, 35tl, 35tc, 35tr, 38/9, 38t, 38bc, 38/9b, 39tc, 39tr, 74t, 74cl, 74crt, 75tl, 75tr, 75cr, 76cl; **Solidere** 146/7, 147cr; **South African Tourism** 136tl, 164cr, 165cl; **Taipei City Government** 130t, 130bc, 131tr, 131cr; **Tallin City Tourist Office & Convention Bureau/Toomas Volmar** 76t, 76br, 77tc, 77tr, 77c, 77cr; **Topfoto** 38cl, 100cl, 166cl; **Tourisme Montréal** 197c (Régie des installations olympiques), 197cr (Stephán Poulin); **Turisvision** 206t, 206br, 207tr, 207cr; **Visit Reykjavik** 64t, 64c, 64/5, 64cr, 65tr, 65cl, 65c, 65b; **World Pictures** 35cr, 72t, 73cr, 74crb, 75, 111c, 111cr, 111tr, 142c, 142b/g, 143tr, 156/7, 156c, 170/1, 170t, 171bc, 175tcr, 178cl, 178/9, 179tr, 180/1t, 180/1b, 180cl, 180ccl, 180cr, 208/9, 208cl, 212t, 212/3, 212cr, 213tr; **Zürich Tourism** 86t, 86bc, 86br, 87bl, 87tr, 87cr.

The remaining photographs are held in the Association's own photo library (AA World Travel Library) and were taken by the following photographers:
P Aithie 4bi, 162/3, 162t, 162cl, 162bc, 172bc, 173tr, 173cr; **H Alexander** 148tr, 150bc, 151bl; **F Arvidsson** 96br, 106b/g, 106t, 106cl, 106ct, 106c, 106b, 107, 107tr, 107cr, 114t, 115tl, 115tr; **J Arnold** 55cr, 55tr, 70ct; **B Bachmann** 112/3t, 112/3b, 112t, 112cl, 113tc, 113c, 113tr, 113cr; **A Baker** 52/3, 52t, 52cl; **A Belcher** 88tr, 90/1, 90ccl, 91tr; **P Bennett** 4biv, 5br, 7tcr, 26/7, 26t, 26b, 27tr, 27cr, 36br, 37bl, 194t, 194/5, 194bcl, 194bc, 195tc, 195tr, 195cr, 218c, 218bc; **I Burgum** 154/5, 154cl, 155tr, 155bl, 168t; **D Buwalda** 103tr; **M Chaplow** 12br, 50, 50t; **G Clements** 89tr, 94cl, 94c, 94/5, 95tr, 95cr, 122t, 122cl, 122br, 123c, 123tr; **C Coe** 4tr, 4vi, 4bcr, 5r, 136tcl, 137tr, 140c, 140cr, 141tr, 149, 150/1, 150tl, 150c, 150br, 151tr, 151c, 176t, 176ccl, 176/7, 177cl, 177tr, 177cr, 218 b/g, 218cl, 218bcl, 219tr, 219cr; **D Corrance** 88tl, 89tcr, 97, 97bl, 97tr, 97c, 97cr, 132cl, 132c, 133cl, 133tr, 203bl; **B Davies** 5br, 102/3, 102t, 102br, 103c, 120t, 121tl; **J Davison** 4tc, 174tr, 194cl, 195tcl, 216b, 216ctr, 217tr, 217cr; **S Day** 5ct, 5vi, 6tl, 12/3, 12l, 12bc, 13bl, 24cl, 24br, 24cr, 126l, 127t, 128c; **L Dunmire** 186t, 186l, 187cr; **R Elliott** 28bc; **D Forss** 5viii, 7tr, 40/1, 40cl, 41tr; **J Gocher** 96t, 96cl, 96bc; **T Harris** 10t, 30t, 44t, 44cl, 45bl, 93cr, 99tr, 99bc, 116r, 132t; **D Henley** 5tccl, 89tl, 92/3, 92t, 92c, 93tl, 93tc, 93tr, 98/9, 98t, 98cl, 98bc, 98br, 99cl, 99c, 184t, 184cl, 184c, 184bc; **N Hicks** 101ccl, 101ccr, 101cr, 101tr; **J Holmes** 66bc; **M Jourdan** 5tcr, 7tl, 8bl, 9c, 12t, 13tr, 13br, 48cl, 49cr, 50cl, 51bl, 51c, 51cl, 51tr, 56t, 57cr, 61cr, 61bc, 190t, 190cl, 190cr, 191cl; **J W Jorgensen** 40t, 41tc, 41br; **P Kenward** 36/7, 49, 90t, 128br, 152c, 170bl, 170bc, 171tr; **A Kouprianoff** 5bl, 5brl, 6tcl, 8tl, 18/9, 18t, 18cl, 19tl, 19tr, 19b, 20t, 20cl, 20c, 20cr, 21, 21cl, 21c, 21cr, 21tr, 42cl, 44/5, 45cr, 66t, 94t, 124bl; **M Langford** 4cr, 89tcl, 90ccr, 90cr, 91t, 91cr, 118/9, 118t, 118cl, 118c, 118cr, 119c, 119ccr, 119cr, 119tr, 126b, 126/7, 128/9, 128l, 128b, 129tr, 224tcl; **J Loader** 5tcl, 137tcl, 162c, 163tr; **D Lyons** 195tcl; **E Meacher** 23tr, 170cl, 171cr; **S McBride** 4bii, 5tr, 14/5, 15tr, 24/5, 24t, 25c, 25cr, 31tr, 62cl, 62bcl, 63, 66cl, 66bl, 67tr, 78/9, 78bc, 80cl, 136tcl, 152cl, 164/5, 164ccl, 164c, 165tr, 165cr, 168/9, 168ct, 168cl, 168c, 168cr, 169tr, 169bc, 169cr, 202br, 203br; **D Miterdiri** 5cb, 81tl, 81cl, 81cr; **A Mockford & N Bonetti** 44c, 45tc, 45tr, 45c; **I Morejohn** 94/5; **K Paterson** 4biii, 4v, 7tcl, 8cl, 8br, 8/9, 9tr, 22/3, 22bl, 22tr, 23bl, 23br, 28t, 29tr, 29cr, 29b, 30/1, 31tr, 54/5, 54t, 54cl, 55cl, 55cc, 70cl, 70c, 70b, 71, 71c, 71tr, 108, 108cr, 108br, 124c, 124br, 125tr, 125br, 174tl, 210/1, 210cl, 210bcl, 210bc, 211tr, 211cl, 211c, 211cr, 224tl; **J F Pins** 196t, 196/7, 196bc, 197cl, 197tr, 204t, 204/5, 204ccl, 204cr, 205tr, 205cr, 216/7; **B Rieger** 60t, 60b; **E Rooney** 5bi, 175tr, 200br, 201, 203tr; **C Sawyer** 4bl, 4viii, 5tl, 5bii, 5vii, 6tr, 15b, 31cr, 36t, 36bc, 37bc, 37tr, 49cl, 49tr, 53tl, 53tr, 53br, 57tc, 57tr, 57c, 60cl, 61tr, 62t, 63tr, 66br, 67bl, 67c, 67cr, 78cl, 79, 80/1, 80tl, 81c, 84c, 85b, 137tl, 137tcr, 152/3, 152t, 152b, 153tr, 153c, 153tcl, 153bc, 174tcl, 175tl, 175tcl, 176 b/gl, 176c, 176ccr, 177, 184/5, 185tr, 185c, 185cr, 190bc, 191tl, 191tr, 191bc, 192t, 192b/g, 192cl, 192ctr, 192cbr, 193tl, 193, 193tl, 193c, 193cr, 200l, 200tr, 201br, 202/3, 202tl, 202tr, 202bc, 219l, 220t, 220b/g, 220ctr, 220cbr, 221l, 221tr, 224tr; **Neil Setchfield** 88tcr, 108t, 108cl, 109l, 109tr, 109cr, 124/5, 124t, 124cl, 125bc; **M Siebert** 84t; **J Smith** 6tcr, 14t, 16t, 16tr, 17tr, 17c, 28cl, 28br, 29tc, 42/3, 42t, 42c, 43tl, 43tr, 43cr, 58/9, 58cl, 59tl, 59tr, 68/9, 68cl, 82/3, 82t, 82cl, 83tr, 83bc, 84/5, 84br, 85tr; **T Souter** 14br, 37br, 163cr; **R Strange** 148cl, 148b; **N Sumner** 204c, 216t, 216cl, 216cbr, 217tl, 217cl, 217c; **R Surman** 5biii10, 11; **J A Tims** 3, 4trb, 214tl, 214t, 214 b/g, 215, 215tl, 215cr; **M Van Vark** 186 b/g; **W Voysey** 48t, 48c, 60/1; **P Wilson** 10c, 10cr, 11bl, 11tr, 11br, 22t, 67, 182t, 182b/g, 182cl, 182bl, 182br, 183l, 183tr, 183c, 183cr, 190/1, 191cr; **S Whitehorne** 24bl, 25tr, 28/9; **J Wyand** 62bc, 63tc.

1	Amsterdam	11	Edinburgh	21	London	31	Salzburg	41	Bangkok
2	Athens	12	Florence	22	Madrid	32	St. Petersburg	42	Beijing
3	Barcelona	13	Geneva	23	Monte Carlo	33	Sofia	43	Delhi
4	Berlin	14	Helsinki	24	Moscow	34	Stockholm	44	Ho Chi Minh
5	Bratislava	15	Istanbul	25	Munich	35	Tallinn	45	Hong Kong
6	Bruges	16	Kiev	26	Oslo	36	Venice	46	Jakarta
7	Brussels	17	Copenhagen	27	Paris	37	Warsaw	47	Kathmandu
8	Budapest	18	Krakow	28	Prague	38	Vienna	48	Kolkata
9	Dublin	19	Lisbon	29	Reykjavik	39	Zurich	49	Kuala Lumpur
10	Dubrovnik	20	Ljubljana	30	Rome	40	Auckland	50	Lahore

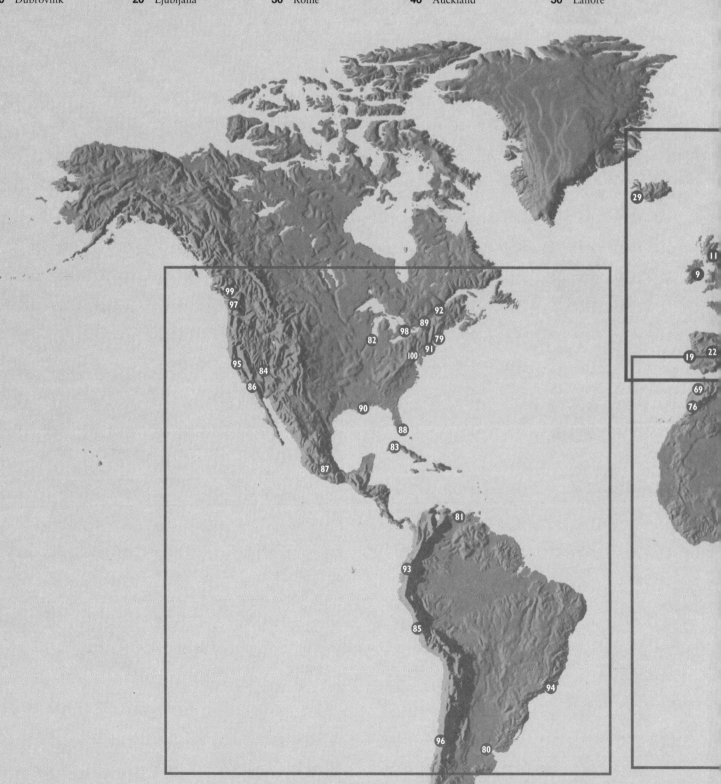